TRANSFORMATIONS IN AFRICA

ESSAYS ON AFRICA'S LATER PAST

EDITED BY
GRAHAM CONNAH

LEICESTER UNIVERSITY PRESS
LONDON AND WASHINGTON

LEICESTER UNIVERSITY PRESS
A Cassell imprint
Wellington House, 125 Strand, London WC2R 0BB, England
PO Box 605, Herndon, Virginia 20172-0605, USA

First published in 1998

British Library Cataloguing in Publication Data
A catalogue record for this book is available from the British Library.
ISBN 0 7185 0137 3 Hardback
    0 7185 0138 1 Paperback

Library of Congress Cataloging-in-Publication Data
Transformations in Africa: essays on Africa's later past/edited by
    Graham Connah.
        p.   cm.
    Ten essays, seven of which are rev. papers of a conference held in
the Humanities Research Centre, at the Australian National
University, Canberra, in June 1995.
    Includes bibliographical references and index.
    ISBN 0-7185-0137-3 (hb). — ISBN 0-7185-0138-1 (pb)
    1. Africa—History—Congresses.   I. Connah, Graham.
DT1.5.T73 1998
960—dc21   97-27703
                                                                CIP

Typeset by BookEns Ltd, Royston, Herts.
Printed and bound in Great Britain by
Biddles Ltd, Guildford and King's Lynn

CONTENTS

LIST OF FIGURES

LIST OF TABLES

NOTE

In this book the convention has been followed of stating uncalibrated radiocarbon dates as years bc, ad, or bp but using BC, AD, and BP for calibrated radiocarbon dates and dates based on historical sources. BP and bp stand for 'before present,' conventionally fixed at 1950.

THE CONTRIBUTORS

Graham Connah is an archaeologist who has conducted field research in Britain, Nigeria, Egypt, Uganda, and Australia. He holds an MA from the University of Cambridge, and a DLitt from the University of New England, Armidale, New South Wales. He is also a Fellow of the Society of Antiquaries, of the Royal Anthropological Institute, and of the Australian Academy of the Humanities. Now an Emeritus Professor of the University of New England, he is at present a Visiting Fellow in the Department of Archaeology and Anthropology at the Australian National University, in Canberra. He has been involved in later African archaeology since 1961 but since the mid-1970s has also been active in the field of Australian historical archaeology. His main publications include: *The archaeology of Benin* (1975), *Three thousand years in Africa* (1981), *Australian field archaeology: a guide to techniques* (ed. 1983), *African civilizations* (1987), *The archaeology of Australia's history* (1993), and *Kibiro: the salt of Bunyoro, past and present* (1996).

Richard B. Lee (BA and MA University of Toronto; PhD University of California, Berkeley) is a Professor of Anthropology at the University of Toronto and past Chair of the African Studies Program. He has held academic appointments at Harvard, Rutgers, and Columbia Universities and research positions at the Center for Advanced Studies in the Behavioral Sciences, Stanford, and the University of British Columbia. He has lectured at universities on four continents; in 1995 he was a visiting lecturer in the Department of Archaeology and Anthropology at the Australian National University, Canberra. His current research interests are in ecology, history, African Studies, Marxist theory and the politics of culture. He is internationally known for his studies of hunting and gathering societies, particularly the Ju/'hoansi-!Kung San of Botswana, with whom he has worked since 1963. Studies of foragers have also taken him to Tanzania, Namibia, Alaska, Northern Canada, Australia, and Japan. His books include *Man the hunter* (1968), *Kalahari hunter-gatherers* (1976), *The !Kung San* (1979), *Politics and history in band societies* (1982) and *The Dobe Ju/'hoansi* (1993). A Fellow of the Royal Society of Canada and past-president of the Canadian Anthropology Society, he was awarded an honorary Doctorate of Letters in 1990 by the University of Alaska, Fairbanks, for his research and advocacy on behalf of the foraging peoples.

Robert K. Hitchcock is Associate Professor and Chair of the Department of Anthropology at the University of Nebraska–Lincoln, as well as Coordinator of African Studies. He received his BA in anthropology and history from the University of California, Santa Barbara (1971) and his MA and PhD in anthropology from the University of New Mexico in Albuquerque (1977, 1982). He is the author of a number of books and articles on indigenous peoples' rights and development, including the recent *Kalahari communities: Bushmen and the politics of the environment in Southern Africa*. He has published recently in *Human Ecology, The Colorado Journal of International Environmental Law and Policy*, and *Development and Change*. A founding member of the Committee for Human Rights of the American Anthropological Association, he currently is working on San and other indigenous peoples' rights and socioeconomic development in Southern Africa, in addition to teaching.

Joanna Casey is Assistant Professor of Anthropology at the University of South Carolina, in the USA. She did her BA and MA in the Department of Archaeology at Simon Fraser University in Western Canada, and her PhD in the Department of Anthropology at the University of Toronto. She is currently directing an archaeological project in Northern Ghana that is investigating later prehistoric occupations. Her other research foci concern ethnographic investigations on women's businesses and the use of wild resources in Northern Ghana. Her publications include papers on the prehistory of Northern Ghana, gender issues, and lithic analysis.

K. C. MacDonald received his PhD from Cambridge University in 1994, where he studied with David Phillipson and Geoff Bailey, and his BA (Hons) in 1989 from Rice University, where he was a student of Roderick and Susan McIntosh. He began his fieldwork in West Africa in 1989, and has continued excavation, survey, and laboratory projects in Mali on a yearly basis up to the present. His research in Africa has been carried out in collaboration with Dr Téréba Togola, of the Malian Institut des Sciences Humaines. They have worked together in the Méma and Gourma regions, although Dr MacDonald has also worked on shorter projects elsewhere in Mali. Appointed Lecturer in African Archaeology at the Institute of Archaeology, University College London, in 1994, his research interests include the Holocene recolonization of the Sahara, the origins of African livestock, and the development of complex societies in Africa – particularly the Empire of Ghana.

Roland Fletcher was educated at Cambridge University, completing his PhD there in 1975. His doctoral research was on the organization of space in small-scale communities both in modern Ghana and New Kingdom Egypt. He specializes in the analysis of human spatial behavior, especially the growth of settlements, and has recently published a book with Cambridge University Press on the limits of settlement growth. His other major research interest is the nature of archaeological theory.

Between 1970 and 1972 he taught at the University of Ghana (Legon) and moved to the University of Sydney in 1976, where he is currently an Associate Professor. From 1993 to 1995 he was an Associate Dean of the Faculty of Arts. He teaches human behavioral evolution and the introductory course for archaeology, as well as his research specialities. With Ian Johnson he established the Archaeological Computing Laboratory, which is now a node of the University's advanced computer visualization laboratory, and he has chaired the University committees on information technology and information resources.

George E. Brooks, AB Dartmouth College, AM and PhD Boston University, is Professor of History at Indiana University, where he has taught African history and world history since 1962. He first undertook research in West Africa in 1961, and has returned to the region a number of times. He visited South Africa and Lesotho in 1979, was a Fulbright Professor at the University of Zimbabwe in 1984, and has visited countries in Central and Southern Africa on several occasions since. His publications include: *Yankee traders, old coasters and African middlemen* (1965); *The Kru mariner in the nineteenth century* (1970); *Landlords and strangers: ecology, society, and trade in Western Africa, 1000–1630* (1993); and he has recently completed a world history text that focuses on the 80 percent of the world's inhabitants who live in 'less-developed countries' as defined by the more affluent 20 percent. His current project is a monograph on Eur-African families and trading groups in Western Africa between the seventeenth and nineteenth centuries. He is a Fellow of the African Studies Association and a member of the American Historical Association, World History Association, MANSA/Mande Studies Association, and a member of the Advisory Board of the *International Journal of African Historical Studies*.

James Woodhouse is a mature student currently studying at the Institute of Archaeology, University College London. Prior to this he worked in commercial archaeology as a contract excavator in England and Wales. Since joining the Institute of Archaeology he has been involved in research projects in England, Barbados, and Mali in West Africa. Most recently, he has been working with the Southern Gourma Project in Mali, as supervisor of excavations at the occupation site of Windé Koroji, and of mapping, geophysical survey, and excavation at the settlement mound of Tongo Maaré

Diabal. As part of this project he directed excavations, and has undertaken the analysis, of the iron-smelting site of Boata, 5 kilometers north of Tongo Maaré Diabal. Currently he is working on the analysis of metallurgical material from Tongo Maaré Diabal, linking iron production processes in the region.

Henry W. Mutoro holds a BEd (Hons) and an MA (Archaeology) from the University of Nairobi. He also has a CPhil and a PhD from the University of California, Los Angeles. His MA thesis was on the origins and development of the Swahili settlements on the East African coast, with particular reference to the Takwa ruins in the Lamu Archipelago, on the north Kenya coast. His PhD was on an archaeological study of the Mijikenda Kaya settlements in the Kenya coastal hinterland. He is interested in computer and Geographical Information Systems applications in archaeology and is currently coordinating a SARDC (Swedish Agency for Research with Developing Countries) sponsored project on Human Responses and Contributions to Environmental Change in Africa during the Holocene, and is himself investigating the Tana River and its environs in Kenya. He is a Professor of History in the University of Nairobi, where he is also currently Dean of Arts.

George H. O. Abungu completed his undergraduate degree in archaeology at the University of Nairobi, and subsequently was employed by the National Museums of Kenya. In 1985 he was awarded a scholarship by the University of Cambridge to pursue his Masters and Doctorate degrees in archaeology. He completed his PhD in 1989 on an archaeological study of communities on the River Tana, in Kenya, during the period AD 700 to 1890. He then returned to Kenya where he was appointed Head of the Department of Coastal Archaeology at Fort Jesus Museum. In 1992 he was appointed the Head of the Coastal Museums Program in the National Museums of Kenya. He has over ten years of fieldwork experience in Kenya and has also carried out shorter assignments in Zimbabwe and Sweden. Recent work on the Kenyan coast includes a two-year-long survey of all coastal sites. He has traveled widely, presented papers at many international conferences, and has a number of publications concerning East African archaeology to his credit.

Christopher R. DeCorse is currently an Associate Professor of Anthropology at Syracuse University. He completed his Bachelor of Arts at the University of New Hampshire and his graduate training at the University of California, Los Angeles. His research interests include ethnohistory, culture change, and public education and archaeology. He has excavated at a wide variety of sites in the United States, the Caribbean, and Africa. His most recent archaeological research has focused on the African settlement at Elmina, Ghana, the site of the first and largest European trade post established in sub-Saharan Africa.

PREFACE AND ACKNOWLEDGMENTS

Seven of the ten essays in this book originated as papers presented at a conference held in the Humanities Research Centre, at the Australian National University, Canberra, in June 1995 but have been revised for publication here. I am most grateful for the interest and initiative of the Humanities Research Centre in organizing that conference and for permitting the publication of a selection of its papers in this form. I would also like to express my thanks to the Centre for its help in a number of ways during the preparation of this book.

An earlier version of the essay by Christopher DeCorse has been published under the title 'Culture contact and change in West Africa,' in *Studies in culture contact: interaction, culture change, and archaeology*, edited by James G. Cusick, Center for Archaeological Investigations, Occasional Paper No. 25, Southern Illinois University, Carbondale, copyright 1998 by the Board of Trustees, Southern Illinois University. I am most grateful for permission to include this here, in a revised, expanded, and more heavily illustrated form.

I also wish to acknowledge the permission of the Cambridge University Library to reproduce the illustration on the cover of this book, which was photographed from Le Capitaine Binger's publication of 1892: *Du Niger au Golfe de Guinée: par le pays de Kong et le Mossi*, Hachette, Paris, Volume 1, page 171. All other necessary illustration acknowledgments are contained in the figure captions.

Finally, I wish to thank Douglas Hobbs of the Department of Archaeology and Palaeoanthropology in the University of New England, for his skillful improvements to some of the figures published here, and Beryl Connah for many long hours of editorial assistance.

Graham Connah
Canberra, April 1997

Dedicated to the memory of
Umaru Gol
who helped to
recapture Africa's history

CHAPTER 1

STATIC IMAGE: DYNAMIC REALITY

Graham Connah

Africa's later past, here defined as the last 20,000 years or so, has often received inadequate attention from archaeologists. Prehistoric archaeologists have tended to concentrate on earlier periods and archaeologists interested in socially complex literate societies have tended to ignore Africa altogether, with the exception of Ancient Egypt which they have treated as a separate entity. The result has been the creation of a static image of Africa's later past, a notion that little of significance happened during this period until the advent of European contact, a notion that still exists at least in the public mind in many parts of the world outside of Africa. Despite the very existence of African history being at one time questioned, it was perhaps historians who led the way in breaking down this image, and archaeologists have been quick to follow. Although the latter are still hampered to some extent by an outdated epochalistic model of Africa's past, the dynamic reality of its later periods is rapidly being made apparent. This book presents a series of examples of the transformations that did indeed take place during these supposedly static centuries. Its contributors discuss the adaptive abilities of African hunter-gatherers, the origins of food production and of social complexity in West Africa, the character of precolonial urbanism, the interrelationship of climatic change and historical change, the development of African metallurgy, the trading systems of both the East African interior and the East African coast, and the impact of initial European contact in West Africa. These are an important sample of the transformations that characterized Africa's dynamic later past.

In 1961 the late Grahame Clark, one of the leading prehistorians of his day, published his *World prehistory: an outline*, an attempt at a world synthesis that many of his contemporaries had thought impossible. It was a book that was to enjoy considerable success and go through two further editions (Clark, 1961, 1969, 1977). In that first edition, less than seven out of a total of 261 pages were devoted to what was called 'the later prehistory of Africa,' and within those few pages Africa was referred to as '... a continent that had already during Late Pleistocene times slipped far behind in the race of progress' (1961: 112). Almost four decades later such a view at best seems quaint and dated, at worst Eurocentric and prejudiced, but it was indicative not only of the lack of research into Africa's later past at that time but also of an attitude that still exists, at least in the public mind, in many parts of the world outside of Africa.

As a specialist in European prehistoric archaeology, although one remarkable for training archaeologists who subsequently worked in other parts of the world, Clark should perhaps be forgiven. Far more difficult to understand is the extent to which those who were specialists in African prehistoric archaeology also, for a long time, tended to ignore the physical evidence of the last few millennia in Africa (Shaw, 1989: 10). Alimen's *The prehistory of Africa*, first published in French in 1954 and then in English in 1957, and one of the earliest attempts at a continent-wide synthesis, is particularly revealing. Most of the book is about stone artifacts and is focused essentially on prehistoric hunter-gathers to the exclusion of nearly everything else (Alimen, 1957). Even as late as 1970 the situation was much the same, when Desmond Clark published his *The prehistory of Africa*. Only 37 out of a total of 223 pages were concerned with what were called 'farmers and present-day people' (Clark, 1970). Indeed, it would seem that such unbalanced coverage was not unusual up to about this time: perusal of the various published proceedings of the Pan-African Congress on Prehistory, for example that for the Livingstone Congress of 1955 (Clark, 1957), reveals a similar tendency to emphasize prehistoric hunter-gatherers or at least prehistoric societies with lithic technologies, although it is a tendency that diminishes as time goes on. One gets the impression that it was almost as if most Africanist prehistoric archaeologists thought that the later African past was not their concern, the problem was that at one time it did not seem to be anybody else's either. It is important to consider how this situation could have come about.

Prehistory was in origin a nineteenth-century European concept. It was essentially concerned with the times before the establishment of Roman control over much of Western Europe, a remote preliterate past about which little could be known except by archaeological investigation (Daniel, 1964). Crucial to the initial acceptance of this concept was the recognition of stone artifacts as humanly shaped, suggesting a great antiquity for humankind. Therefore, when such artifacts began to be found in other parts of the world, including Africa, there was a tendency for them to dominate the attention of prehistoric archaeologists. In the African continent this became still more the case when the remains of early humans and their apparent ancestors also began to be found during the present century. If Africa had indeed been the home of humankind, then the earlier archaeological evidence was so important that its investigation must inevitably eclipse any interest in later periods. So much did this become the case, that as recently as the 1950s, very little was known about the archaeology of the later African past. From not knowing, to assuming that there was really not very much to know, because not very much had happened, was an all too easy step. In the imagination of far too many people in the

Western world, Africa was a continent of farming villages which had only been woken from a timeless sleep by the intrusion of European travelers, traders, missionaries, colonists, and officials. Given the wide acceptance of such a static image, it is hardly surprising that Grahame Clark should think of Africa as having 'slipped far behind in the race of progress.'

Archaeology, however, had roots other than those provided by the nineteenth-century idea of prehistory. It grew also out of the fascination for investigating ancient Eurasian literate societies that was ultimately a product of the European Renaissance. First Greece and Rome, then Egypt and Mesopotamia, still later the Indus Valley and the Yellow River: excavation in these and other places produced physical evidence that was technically and artistically impressive and yielded written material which usually, after some endeavor, could be read. In the highly literate scholarly tradition of Western Europe it was, not surprisingly, the existence of such writing that was thought to principally characterize that high level of social complexity that became identified by the word 'civilization' (Childe, 1942). Daniel (1968: 142–3) claimed that he 'once tackled Childe about his neglect of the civilizations of Nuclear America, and he dismissed my question with the words, "Never been there – peripheral and highly suspect."' In such an intellectual climate, what chance had Africa?

What chance indeed, when even the African origins of Pharaonic Egyptian society were denied by some scholars, who sought to explain the emergence of this remarkable ancient culture as at least partly the result of influences from South-West Asia (Frankfort, 1951)? Generated from the bounty of Africa's greatest river and confined by some of its most forbidding deserts, here was a major African achievement which European scholarship treated as something divorced from Africa. Ancient Egypt came, in fact, to fill a place in the European consciousness that at times almost eclipsed Greece and Rome. There must be other archaeologists who, like myself, have never really understood this. In the summer of 1996 I spent some time in the British Museum in London, not so much looking at the exhibits with which I was anyway familiar, but watching the dense mass of people who daily packed its galleries. There was no doubt at all what the greatest number of visitors most wanted to see – it was the Egyptian displays. As a result of anachronistic teaching, even Australians are still likely to show more interest in Ancient Egypt than in the human history of their own continent.

Given such a mind-set, it is surely no surprise that some Europeans should have tried so desperately to attribute Great Zimbabwe to the Phoenicians (Garlake, 1973: 72), the Ife bronzes to Ancient Greeks (Willett, 1967: 14), and the origins of the Swahili cities to Arab colonists (Chittick, 1971: 136). Quite understandably, African scholars now regard such ideas as the result of blatant racism but ignorance and stupidity were probably more important factors.

There was also the more fundamental matter of what I would call 'the image of Africa.' The habit, particularly prevalent around the 1960s, of referring to 'Africa South of the Sahara' or 'Subsaharan Africa' or even 'Black Africa' hints at the character that this image has sometimes assumed: Africa was to be denied parts of itself, its northern extremes being regarded as more Mediterranean than African and, as we have already seen, Egypt being thought of as more Near Eastern (in itself a most revealing term). It was as a deliberate challenge to the notion of 'ancient civilizations' that never seemed to include Africa, except Egypt that was always isolated from it (see for example Cotterell, 1983), that during the 1980s I provocatively gave the title *African civilizations* to my book about precolonial cities and states in tropical Africa (Connah, 1987). My concern was with some of the many people that Europe had forgotten.

In the view of some European historians, however, there was not really anything to remember. Early in the present century, one of them actually claimed that Africa had no history (Newton, 1923), and in so doing indicated an attitude that was to remain common for some time. Nevertheless, it was perhaps historians who did most to attract attention to the study of Africa's later past. Significantly, of the major relevant journals, *The Journal of African history* first appeared in 1960, but *The African Archaeological Review* not until 1983. In the very year that Grahame Clark was giving such scant attention to what he called 'the later prehistory of Africa,' Roland Oliver of the University of London published an edited book called *The dawn of African history*, which, although brief, devoted most of its 103 pages to later African societies (Oliver, 1961). This had originated as a series of talks that had been broadcast by the General Overseas Service of the BBC in 1958. In his foreword to this book, Oliver put his finger on the key problem of studying Africa's later past: the diverse nature of the sources.

> The history of Africa is a neglected subject, not only because the evidence for it is thin, but also because such a variety of skills is necessary to master what evidence there is. The written sources of African history are in English, French, Arabic, Portuguese, Dutch, German, Italian, Afrikaans, Amharic, Greek, Latin and Ancient Egyptian, to name only the most important. The unwritten lore of pre-colonial times has to be recovered from peoples speaking some six or seven hundred other languages. The archaeological approach, beginning with man's origins and before, and continuing right up to the eve of the colonial period, requires as many skills as the historical. In such a situation co-operative work is almost essential, both in research and presentation. (Oliver, 1961: iii)

This early recognition that the study of the later African past must involve written sources, oral traditions, and the interpretation of archaeological data, was most important. It was evident that researchers in any of these fields should not work in isolation. In that case the concept of prehistory, so appropriate in Europe where in many areas there was a fairly sharp divide between the remote preliterate past and the literate past, did not fit so well to the African situation. How could one write the later prehistory of a continent in which some areas lacked literacy till the late nineteenth century AD, others had at least two millennia of written records, still others had brief periods of documentation followed by silence, and many had detailed oral traditions? It seemed that both the chronological and the geographical interdigitation of prehistory and history was so complex in the African case, that their separation was pointless. In addition, the archaeologist working on later periods in Africa was often not dealing with a remote and dead past, as prehistoric archaeologists in Europe had to do, but with physical evidence relating to the predecessors of living peoples who could be or had been recorded both anthropologically and ethnographically. This was so much nearer the North American archaeological experience than the European one, that from the 1960s onwards there were increasing influences from that source, brought to Africa not only by visiting researchers from the United States and Canada, but also by the growing number of archaeologists from African countries who had been trained there. At last the static image of the later African past was beginning to disintegrate.

But not quite. A legacy was left which manifested itself in several ways. One was the concept of the archaeological culture and the emphasis on cultural history, that so characterized European (particularly British) prehistoric archaeology from the 1930s till the 1950s. Examples in the older literature for Africa's later periods include such things as the Uitkomst Culture in South Africa (Mason, 1969), the Kalomo Culture in Zambia (Fagan, 1967), the Stone Bowl Culture in Kenya (Cole, 1954), and even the poorly defined Nok Culture in Nigeria (Fagg, 1959). Such nomenclature and the ideas that gave rise to it now sound remarkably old-fashioned, but another legacy of the static past image has not been laid to rest so successfully. This is the nineteenth-century epochalistic thinking that gave rise to such terms as 'Late Stone Age,' 'Neolithic,' and 'Iron Age.'

At the 1995 Congress of the Pan-African Association for Prehistory and Related Studies, held in Harare, Zimbabwe, 64 out of the 192 abstracts available at the conference, that is 33 percent, made use of some form of epochalistic terminology, and the subject matter of some papers should really exclude them from the overall total as irrelevant to this particular issue. The 64 abstracts in question ranged over the full spectrum of Africa's past, of course, not merely its later periods that are under discussion here, but it did seem that the prospect of perceiving the past in new and meaningful ways was being inhibited by outmoded ideas. At the brink of the twenty-first century, a surprising number of scholars were still clinging to the concepts of the nineteenth. Interestingly, a small group of delegates were so concerned about this that they submitted a proposed resolution to the Plenary Closing Session of the conference. In it they stated that 'the increasing pace of archaeological data recovery in Africa has made it clear that the diversity and complexity of Africa's past cannot be accommodated adequately in many regions by Eurocentric "age and stage" terminology' and that it was therefore 'preferable to characterize sites descriptively in such a way as to distinguish clearly among chronology, material culture, subsistence economy, and all higher-level socio-political references.' When this proposed resolution was read out to the assembled delegates there was a shocked silence, compounded, it would appear, of disbelief by some that their cherished ideas should be challenged, and of doubt by the rest of us that we would get away with it. Nobody should have worried; in the best tradition of international gatherings, it was decided to do nothing. Speedily, someone put a motion that the proposed resolution be withdrawn and, of course, this motion passed. Subsequently, I submitted a note on this subject to the editor of one of the leading journals on African archaeology, but publication was refused (after a delay of over a year) on the grounds that the subject needed 'to be treated in a more appropriate format.' Static images take a long time to get rid of; as long ago as 1943, Glyn Daniel referred to the Three-Age System, as he knew it, as 'a mill-stone hanging around the necks of future archaeologists' (Daniel, 1943: 60).

Times are changing, however, and it is most encouraging to find evidence of a growing tendency to abandon epochalistic terminology and the concepts that gave rise to it. In his major synthesis of African archaeology, for instance, David Phillipson (1985, 1993) has successfully broken with tradition, and on this subject has remarked as follows:

Since more plentiful data relating to absolute chronology are now available than could be employed by the writers of previous syntheses, and in view of the evidence ... for disparate rates of development in different areas, this book does not employ the conventional terminology based upon broad technological/chronological subdivisions such as 'Late Stone Age', 'Neolithic' or 'Iron Age.' It has long been recognised that such terms cannot be precisely defined, but their informal use has continued, often at the expense of clarity; they are avoided in this book. (Phillipson, 1993: 5)

In my view, Phillipson is correct on this issue, and in my own writings I have avoided such terminology for almost two decades (see for example Connah, 1981, 1987, 1996). In this present book it has, I think quite rightly, been left to the individual contributors to decide such matters for themselves, but some evidence of the move away from the epochalistic legacy is nevertheless apparent.

Yet another legacy of the static image has been the extent to which writers about the later African past have used diffusion from external sources as an explanation for culture change. Thus a great deal of ink has been expended on the supposed diffusion of food production, of iron technology, of the idea of state formation, and of other things. It would be unrealistic to claim that diffusion did not occur to some extent during the last few millennia in Africa, just as it also occurred in other parts of the world, but it seems most unlikely that it was the major cause of change as was previously thought. It is now being realized that indigenous developments within the African continent were a far more significant factor than external influences, important though these sometimes were.

Perhaps also arising from the old static image was a tendency to compartmentalize the later African past. For example, there was the prehistoric past (whatever that meant), the ethnohistorical past, the historical past, and the ethnographic 'present' (often at some distance in the past). In addition, there were the inevitable differences stemming from the different disciplinary orientations of the archaeologist, the historian, the oral traditionalist, the art historian, the linguistics specialist, the ethnographer, the social anthropologist, the sociobiologist, the paleoecologist, and so on. In the new and more dynamic approach to the later African past, there seems to be a more seamless view of the past, so that archaeologists, for instance, are as likely to study the physical evidence of European colonialism as they are to investigate the origins of African iron-smelting, and any synthesis of the last few millennia in Africa has to strive for a holistic rather than a reductionist methodology, so far as different disciplinary contributions are concerned.

The series of essays presented here are important reminders of the dynamic character of Africa's later past. By the phrase 'later past,' which is deliberately vague, is meant the last twenty thousand years or so, but the main interest here is in only the last few thousand years. Most of these essays originated from papers presented at a conference that was held at the Humanities Research Centre of the Australian National University, Canberra, in June 1995, although they have been revised since then, in some cases substantially, and several have been added that were not given at the conference. The conference was the first of three held during 1995, all on the subject of Africa. The other two dealt, respectively, with African history (not yet published) and with contemporary Africa (Alexander, Hutchison and Schreuder, 1996), and as convenor of the first conference I was originally invited to run a conference called 'Ancient Africa.' This I declined to do, because the sheer enormity of such a subject, embracing everything from early hominids to Great Zimbabwe, made it an impractical proposition with only three days and limited resources. Instead, the conference was focused on later periods and was called, perhaps not very appropriately, 'Africa: precolonial achievement' (Connah, 1995). The invited speakers were asked to examine selected aspects of Africa's more recent past, aspects that demonstrated the dynamic complexity that actually existed in the continent before colonial contact. They were free, however, to interpret this invitation in whatever way they pleased. The result challenges yet again the former notion among scholars that little of significance happened during the later African past: we are given a series of insights into major elements of change over the last few thousand years and some indication of the interplay of change and continuity during that period. In the closing discussion at the conference, one of the African delegates present argued that outside of Africanist scholarship there is still a notion that African societies have changed little over the last twenty thousand years or so, and as a result the idea that Africa has no history has become ingrained in Western thought, with serious consequences, for instance, for international development policies. In actual fact, this speaker pointed out, the conference had reminded us how numerous and how complex were the transformations of African societies over the last few thousand years. It is from this remark that has come the title of this book, for in the new dynamic view of Africa's later past we are indeed principally concerned with transformations in Africa.

As Richard Lee and Robert Hitchcock demonstrate in their contribution, even the hunter-gatherers of Africa, who in the popular imagination have been thought of as the epitome of changelessness, have adapted and adjusted to the changing world around them during the last two millennia. Some have adopted pastoralism, others cultivation, and in recent times some have become a part of industrial society, while the remainder have often maintained complex and flexible interrelationships with farmers, cultivators, and industrial communities. Lee and Hitchcock show that these changes are still in progress, as African hunter-gatherers continue to renegotiate their relationships with those around them. Thus, for example, some of the modern representatives of Africa's oldest subsistence economy are now playing an active part in the identity politics of the new South Africa.

One of the most important transformations that has taken place in Africa during the last 7000 years or so is the adoption of food production, involving a major subsistence change whose mechanism is still not fully understood. As Joanna Casey points out in her chapter, one of the problems is that we still lack sufficient primary evidence to explain how and why this transition occurred. She examines the case of West Africa, where some of the earliest significant developments took place, and suggests that ecological factors could have played an important part in their timing and character. In particular, she suggests that the appearance of the wet and dry seasonal regime about 7500 years ago played a vital role in the development of plant food cultivation. It both necessitated and made possible the storage of seasonal products, and encouraged a tripartite subsistence system involving the interlocking seasonal activities of herding, harvesting, and fishing.

The development of social complexity in Africa, leading to the emergence of its first states and, although not necessarily related, the appearance of its first cities, implies sociopolitical changes of substantial magnitude. In the search for the origins of such changes, influences either external to Africa or from some other part of the continent have often been suggested as triggering mechanisms. In Kevin MacDonald's chapter he searches for the antecedents of Ghana, the earliest recorded state in West Africa, and finds them not in any external stimulus but in the premetallurgical pastoral societies of the Sahel about 6000 years ago. He discusses archaeological evidence that suggests the transitory appearance of what he terms 'Mobile Elites,' resulting from pastoral wealth and power accumulation. In cases where there were additional climatic or cultural stimuli semisedentary 'Chiefdoms' developed, such as Dhar Tichitt-Oualata in Mauritania and Kerma in the Sudan.

The advent of urbanization in Africa, challenging as it does the long-standing Eurocentric image of precolonial Africa as a continent of villages, was clearly a transformation of very great significance. Roland Fletcher examines the diversity of indigenous African urban settlements, which ranged from small compact entities to massive, dispersed ones. He discusses the relationship between areal extent and residential density within these settlements and considers how those which made little or no use of literacy were able to function. It is apparent that residential mobility played a significant role in these urban developments, with entire communities moving seasonally in some cases, as in Ethiopia, and substantial numbers of people moving in and out of urban settlements episodically and seasonally in the case of the West African forest regions.

Significant changes in African societies over the last few thousand years have taken place against a background of ecological change, brought about by changing rainfall patterns. Particularly is this the case in West Africa, where the interaction of ecological change and human response has had such profound consequences that George Brooks suggests that alternating wet and dry phases may be used to demarcate historical periods. He identifies and discusses seven such ecological–historical periods between approximately 18,000 BC and about AD 1860. His climatic information is drawn from a literature that is large, complex, and at times contradictory, and he stresses that much remains to be learned of West African rainfall patterns and their consequences. Nevertheless, his approach is important because it provides us with a periodization of West Africa's later past independent of European-derived chronologies, a periodization generated within Africa itself.

There must be few subjects concerning precolonial Africa that have generated as much discussion on the basis of slender evidence as the introduction of metallurgical technology some 2000 or more years ago. Here was a change that was ultimately to have widespread and profound socioeconomic and political consequences, and yet we still know relatively little about how it happened. James Woodhouse was not at the Canberra conference but I invited him to examine the relevant evidence and the theories which have been based on it. He discusses the weaknesses in the traditional view that iron metallurgy could not have developed independently in Africa because of the apparent lack of a previous pyrometallurgical tradition in copper. He shows how the case for diffusion from outside of Africa has weakened as our knowledge of the chronology of early iron-smelting has improved, but how evidence suggesting an indigenous development is still beset by problems. It appears that the jury is still out on this issue and that we do indeed have, as his title says, a case of 'metal from nowhere.'

Long-distance trade, with markets outside of Africa, has often been suggested as a major cause of change within past African societies. The complex and widespread trading systems of the African interior have had less attention and yet probably played a more immediate role. Henry Mutoro considers the precolonial trading systems of the East African interior, involving both subsistence-oriented and nonsubsistence-oriented trade. These were of great antiquity but the nonsubsistence-oriented trade, particularly in ivory and slaves, was stimulated over the last 1000 years or so by the growing demands of the coastal settlements striving to satisfy expanding markets in Europe and the Orient. Nevertheless, ultimate control of trade in the interior remained in the hands of the societies of the interior, or rather of their rulers, who were thus able to supplement traditional commodities with cloth, beads, and other exotic items. This trade also brought about considerable interaction both among the peoples of the interior and between them and the people of the coast. However, because of the character of the trade, it ultimately destroyed the economic infrastructures of the communities involved.

Among the major cultural developments of Africa's later past, along with those of Meroë and Aksum, must be considered the emergence of the Swahili city states of the East African coast. These are discussed by George Abungu, who examines the documentary evidence dating from early in the first millennium AD and the archaeological evidence dating from later in that millennium. He shows how the people of the coast participated in the Indian Ocean trade and had contact with the Arabian Peninsula, the Indian Subcontinent and South-East Asia. As a result, these East African coastal settlements received both goods and ideas from outside Africa, and showed evidence of such influence in both their architecture and their Islamic religion. However, these city states were intrinsically African in origin, in people, and in culture. They were essentially gateway communities, whose lives were shaped by the trade between the African interior and the wide world of the Indian Ocean.

It was the arrival of Europeans on the East African coast at the end of the fifteenth century AD that ultimately brought the Swahili city states to an end, and it is transformations in Africa resulting from the initial impact of European contact, trade, and colonization, that are the subject of the final chapter in this book, by Christopher DeCorse. Again, this is an invited chapter, as he was not present at the Canberra conference. He examines the evidence for African–European interaction in West Africa and emphasizes the contextual variation of such contacts, in which Europeans were often confined to the coast and African sociopolitical adjustments to contact could take place independently. He also considers the extent to which acculturation of African societies resulted from contact, and discusses the evidence from his excavations at the African settlement of Elmina, in Ghana, where, in spite of the presence of numerous European artifacts and European building methods, cultural continuity was more apparent than cultural change. Thus even the transformations resulting from initial European contact were in at least some cases African transformations, not European ones.

Overall, the nine chapters presented here, or 'essays' as they are called in the title of this book, can only sample the dynamic reality that was Africa's later past. There are many other aspects of that past that would also challenge the old static image but which it has not been possible to consider here. One such, for instance, is the appearance of city and town walls, and other settlement enclosures, in many parts of Africa over the last 1000 years or so. These structures, of stone, or mud, or earth, were frequently built on a massive scale. The probably fifteenth-century innermost earthwork at Benin City, in Nigeria, for example, was over 17 meters high and had a circumference of 11.6 kilometers (Connah, 1975: 88, 1987: 134), and the mud walls of Kano, also in Nigeria, were recorded by visitors during the nineteenth century as probably 20 meters high, flanked by a ditch approximately 15 meters deep (Staudinger, 1889 translated by Moody 1990, Vol. 1: 210), and with a circumference of about 24 kilometers (Denham, Clapperton and Oudney, 1826, Clapperton's Narrative: 50). Apart from being impressive in themselves, such structures have a great deal to tell us not only about the size and shape and character of the settlements that they contained, but also about surveying, engineering, and building skills, as well as about the existence of centralized direction or collective effort, and about labor availability. They are eloquent of an African past very different from that of the old Eurocentric popular image. As a visual reminder of the dynamic quality of Africa's later past, the cover of this book reproduces a late nineteenth-century drawing of the walled city of Tiong-i in southern Mali (Binger 1892, Vol. 1: 171). At first glance it looks like something from medieval Europe, and that in itself should make us think.

In one of the discussions at the Canberra conference, Julian Cobbing of Rhodes University, in South Africa, contrasted what he called the 'box categories,' that we so often use in our discussion of the African past, with what he called the 'fluidity of reality,' and suggested that the crucial point at issue was 'the fluidity of how we conceive things.' In attempting to identify and understand some of the major transformations of Africa's later past, it is worth keeping this in mind if we are to avoid merely creating a new static image that could obscure the dynamic reality that we actually seek.

BIBLIOGRAPHY

Alimen, H. (1957) *The prehistory of Africa*. Translated by Brodrick, A.H. London, Hutchinson.

Alexander, P.F., Hutchison, R. and Schreuder, D. (1996) (eds) *Africa today: a multi-disciplinary snapshot of the continent in 1995*. Canberra, The Humanities Research Centre, Australian National University.

Binger, Le Capitaine (1892) *Du Niger au Golfe de Guinée: par le pays de Kong et le Mossi*. 2 vols. Paris, Hachette.

Childe, V.G. (1942) *What happened in history*. Harmondsworth, Penguin.

Chittick, H.N. (1971) The coast of East Africa. In Shinnie, P.L. (ed.) *The African Iron Age*. Oxford: Clarendon, pp. 108–41.

Clark, J.D. (1957) *Third Pan-African Congress on Prehistory, Livingstone 1955*. London, Chatto & Windus.

Clark, J.D. (1970) *The prehistory of Africa*. London, Thames and Hudson.

Clark, G. (1961) *World prehistory: an outline*. Cambridge, Cambridge University Press.

Clark, G. (1969) *World prehistory: a new outline*. Cambridge, Cambridge University Press.

Clark, G. (1977) *World prehistory: in new perspective*. Cambridge, Cambridge University Press.

Cole, S. (1954) *The prehistory of East Africa*. Harmondsworth, Penguin.

Connah, G. (1975) *The archaeology of Benin: excavations and other researches in and around Benin City, Nigeria*. Oxford, Clarendon Press.

Connah, G. (1981) *Three thousand years in Africa: Man and his environment in the Lake Chad region of Nigeria*. Cambridge, Cambridge University Press.

Connah, G. (1987) *African civilizations: precolonial cities and states in tropical Africa: an archaeological perspective*. Cambridge, Cambridge University Press.

Connah, G. (1995) Africa: precolonial achievement. A conference held 10–12 June 1995 at the Humanities Research Centre, Australian National University, Canberra. *Australian Historical Association Bulletin* 81: 35–9.

Connah, G. (1996) *Kibiro: the salt of Bunyoro, past and present*. London, Memoirs of the British Institute in Eastern Africa, No. 13.

Cotterell, A. (ed.) (1983) *The encyclopedia of ancient civilizations*. London, Macmillan.

Daniel, G. (1943) *The three ages*. Cambridge, Cambridge University Press.

Daniel, G. (1964) *The idea of prehistory*. Harmondsworth, Penguin.

Daniel, G. (1968) *The first civilizations: the archaeology of their origins*. London, Thames and Hudson.

Denham, D., Clapperton, H. & Oudney, W. (1826) *Narrative of travels and discoveries in Northern and Central Africa, in the years 1822, 1823, and 1824*. London, Murray.

Fagan, B.M. (1967) *Iron Age cultures in Zambia, Vol. I: Kalomo and Kangila*. London, Chatto & Windus.

Fagg, B.E.B. (1959) The Nok Culture in prehistory. *Journal of the Historical Society of Nigeria* 1(4): 288–93.

Frankfort, H. (1951) *The birth of civilization in the Near East.* London, Benn.

Garlake, P.S. (1973) *Great Zimbabwe.* New York, Stein and Day.

Mason, R. (1969) *Prehistory of the Transvaal.* Johannesburg, Witwatersrand University Press.

Newton, A.P. (1923) Africa and historical research. *Journal of the African Society* 22(88): 266–77.

Oliver, R. (1961) *The dawn of African history.* London, Oxford University Press.

Phillipson, D.W. (1985) *African archaeology.* Cambridge, Cambridge University Press.

Phillipson, D.W. (1993) *African archaeology.* 2nd edn, Cambridge, Cambridge University Press.

Shaw, T. (1989) African archaeology: looking back and looking forward. *African Archaeological Review* 7: 3–31.

Staudinger, P. (1889) *Im Herzen der Haussaländer.* Berlin, Landsberger. Translated by Moody, J. (1990) *In the heart of the Hausa states.* 2 vols. Athens, Ohio, Ohio University Center for International Studies.

Willett, F. (1967) *Ife in the history of West African sculpture.* London, Thames and Hudson.

CHAPTER 2

AFRICAN HUNTER-GATHERERS: HISTORY AND THE POLITICS OF ETHNICITY

Richard B. Lee and Robert K. Hitchcock

When exploring Africa's considerable precolonial achievements, the focus has tended to be on the great kingdoms of the Sudan and upper Nile, or on the great migrations of the Iron Age peoples. Less heralded (and at times virtually ignored) are the African peoples who pursued a hunting and gathering way of life, first in isolation and then as neighbors (and clients) of the agricultural peoples. Ninety percent of the human history of the African continent is a history of hunting and gathering (the same is true of course in Europe and Asia). The legacy of the hunters and gatherers can be seen everywhere in Africa. Their rock art speaks across the centuries of an older African spirituality. Their history of interaction and assimilation with other African peoples is inscribed, for example, in language with the click sounds used by millions of Zulu and Xhosa speakers.

The archaeology of Africa's hunter-gatherer peoples is a rich and complex story. And in spite of the waves of migrants, the hunter-gatherers have shown astonishing resilience. They have maintained their identity in over a dozen African countries, from Uganda, Kenya, and Tanzania in the east, to Gabon and Cameroon in the west, to Botswana, Namibia, and South Africa in the south.

Some current theories have tended to portray the hunters as dominated for centuries by powerful Iron Age overlords. While this view certainly holds for some peoples — for example the Twa of Rwanda — this cannot be generalized. As recent scholarship has shown, in many areas hunters and gatherers met their agricultural neighbors on the basis of relative equality, and were able to maintain a degree of autonomy well into the present century. Studies of contemporary African hunter-gatherers such as the Hadza, Mbuti, Okiek, /Gwi, and Ju/'hoansi illustrate both the integrity of their lifeways and the histories of their articulation with other societies.

One of the most interesting social phenomena of the post-Apartheid era has been the rediscovery of their 'Khoisan' roots by students and intellectuals of the 'Colored' population in South Africa. Led by historians of the University of the Western Cape, this movement seeks to 'recapture' a history which has been submerged by missionization and forced acculturation. The Khoisan revival promises to bring new energy into the identity politics of the region, and new perspectives on the study of southern African hunters and gatherers.

When exploring Africa's considerable precolonial achievements, one rarely focuses on the hunter-gatherers. Yet it was they who had sole dominion over the continent for millennia before the advent of agriculture, the Bantu expansion, and the rise of the great kingdoms of the savanna and Sudan. Africa is the cradle of humankind, and ninety percent of human history in Africa and elsewhere is the history of hunting and gathering. The legacy of Africa's hunter-gatherers can be found in the magnificent rock art of the Sahara and the eastern and southern part of the continent and the widespread remains of ancient sites. The hunter-gatherer legacy is more subtly inscribed in the click sounds found in Hadza and San languages in eastern and southern Africa and in Zulu and Xhosa spoken by millions of contemporary South Africans. The hunter-gatherer presence in Africa is woven into the fabric of life as well as the myths, stories, placenames, and the cultural imagination of the continent's peoples, both black and white.

Africa today is a continent of city folk, traders, wage workers, farmers, and herders. Yet even in the 1990s, over 400,000 of Africa's people would identify themselves as foragers or former foragers (Table 2.1). Two hunter-gatherer groups, the San and the Pygmies, represent classic cases in the ethnographic canon (Murdock, 1959; Burger, 1987: 171–4). In addition, there are a number of other groups like the Hadza, the Okiek, and the Boni, that are less known but of equal interest.

The archaeology of Africa's hunter-gatherer peoples provides some of the earliest traces of human presence anywhere in the world. Hilary Deacon has reported fully human remains dating 90,000–120,000 BP at the Klasies River Mouth site in the eastern Cape of South Africa. And John Yellen, Alison Brooks, and their colleagues have found what is arguably the earliest example of an aesthetic impulse in the making of a tool, a bone harpoon some 60,000 years old from the Semliki Valley of eastern Democratic Republic of Congo (Yellen et al., 1995; Gibbons, 1995).

Our purpose here, however, is not to go into the deeper archaeological time-depths. The focus will be on the contemporary hunter-gatherers of Africa, their contributions to African civilization, and their attempts to preserve or rediscover their political and cultural identities in a continent besieged by crisis.

During the last few millennia the encounter between resident hunter-gatherers and incoming farmers and herders has formed one of the key themes in African history and oral traditions (Kopytoff, 1987; Smith, 1992). The nature of this interface between foragers and others has become an area of lively debate in anthropology and archaeology (Clark and Brandt, 1984; Schrire, 1984; Wilmsen, 1989). The prevailing view that African hunter-gatherers had been relatively autonomous societies until recently has required revision. The appearance of farming and herding in parts of southern Africa, for example, has been steadily pushed back, to the early first millennium AD. How these earlier

Table 2.1 Population sizes of African indigenous peoples who are or were hunter-gatherers

Name of group	Location	Population size	References
Bushmen	Angola	8000	de Almeida (1965); Burger (1987: 166)
Bushmen	Botswana	48,220	Hitchcock (1996)
Batwa (Pygmies)	Central Africa	200,000	Turnbull (1961, 1983); Cavalli-Sforza (1986)
Aka		30,000	Bahuchet (1988, 1991); Hewlett (1996)
Baka		30,000	Hewlett (1996)
Mbuti		27,000	Ichikawa (1978, 1983)
Efe		3000	Bailey (1991)
Boni (Aweer)	Kenya	2000	Stiles (1981, 1993a)
Dahalo	Kenya	5200	Stiles (1981, 1993b)
Okiek (Dorobo)	Kenya	40,000	Blackburn (1974, 1982, 1996); Kratz (1994)
Wata	Kenya		Stiles (1981, 1993b)
Mikea	Madagascar	1000	Stiles (1991, 1993b); Kelly and Poyer (1993)
Ovatjimba	Namibia	500	MacCalman and Grobbelaar (1965); Jacobsohn (pers. comm.)
Bushmen	Namibia	38,000	Marshall (1989); Gordon (1992); Hitchcock (1992, 1996); Biesele (1994)
Eyle	Somalia	450	S. Brandt (pers. comm.)
Kilii	Somalia	1500	Stiles (1981, 1993b)
Bushmen	South Africa	4200	Southern African San Institute (pers. comm.)
Okiek	Tanzania	2000	Blackburn (pers. comm.)
Hadza	Tanzania	1000	Woodburn (1964, 1968); Ndagala (1988, 1993); Blurton Jones *et al.* (1989, n.d.); Kaare (1994)
Kwandu	Zambia	5500	Clark (1951); Reynolds (1972a, 1972b)
Bushmen (Tyua)	Zimbabwe	1000	Hitchcock (1995, 1996); G. Haynes (pers. comm.)
Doma (VaDema)	Zimbabwe	500	C. Cutshall, M. Murphree (pers. comms)
TOTAL		438,670	

Note: Data for this table were also obtained from researchers, community institutions, development agency files, nongovernment organizations, censuses, government reports, and national, church, and private archives.

dates are to be interpreted, however, has been contested. Some analysts have taken the earlier dates as evidence that hunters were everywhere dominated by powerful Iron Age overlords (Wilmsen, 1989; Wilmsen and Denbow, 1990). Others have argued for the persistance of relative independence of at least some foragers up to the present (Solway and Lee, 1990; Lee and Guenther, 1991, 1993, 1995).

It is difficult to generalize across the continent. In fact, hunter-gatherers in Africa today are strikingly diverse socially, ethnically, and economically. They range from forest foragers and part-time foragers living symbiotically close to agricultural villagers (such as the various groups of Pygmies), to relatively independent communities only recently incorporated into regional and international economies and polities (like the Hadza and some San).

Despite a diversity of origins and present circumstances, a few general points can be made. In some ways African foragers display the characteristics common to other societies in their regions, speaking local languages and adopting local customs. In other important ways they have maintained distinct identities. Most of the hunter-gatherers exhibit a pattern of flexible and relatively egalitarian band organization common to hunter-gatherers elsewhere. In their internal sociopolitical organization they have tended to be far less rigid and hierarchical than the norm of their agricultural and pastoral neighbors.

Their flexibility and mobility work both to their advantage and disadvantage. In the event of war or famine, they have the desert or the rainforest to fall back on. They have the ability to survive outside the system. On the other hand, their lack of hierarchy meant that when outsiders exerted sufficient political or military force, the foragers could not easily resist and sooner or later came to be dominated by others.

A third characteristic common to all African hunters and gatherers is in land tenure. In most of Africa land has been held communally, with little overall tendency for the consolidation of land rights in the hands of a few. Instead, varied rights over land with multiple forms of control and access existed. In important ways these forms of tenure have preserved a space for foragers to maintain access to traditional resources. However, recent land reform efforts of many governments have led to dispossession of foragers and their neighbors, for example, in Tanzania, Kenya, Somalia, Botswana, Zimbabwe, and South Africa (Hitchcock, 1993, 1995; Miller, 1993; Veber et al., 1993).

The status of forager groups in several countries has declined so seriously that a number of them have sought assistance from development agencies, church groups, or philanthropies. Others have become environmental activists, protesting against ill-advised development projects such as the ranching, mining, and irrigation schemes initiated by governments and international donor agencies (Durning, 1989, 1992; Miller, 1993). Still others have initiated their own self-help efforts, as is the case with the Ju/'hoansi of northeastern

Namibia and their Nyae Nyae Farmers Cooperative (Biesele, 1990, 1994; Lee, 1993).

With the rise of Green politics and the growing interest in the plight of indigenous peoples, hunter-gatherer populations in Africa have become an important political focal point in recent years (Burger, 1990; Miller, 1993; Veber et al., 1993). A number of advocacy groups support African hunters and gatherers in their struggles to find their place (Hitchcock, 1993, 1996; Hitchcock and Holm, 1993, 1995). Concern about their survival has heightened as a result of the rising number of reports of violations of their civil, political, and socioeconomic rights (Amnesty International, 1992; Gurr, 1993; Hitchcock, 1994). Despite this, it went largely unnoted, for example, in the media coverage of the recent Rwanda tragedy that as many as three-quarters of Rwanda's 30,000 Batwa Pygmies allegedly were killed during the genocidal actions that occurred there between April and July, 1994 (New York Times August 25, 1994). The problems faced by San in Botswana who allegedly were tortured and who died at the hands of wildlife officers and police received somewhat more attention, but relatively little was done in the way of official investigations into the charges (Mogwe, 1992; U.S. Department of State, 1993: 13–14; Washington Post December 18, 1995).

AFRICAN HUNTER-GATHERERS AS DISCOURSE

Writing about hunter-gatherers today has to deal with a century of discourse. Some of this discourse is rooted in European and African notions of 'difference' and race, other discourse springs from European ideas of 'natural man'. All of these are closely bound up in complex discourses that accompanied European colonialism and imperialism (Wolf, 1982). These ideologically saturated discourses form an implicit background of unstated assumptions, predispositions, and prejudices. Nineteenth-century European settlers in the main regarded the hunter-gatherers with thinly veiled contempt, as incorrigible bandits speaking scarcely intelligible tongues. The South African San along with the Khoikhoi ('Hottentots') were positioned on the bottom rung on the scala natura of humanity, serving as a symbol for ruminations on who may or may not be part of the human family (Moodie, 1976; Thompson, 1985; Gordon, 1992). A more nuanced view of the hunter-gatherers was expressed by their agricultural and pastoral neighbors, who while according them an inferior social position, nevertheless regarded them with a mixture of paternalism and condescension, fear and respect (Grinker, 1990, 1994).

European attitudes in this century have undergone an almost complete reversal; witness the idealization of the Bushmen as the embodiment of noble virtues in the writing of Laurens van der Post (1958, 1961) and Jamie Uys' film

The gods must be crazy (Uys, 1980). Conservationists, indigenous rights advocates, and ethnographers have written about the hunter-gatherers in largely positive ways (Burger, 1987, 1990; Durning, 1992; Kent, 1996). The European public continues to see in the Bushmen and Pygmies images of the good and simple life lived close to nature. Although attitudes of African peasant neighbors of the hunter-gatherers have not changed radically, among elites 'racial' attitudes have hardened, as can be seen in the negative views of the San (Basarwa) among Botswana's political class (Mogwe, 1992; Hitchcock and Holm, 1993).

In the 1990s, the hunting and gathering peoples of Africa face a number of serious problems: conflict with neighbors over a shrinking land base, pressures to subordinate themselves to state policies that limit their mobility and freedom of action, and strong pressures to assimilate to the cultural practices of their neighbors (Hitchcock, 1993, 1995; Veber *et al.*, 1993; Kent, 1996). In some ways, situations have worsened as conflicts over resources have increased and states, companies, and individuals have expanded into remote areas to exploit resources ranging from timber to medicinal plants. In a few cases, notably Rwanda, foraging Pygmies (Twa) have been subjected to genocidal actions (Human Rights Watch, 1996). The socioeconomic deterioration that occurred in the interior of Somalia in the 1990s had spillover effects on Eyle peoples (Mohamed Farah, personal communication).

The 1990s have also seen rising political mobilization among African former foraging peoples, with meetings being held in Africa as well as elsewhere (e.g. Europe, North America) in which problems facing African populations were addressed (Veber *et al.*, 1993; Hitchcock, 1996). These meetings came up with a whole series of recommendations about how improvements could be made by states, international agencies, and African communities so that local people's standards of living were enhanced. After a brief survey of African hunter-gatherers, we explore in more detail how themes of hunter-gatherer pasts are woven into contemporary political consciousness, particularly in post-Apartheid South Africa and its neighbors.

AFRICAN HUNTER-GATHERERS: NATIONS WITHIN NATIONS

The historical status of African hunters and gatherers is a subject of ongoing discussion among archaeologists, anthropologists, and ethnohistorians (Elphick, 1977; Clark and Brandt, 1984; Schrire, 1984; Wilmsen, 1989; Gordon, 1992; Barnard, 1992a, 1992b; Kent, 1996). At least some contemporary foragers are linked by archaeology, rock art, and oral traditions to ancient hunter-gatherers (Dowson, 1992). Others may represent more recent readaptations to hunting and gathering. At times of civil strife and

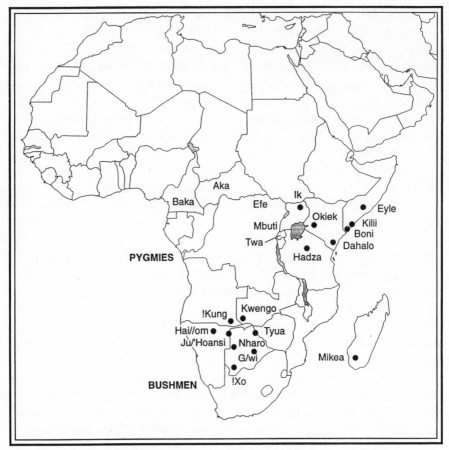

Fig. 2.1 African hunter-gatherers.

rapid change hunter-gatherer groups may have functioned as refuges from war and famine.

African foragers group themselves into three regional supercategories in central, east, and southern Africa: the 200,000 pygmies of central Africa, the 100,000 east African hunter-gatherers from a variety of locales, and the approximately 100,000 Bushmen/San of the semiarid savannas of southern Africa (Fig. 2.1). The Pygmy groups reside in the rain-forest regions of eight and possibly nine countries: Cameroon, Central African Republic, Congo, Gabon, Guinea, Rwanda, Uganda, Zambia, and perhaps Angola (Cavalli-Sforza, 1986; Bailey and DeVore, 1989). Non-Pygmy hunter-gatherers are found in six East African countries: Rwanda, Uganda, Tanzania, Kenya, Somalia, and Ethiopia (Stiles, 1981; Blackburn, 1982, 1996; Kratz, 1994). While Bushmen currently reside in six as well: Angola, Botswana, Namibia, South Africa, Zambia, and Zimbabwe (Hitchcock, 1996).

CENTRAL AFRICA

The Pygmies, considered the classic 'forest peoples' in the writings of the late Colin Turnbull (1961, 1965, 1983), have made their home in the tropical rain forest, one of the world's most challenging environments (Bailey, 1991; Bailey and DeVore, 1989; Cavalli-Sforza, 1986; Harako, 1981). Until recently archaeologists assumed that the Pygmies were the 'original' inhabitants of the rain forest where they had lived for millennia as hunters and gatherers before the arrival of agricultural peoples. But current opinion varies on whether humans indeed *can* live exclusively by foraging the wild products of the rain forest, or whether some form of symbiosis with farmers is a necessary part of the pygmies' adaptation (Bailey *et al.*, 1989; Bahuchet, 1991; Bahuchet, McKey and de Garine, 1991). Whatever the answer, Pygmies identify closely with the forest; they live partially but not exclusively on the wild products of the rain forest ecosystem; and they make the forest the center of their intellectual and spiritual life.

All Pygmy populations relate in complex ways to non-Pygmy village peoples for whom they work or with whom they exchange goods and services (Turnbull, 1965, 1983; Hewlett, 1996). These diverse interactions range from relative autonomy with occasional contact, to long-term hereditary servitude. Today some Pygmies do live self-sufficiently, but not strictly on the forest itself; rather, they subsist on a combination of wage labor, barter, food production, and wild resource exploitation (Bahuchet, 1988, 1991; Bahuchet, McKey and de Garine, 1991; Hewlett, 1993, 1996; Grinker, 1994).

Colin Turnbull's thoughtful studies of the Mbuti pygmies made this group famous to thousands of readers. Turnbull noted how diffident the Mbuti were towards outsiders when residing in the villages, and how their demeanor changed and their personalities blossomed when they entered the forest for a period of extended foraging. The non-Pygmy villagers feared the forest and rarely entered it, while the Mbuti regarded it with great affection as the source of their well-being, and celebrated it in their myths and ceremonials (Turnbull, 1961, 1965, 1983).

All contemporary Pygmy populations either speak Bantu and Sudanic languages related to those of their farming neighbors, or else they can communicate with their neighbors through lingua francas such as Lingala, the national language of the Democratic Republic of Congo, or KiNgwna, a dialect of Swahili (Cavalli-Sforza, 1986; Grinker, 1994). While the Pygmy hunters still obtain a significant portion of their subsistence from wild foods, the bulk of the diet today is obtained from agricultural sources. They receive payments in kind for the work done for villagers, as well as tending their own gardens, and from the sale of forest products and crafts.

In the case of the Dzanga-Sangha forest special reserve in the Central African Republic (CAR), Baka Pygmy communities are being assisted in economic development and conservation promotion by an interdisciplinary team composed of ecologists, social scientists, and health and rural development workers. This project, which is sponsored in part by the World Wildlife Fund (USA) and the US Agency for International Development (USAID), supports self-help activities and assists in the establishment of both formal and informal village associations. Some of the Baka are working as tourist guides while others are selling goods on the commercial market that they obtain from the forest or manufacture themselves. Health workers do immunizations, provide first aid assistance, and practice preventative medicine (Kretsinger, 1993). Conservation efforts are promoted through limiting the number of trees extracted in timbering activities, setting upper limits on the number of tourists visiting the area, and enforcing game laws.

It is interesting to compare the Baka in the Dzanga-Sangha Dense Forest Reserve with those involved in other kinds of rural development projects that involve Pygmy populations in central Africa. The Baka Pygmies in Cameroon have been affected by a number of sedentarization programs that include the establishment of permanent village settlements and agricultural projects since the 1960s (Hewlett, 1993). The Ministry of Social Affairs of the Government of Cameroon (GOC) established a program aimed at enhancing the living conditions of marginalized groups in 1975. Some of the funding from this program was utilized to conduct studies of the Baka and Bakola Pygmies. The Cameroon government also coordinated the activities of various nongovernment organizations such as SNV (The Dutch Assistance Program) and the French Association of Volunteers for Progress, as well as Catholic missionary groups. Impacts of the programs included enhancing the degree of dependence on food production efforts, raising literacy rates, and increasing health and nutritional status. Similar kinds of efforts have been undertaken among a number of other former foragers in central and eastern Africa (Ndagala, 1988, 1993; Hitchcock, 1993; Kaare, 1994).

EAST AFRICA

Sizable numbers of hunter-gatherers still exist in and near the Rift Valley (Okiek and Hadza), along the East African Coast (the Dahalo as well as Degere and Wata), and around the Juba and Tana rivers near the Kenya–Somali border (the Boni, Kilii [Aweer], and Eyle). The Okiek (Dorobo) of Kenya and Tanzania occupy forested areas in or adjacent to the Rift Valley of central Kenya south to northern Tanzania (van Zwandenberg, 1976; Blackburn, 1982, 1996; Kratz, 1994). Today the majority of Okiek have taken up farming, livestock production, and wage labor; they also participate extensively in exchanges and entrepreneurial activities of various kinds such as bee-keeping and manufacturing of implements.

Because the Okiek were not recognized officially by either colonial or postcolonial governments, they frequently were denied land or resource access rights. Eviction from their traditional areas was common since their land was sometimes gazetted for game reserves; destruction of their forest habitat has followed as a result of agricultural expansion or overgrazing (Rod Blackburn, personal communication).

Like the Bushmen, the Hadza are click-speaking peoples who differ significantly from their neighbors both linguistically and socioeconomically. The 1000 Hadza (Hadzabe) of the region around Lake Eyasi in northern Tanzania are foragers who, despite interactions with their neighbors, have maintained a fierce independence, owning few livestock, not cultivating crops, and remaining in remote areas (Woodburn, 1964, 1970; Blurton Jones, Hawkes and O'Connell, 1989, n.d.). At various times the government of Tanzania has made attempts to contact the Hadza and settle them, usually with disastrous results; the Hadza then returned to the life in the bush (McDowell, 1981a, 1981b; Ndagala, 1988). The Hadza have also been affected by the expansion of herders and farmers into their area, the imposition of wildlife laws, and the expanding tourism and contract farming industries (Ndagala, 1993; Kaare, 1994; Blurton Jones, Hawkes and O'Connell, n.d.).

A major comparative question is why the Hadza have repeatedly deserted the settlements, while other African foragers, like the San and Okiek, have involved themselves quite extensively and voluntarily in economic and other interactions with their herder neighbors.

There are several different hunter-gatherer groups in southern Somalia, including the Kilii (Aweer) and the Eyle (Stiles, 1981a, 1981b). Both groups were affected by the traumas of recent Somali history, including famine, militarization, civil war, and relief operations. The Somali hunter-gatherers underscore the fact people may become foragers either out of choice or necessity. In some instances, individuals turned to foraging because their domestic subsistence base was destroyed. In others, people chose to be foragers to avoid being caught in the crossfire of feuding subclans. Still others assumed Eyle or some other hunter-gatherer group's identity so as to remain unnoticed in a complex sociopolitical situation in which Somali clan members were being targeted by members of other clans.

SOUTHERN AFRICA

The hunting and gatherering San (Bushmen, Basarwa, Khwe) share physical traits and linguistic affinities with the pastoral Khoikhoi (Schapera, 1930; Elphick, 1977; Nurse and Jenkins, 1977). Together they form the *Khoisan* cultural/linguistic grouping (Lee and DeVore, 1976; Barnard, 1992a). Known to millions as leather-clad foragers, the San peoples of southern Africa, numbering slightly over 100,000, display the same range of social conditions as other African hunter-gatherers. San are found on white-owned freehold farms working as laborers, on the ranches and cattle posts of Tswana and Herero livestock owners, and on the peripheries of game reserves where they work as guides (Hitchcock, 1996). Some of them live in the major towns of Botswana, Namibia, and Zimbabwe where they do a variety of activities ranging from working as domestic servants to gardening and from car, truck, and tractor repair to practicing as traditional healers. Representations of San history show a similar range (Lee, 1979, 1993; Lee and DeVore, 1976; Wilmsen, 1989; Gordon, 1992).

To some South African whites the San have assumed iconic status, cast in the role of 'Urmenschen' in a vision of pristine Africa, while in Botswana, elite Africans see the 'Basarwa' as quite the opposite: a social problem, a feckless underclass standing in the way of progress. (It is striking how closely these contemporary African elite views mirror those of white settlers of the last century.)

The changing nomenclature over the last 30 years reflects some of these issues. In the late 1960s, the term 'Bushmen', considered perjorative, was replaced in scholarly circles by the seemingly more neutral indigenous term 'San,' introduced by Monica Wilson and Leonard Thompson in their *Oxford History of South Africa* (Wilson and Thompson, 1968). But the term 'San' was not without its detractors. Meaning 'aborigines or settlers proper' in the Khoi language (Hahn, 1881), it also had the connotation of 'worthless vagabond.' In 1992, when a group of literate 'San' (Namibian Ju/'hoansi) were asked to comment on the terms 'San' and 'Bushmen,' they said they preferred the latter; 'San' meant nothing to them and 'Bushmen,' though perjorative, could be reinvested with a more dignified meaning (Biesele, 1993; Hitchcock, 1996). In solidarity, scholars reintroduced the term 'Bushmen' in the 1990s, though many continued to use the term 'San'.

At a Basarwa Research Conference held in Gaborone, Botswana, in August 1995, it was noted that the various groups in Botswana are today referring to themselves collectively as 'Basarwa,' the Setswana term for Bushmen. John Hardbattle, one of the founders of the advocacy group Kgeikani Kweni (First People of the Kalahari) suggested the use of the term N/oakwe. Subsequently, the term 'Khwe' was employed by members of Kgeikani Kweni for all indigenous southern African peoples known also as 'Basarwa,' 'Bushmen,' and 'San.' In October, 1996, at a meeting held in South Africa, it was decided 'once and for all,' to adopt the term 'San' and the new South African advocacy organization supporting indigenous peoples who were former foragers is known as the South African San Institute (SASI) (Roger Chennels, Axel Thoma, Braam LeRoux, personal communications).

In the past the San occupied most of the subcontinent south of the Zambezi

River; archaeologically their presence is attested to in the hundreds of rock painting and engraving sites associated with Later-Stone-Age tool assemblages, a legacy of world–historic proportions (Lewis-Williams, 1981; Dowson, 1992). At the Klasies River Mouth, site of the earliest known appearance of modern human beings (at *c.* 120,000 years ago), Hilary Deacon (personal communication) argues that the resident populations were lineal ancestors of the modern Khoisan peoples.

With the entrance of domestic sheep and pottery, and, later, iron and cattle, as early as the first century AD, the character of southern African populations began to change (Nurse and Jenkins, 1977; Hall, 1987). But even during the last two millennia the San were the exclusive occupants of significant portions of southern Africa, living as autonomous hunter-gatherers in parts of the Kalahari and Namib Deserts (Solway and Lee, 1990). For much of this period there is evidence of trade relations between the San peoples and their non-San neighbors (Phillipson, 1985; Wilmsen, 1989; Wilmsen and Denbow, 1990). To the southwest they interacted with the closely related Khoi (Hottentot) pastoralists from whom they differentiated linguistically sometime before the first millennium AD; well over half of all the San today speak Khoi languages (Silberbauer, 1981; Tanaka, 1980).

In the east and southeastern parts of South Africa they coexisted, intermarried, and were eventually assimilated to powerful Bantu-speaking chiefdoms which now form the bulk of South Africa's population; the standard explanation for the numerous click sounds found in modern Zulu, Swazi, and Xhosa is the linguistic influence of click-speakers, assumed to be female, intermarrying with Bantu-speakers and passing on the clicks to their offspring, according to linguists.

San peoples played a major role in the colonial history of South Africa. They met the early explorers at the Cape, guided them into the interior and later fought tenaciously to preserve their land in the face of European expansion (Wright, 1971; Marks, 1972; Elphick, 1977; Szalay, 1995). Their art, myth, and folklore became part of the South African historical and literary canon, in the works of such writers as W. H. I. Bleek and Lucy Lloyd (1911), Eugene Marais (1957), and J. M. Stow, George McCall Theal, and Laurens van der Post. And today Bushman themes provide a seemingly inexhaustible source of inspiration for South African artists, poets, filmmakers, and writers like Pippa Skotnes.

How these rich sources of the literary and artistic imagination refract and are refracted by the contemporary social conditions of Bushman/San peoples is an important question. When the San had been hounded almost to extinction in South Africa proper, it was believed, at the turn of the century, that they were a 'dying race.' However, in the Kalahari Desert and surrounding areas thousands of San remained, speaking many different dialects, and existing in a wide variety of socioeconomic situations (Schapera, 1930; Biesele *et al.,* 1989;

Barnard, 1992a; Hitchcock, 1996). Namibia has over 38,000 Bushmen including the Hai//om and Ju/'hoansi, who today are found on white farms, in urban areas, in former government-sponsored settlements such as the famous Tjum!kui located in Bushmanland, and in small communities where people make their living through a mixture of foraging, herding, and rural industries (Marshall, 1976; Marshall and Ritchie, 1984; Biesele, 1990, 1994; Gordon, 1992; Hitchcock, 1992, 1996). Many are living on farms and land that belong to other people, which puts them at a disadvantage in the modern state of Namibia.

The !Kung and Vasekele populations in Angola and Namibia were heavily affected by the long wars waged by the Portuguese and South Africans against African liberation movements (Lee, 1993; Marshall and Ritchie, 1984; Biesele et al., 1989). In addition, a number of Bushmen in Namibia, Zimbabwe, and Botswana were dispossessed as a result of the establishment of game reserves and national parks (Gordon, 1992; Hitchcock, 1995, 1996). Ranching, agriculture, dams, and road projects have also had significant impacts on the well-being of San and other remote area populations (Wily, 1979; Gordon, 1992; Hitchcock, 1995; Hitchcock and Holm, 1993). In spite of the constraints they face, individual San and some San communities have entered the national economies of southern African states as marginally successful food producers and wage workers (Biesele et al., 1989; Hitchcock, 1996). Others remain dependent on the state for support via welfare payments and drought relief (Mogwe 1992; Hitchcock and Holm, 1993). As in Namibia, some Botswana San have become full-time employees of nongovernment organizations that work directly with San peoples.

The Republic of Botswana is unusual in Africa in that it has had a program aimed directly at assisting its indigenous hunting-gathering minority, the Bushmen or, as they are known in Botswana, the *Basarwa* (Wily, 1979, 1982; Lee, 1979, 1993; Guenther, 1986; Hitchcock, 1996; Hitchcock and Holm, 1993). In spite of the Botswana Government's Remote Area Development Program, the socioeconomic status of the 50,000 San has declined considerably in recent years. Regarded by other Africans as ethnically distinct, their current class position is compounded by disabilities of race and ethnicity. Thus the internal politics of the Botswana Basarwa have come to resemble very much a politics of the oppressed (Hitchcock and Holm, 1993, 1995).

Many if not most of the Bushmen of Botswana are seeking at least a certain degree of cultural and political autonomy. They would like land of their own and, as they put it, 'to be left alone so that we can live the way we wish.' As one Kua man put it, 'We are different from the Tswana majority, and we have the right to be different.' The Botswana government, on the other hand, is pursuing a policy of assimilation ('villagization') (Wily, 1979; Hitchcock and Holm, 1993). As some government officials have said, 'We must absorb all of "these people" into the body politic of the nation of Botswana.'

One government official told a review committee in 1990 that: 'There should be no "Bushman Problem" since we are doing everything possible to make sure that they have sufficient economic opportunities.' The problem is that the kinds of strategies that are being attempted have had relatively little effect in increasing decision-making power and social and political rights among San groups, something that concerns San leaders and community members greatly.

Self-determination has not been achieved by the San of Botswana, as indeed is the case for virtually all former foragers in Africa. Some former foraging groups have engaged in armed struggles against the states in which they resided, as was seen among the Tyua ('Amasili') in Zimbabwe (Hitchcock, 1995). While conflicts between indigenous groups and the state are by no means rare in Africa (Clay, 1994; Gurr 1993; Gurr and Harff, 1994; Neitschmann 1994), most former foraging groups have tended to shy away from outright rebellion and war. San generally have sought nonviolent means of opposing state and international agency policies (Hitchcock, 1996). These peaceful means have sometimes achieved significant results, as occurred in 1990–91 when River Bushmen joined other ethnic groups in the Okavango Delta region of north-western Botswana to oppose the establishment of the Southern Okavango Integrated Water Development Project, a project which they contended would have negative effects on their livelihoods.

In most cases, however, San in Botswana generally have little say about the kinds of development activities that affect them. Decisions are often made by outsiders, including the central government, district councils, land boards, companies, cattle owners, and even members of the Remote Area Development Program (RADP), the institution established by the government of Botswana in 1974 to meet the needs of Bushmen and other remote area groups (Wily, 1979; Hitchcock and Holm, 1993).

Some San have called for the rights to make their own decisions about development while others have requested land of their own (Wily, 1979, 1994; Mogwe, 1992; Hitchcock, 1996). This does not mean, however, that they are seeking to secede from Botswana or that they want a separate country for themselves. Rather, Bushmen want the right of political participation and the opportunity to have a say in matters relating to their own internal and local affairs, including access to land, information, education, health services, development assistance and pursuit of their own types of cultural and religious activities.

KHOISAN MARGINALITY: HISTORICAL PERSPECTIVES

The current disadvantaged status of San people in Botswana raises important issues of history. Were they always subordinated to more powerful outsiders, or is their present plight a recent phenomenon, preceded by a longer history of autonomous foraging? Before that question can be addressed, we have to consider a priori, one of the relationship between historic 'Khoi' pastoralists and 'San' hunter-gatherers. Were they ever separate peoples or were the San in the Cape merely impoverished Khoi, who had lost their cattle and sheep? And similarly, could San people adopt cattle husbandry and immediately 'raise themselves up?' Richard Elphick (1977) argued for the fluidity and interchangeability between Khoi and San in the Cape area, and the perspectives he provided have been influential (Schrire, 1984). Whatever the situation in the Cape (and the archaeological evidence is complex), there were certainly many San groups outside the Cape without a history of herding (Smith, 1992). The major issue here is whether the San were autonomous societies precolonially or dominated for a millennium by powerful outsiders. In other words, do those San now seeking to throw off the shackles of ethnic discrimination have to overcome a legacy of a century of domination or is there a far deeper history of oppression stretching into the past? This historical issue is part of what has become known in the last decade as the Kalahari Debate (Solway and Lee, 1990; Wilmsen and Denbow, 1990; Barnard, 1992b; Lee, 1992).

One of us (Lee) had documented the hunting and gathering way of life of the Dobe Ju/'hoansi, a people who, though by no means isolated, lived largely independently on their wild food resources into the 1960s. The archaeological expression of this autonomy has been documented by John Yellen and Alison Brooks (Yellen and Brooks, 1988). Edwin Wilmsen (1988a, 1988b, 1989) disagreed, and put forward the argument that the Ju/'hoansi status as hunter-gatherers was an illusion. Instead, he portrayed them as devolved pastoralists, long dominated precolonially by regional African centers of power. The impact of merchant capital, he argued, was early and devastating, further transforming the Ju/'hoansi, who, having lost their cattle, became hunter-gatherers only in the 1890s (Wilmsen 1989; Wilmsen and Denbow, 1990).

As Solway and Lee (1990), and Lee and Guenther (1991, 1993, 1995) have argued, there are some major problems with this 'revisionist' thesis, especially when it attempts to universalize the subordination of the San. First, the archaeological evidence for *contact* between Iron-Age and Stone-Age peoples is good, but much weaker when one tries to show *domination* of Later-Stone-Age by Iron-Age peoples. As Lee's current research — combining archaeology and oral history — attests, coexistence might be a better word (Lee, 1994). Second, the revisionists have tended to underestimate the sheer diversity of historical circumstances of the Khoisan peoples in the precolonial period. There *were* wretched San peoples in the nineteenth century living in abject poverty; there were also independent cattle-holding San peoples, and a number of very successful San groups who lived by the hunt and who maintained a proud independence.

Williams (1991) among others, has written of the relations between the eighteenth and nineteenth century Ovambo kingdoms of northern Namibia and the Bushmen, who they called the 'Khwankala,' describing the relation as equitable and friendly. They traded on the basis of equality, not as masters and servants. In at least two kingdoms, traditions have it that the royal line was founded by marriages between Ovambo men and hunter-gatherer women.

The German geographer Siegfried Passarge (1907) wrote in detail of the 'Buschmannreich' of the Ghanzi San in western Botswana who, from the 1840s to the 1870s, lived exclusively by hunting and gathering, and who under their paramount leader, the mighty Dukurri, kept all comers at bay and jealously guarded their turf.

In South Africa, there is John Wright's important study of *Bushman raiders of the Drakensberg* (1971) which shows how resilient the San people had been in the face of increasing pressure by both European and other African forces on the Natal frontier from the 1840s to the 1870s. And Shula Marks' (1972) work documented the military resistance by the San peoples to Boer expansion in the seventeenth and eighteenth centuries. Miklos Szalay (1995) examined the situations faced by the San during the colonization of the Cape from 1770 to 1879. Szalay described in detail the processes of San subjugation, incorporation, and acculturation, stressing that they did not sit idly by, allowing themselves to be destroyed physically and culturally but rather engaged in both passive and active resistance.

KHOISAN HISTORY I: ORAL HISTORIES IN NYAE NYAE

Lee's current research in northern Namibia and Botswana illustrates some of these themes and the importance of working *with* local people on projects that are relevant to their own goals. In 1994 Lee initiated, with Andrew Smith, a University of Cape Town archaeologist, a joint project in archaeology, oral history, and cultural resource management. The goal was to evaluate the claim of the revisionists that the Nyae Nyae-Dobe area had been dominated for centuries by powerful outsiders. Smith, a specialist on African pastoralism (Smith, 1992), was also looking for evidence of domesticated animals in the prehistory of the area.

Lee and Smith were both interested in the colonial encounter, the timing and nature of the European presence in the area. All of these questions could be pursued both archaeologically and through the collection of oral histories. The third and equally important component was to get members of a local Ju/'hoan stake-holder group, the Nyae Nyae Farmers Cooperative (NNFC), involved in order to develop expertise *within* the community on the history and prehistory of the area, that could be put to use in finding and preserving other sites as part of the national heritage of Namibia. Eventually this knowledge could be put to use in ecological and cultural tourism projects, in curriculum development, and in teaching local history in the Namibian school system.

We approached the Nyae Nyae Development Foundation of Namibia (NNDFN) and the Nyae Nyae Farmers Cooperative to work with us on an excavation at the Cho/ana site in the Kaudom Game Reserve, in the northern part of what used to be Eastern Bushmanland but is now called Eastern Otjozondjupa, Namibia. Cho/ana had been a well-known center of Ju/'hoan occupation prior to the gazetting of the game reserve in 1975, and it was known historically as an entrepôt where people came together for the purposes of trade both precolonially and in the nineteenth and twentieth centuries.

Fieldwork was conducted in May 1995 with a crew of five Ju/'hoansi seconded by the Farmers Cooperative, including two elders who were acknowledged to be reliable sources on oral history. Work was divided between excavating a Later-Stone-Age site yielding thousands of stone flakes and bone fragments, and conducting oral history interviews. Questions were focused on five subject areas:

1. The history and significance of the Ju/'hoan occupation of the Cho/ana site;
2. The nature and extent of the traditional exchange networks of which Cho/ana was a key node;
3. The ethnography of the region as seen through the eyes of the Ju/'hoansi: the nature and extent of their historical contacts and current relations with over twenty of the surrounding ethnic groups in northern Namibia and Botswana;
4. Ju/'hoan views of their current and past regional subdivisions and how this affected contact, intermarriage and exchange;
5. Ju/'hoan views of their own history, their precolonial culture and economy, and their own accounts of the colonial encounter.

There was no evidence either in the oral traditions or in the archaeological record of the presence of domesticates or of non-Ju/'hoan people resident in the area prior to the latter part of the nineteenth century. This provided corroboration of the Ju/'hoansi's own strongly held views that their ancestors were independent hunter-gatherers, not pastoralists, and that they were not dominated by outsiders. So in at least one key area, the claims of the revisionists for the universal subordination of hunters by farmers is shown to be false.

The interviews provided a valuable adjunct to the archaeological work, providing a social context in which the material could be interpreted. Occasionally there were striking tie-ins attesting to the accuracy of the oral histories. For example, the elders described a kind of white glass bead as one of the earliest of the European trade goods obtained through intermediaries to the north. A few days later precisely such a bead was found in a sealed level in association with a Later-Stone-Age (LSA) industry. This and a piece of bottle glass showing signs of LSA retouching gave a further indication of the involvement of the Cho/ana Ju/'hoansi in trade with their neighbors and the persistence of LSA stone-working techniques into the colonial contact period. Further collaborative research is planned for 1997–98.

Another positive result was the training component of the project. One of the young men, /Ui Keyter /Oma, showed a real aptitude for archaeology. A technical traineeship was arranged for him with the National Museum in Windhoek under the direction of Dr John Kinahan. /Ui is the first person of Ju/ 'hoan background to study archaeology in a professional setting. In July 1995 he accompanied a Southampton University student team under the direction of Dr Thomas Dowson, a well-known rock art authority, on a four-week study tour of Namibian rock art sites. As of this writing /Ui is completing his third six-month stint at the Namibian National Museum with support from the Kalahari Peoples Fund and is planning a career in conservation and cultural resource management.

KHOISAN HISTORY II: SCHMIDTSDRIFT AND KAGGA KAMMA

Though San peoples have continued to flourish elsewhere, by the turn of the twentieth century it was believed that the Bushman peoples inside South Africa were virtually extinct. However, in South Africa today the Bushmen are making something of a comeback, though in a distinctly postmodern way. Two examples should be mentioned.

After the United Nations-brokered peace process and the independence of Namibia in 1989, South Africa was faced with the problem of what to do with the thousands of Bushman soldiers and dependants who had been recruited into the South Africa Defence Force (SADF) from the 1970s forward to fight in the Namibian–Angolan border war. While some San former fighers were repatriated to their respective territories, many elected to travel south with the departing South African military forces.

Today, some 4000 former soldiers and their families reside at Schmidtsdrift, a 36,000-hectare army base near Kimberley (Uys, 1994; Steyn, 1994). Even under the Apartheid regime their status was ambiguous, but with the coming to power of the Mandela government in South Africa in April 1994, their status has become even more problematic. Having fought *against* the allies of the present government, the continued presence of some 550 San former SADF soldiers and their families in post-Apartheid South Africa is an unpleasant reminder of the evils of Apartheid and racial injustice. And because of their cultural and linguistic distinctiveness neither the black nor the white communities have been willing to absorb them. The San remain housed on the Schmidtsdrift base in a temporary military bivouac over eight years after their arrival.

The situation facing the San today is uncertain since the land belonged in the past to Tswana and Griquas who were relocated in 1968 when the army base was established. The !Xuu and Khwe Trust has been attempting to find them some alternative land on which to settle, and efforts have been made to obtain freehold farms so that the San can be resettled yet again. A few of the San have considered going back to Namibia and Angola, but the majority wish to stay in South Africa, a place that they now consider home.

The San in South Africa have not been content to simply sit and wait for government assistance or tourist handouts. Instead, they have formed advocacy organizations aimed at gaining land and resource rights and funding for development purposes. One of these organizations is the !Xuu and Khwe Trust, an organization based at Schmidtsdrift. Over half of the trust board is made up of San drawn from the Schmidtsdrift population. Some of the trust's activities include advocacy efforts; the trust also sponsors community development projects, some of them under the !Xuu and Khwe Cultural Project which includes a craft-makers cooperative, an arts project, an art center, and a living museum. Some of the local hunters at Schmidtsdrift serve in a problem animal control (PAC) unit with the Department of Nature Conservation.

Another example of the tragic consequences of Apartheid and its aftermath for the San people is the Kagga Kamma Bushman group, near Ceres north of Cape Town. The Kagga Kamma people were arguably the last surviving San group in South Africa proper. They lived in the extreme northwestern Cape adjacent to the Kalahari Gemsbok Game Reserve (now a national park), where for a generation they combined foraging and odd jobs with posing for tourist photographs at the park gates (Botha and Steyn, 1995). In the 1980s they were forced to abandon the national park and took up an even more precarious existence as squatters and casual farm laborers on white farms.

Their tragic plight received some media coverage in the early 1990s, when an entrepreneur collected them and brought them to Kagga Kamma, where they became the centerpiece of a Bushman 'theme park' far from their traditional area (White, 1993). Their life today consists of dressing in 'traditional' clothing and presenting themselves before a daily stream of tourists. They make and sell crafts and perform dances for which they receive modest wages and rations. Hylton White (1995) has written a thoughtful and sensitive study of the Kagga Kamma people, reflecting upon their sad history, the white South African public's appetite for 'authentic Africa,' and how the two came together in the incongruous circumstances of Kagga Kamma.

On October 9, 1995, it was reported on the South African Broadcasting Corporation (SABC), that Derek Hanekom, the Minister of Lands of South

Africa, and Anthony Hall-Martin of the Parks Board, met with 30 of the 200 San who live in the vicinity of the Kalahari Gemsbok National Park. The Bushmen there had put forth a claim to at least half of the national park as well as some neighboring farms (Land Claim Committee, Southern Kalahari Bushmen, 1995). The point was made by Minister Hanekom that there was a possibility that the San could perhaps be given the right to co-manage the Kalahari Gemsbok Park with the Parks Board. The rights of the San were thus seen as important by at least some South African government officials. According to some of the San advocacy groups and their supporters, this in itself is a tacit recognition of the significance of the San in the contemporary politics of South Africa.

There are new efforts on the part of local communities and various development agencies and nongovernment organizations to implement community-based natural resource management projects (CBNRMPs, also called Integrated Conservation and Development Projects, or ICDPs) in Africa, including ones in Botswana, Lesotho, Malawi, Namibia, South Africa, Swaziland, Zambia, and Zimbabwe. Many of these activities are being conducted adjacent to, and sometimes inside, conservation areas (Brown and Wyckoff-Baird, 1992; Wells and Brandon, 1992; Barrett and Arcese, 1995). These projects are found in a wide variety of ecological zones, from tropical forests to savannas, and from Afromontane habitats to coastal marine regions. The San and other groups involved in these projects hope that they will serve to enhance their chances of maintaining their rights to their land and resources and facilitate their obtaining income. One way these projects can do this is to provide them with tenure rights over land that in the past belonged to the state, thus enabling them to be the direct beneficiaries of tourism and other kinds of rural industries.

In the past, a major problem with biodiversity conservation programs in Africa was that they tended to dispossess people or to prevent them from pursuing resource procurement activities (Anderson and Grove, 1987; Hitchcock, 1994, 1995). As one Ju/'hoansi woman in the Nyae Nyae region of northeastern Namibia put it, 'Government first took away our right to hunt and then tried to remove us from our n!oresi (traditional territories).' The passage of legislation to control hunting and to set aside parks and reserves generally exacerbated problems of poverty and resource stress among local communities in Africa. This was the case with the Kalahari Gemsbok National Park in South Africa and Botswana, where local San lost their residence and resource access rights and became poverty-stricken and landless peasants on the peripheries (Gordon, 1992). The arrests or shooting of poachers, as has been done in a number of African countries, is a costly strategy that has served to alienate local populations (Anderson and Grove, 1987; Mogwe, 1992; Hitchcock, 1994, 1995).

To be successful, community-based natural resource management projects must be based on principles of social justice and ecological sustainability. They must also incorporate careful planning and design that are participatory in nature and which build extensively on indigenous knowledge of environmental management and community cooperation (Brown and Wyckoff-Baird, 1992; Durning, 1992; Wells and Brandon, 1992).

KHOISAN HISTORY III: NEO-KHOISAN IDENTITIES

From the ongoing strength of tradition in San communities in the north like the Nyae Nyae Ju/'hoansi of Namibia, and the tragic circumstances of the Schmidtsdrift and Kagga Kamma people, must be added a discussion of the broader class and ethnic politics of Khoisan peoples in post-Apartheid South Africa. The issue of African hunter-gatherer marginality gained relevancy and immediacy at a conference on Khoisan studies that Lee attended in Munich, Germany in July 1994. Present were the usual assortment of linguists, historians, and anthropologists and the tone of the meeting was suitably scholarly. But the atmosphere of probity and gravity was jarred on the opening day, when Professor Henry Bredekamp, a historian from the University of the Western Cape (a former 'Coloured' university), rose to address the meeting, with deep conviction:

> This meeting has a great deal of significance for me because I am a Khoisan person. There are millions of South Africans like me who trace their ancestry back to the Khoi and the San peoples. These are *our* histories *our* languages you are discussing. Under Apartheid we lost much of our culture. Now we want to work closely with you in recovering our past and our traditions. (Henry Bredekamp, July 1994)

Bredekamp's intervention energized the meeting and before the group dispersed, it was agreed to hold the next Khoisan studies meeting in Bellville at the University of Western Cape in July 1997. It gives a new lease of life for the field of Khoisan studies and to the study of African hunter-gatherers. An entire new constituency is awakening to the importance of recording the traditions and ways of life of the small cultures of Africa, against the day, as some representatives of former foraging groups noted, when they might be 'rediscovered.'

What are some of the implications for African archaeology and anthropology of these new trends? The great African philosopher-revolutionary, Amilcar Cabral, wrote movingly some 30 years ago that the task before the people of Africa was not only achieving independence but also recapturing history, a history taken from the African peoples by the colonialists (Cabral, 1974). One year after the Munich meeting Lee was at the University of the Western Cape, invited by Henry Bredekamp, where he noted that recovering history appeared to be one of the most important cultural processes underway in post-Apartheid South Africa. In fact it is one of the most significant social movements worldwide in the late twentieth century. Everywhere, it seems, indigenous peoples are rediscovering aspects of themselves that had long been suppressed. Recapturing history has become a major movement in literature, history, and anthropology: the study of colonial discourse, postcoloniality, and the attempts by subaltern peoples to liberate their consciousness from it (see, for example, Smith, 1988).

It goes without saying that the history of the so-called 'non-whites' of South Africa is not a unitary one; diverse historical streams are represented within it. Recapturing histories is not simply a question of reviving old ethnicities; it is also about acknowledging the birth of new ones, ethnicities like those of the people in the University of the Western Cape student body, whose roots could be traced not only to Khoi and San, but as well to Dutch, Malay, Xhosa, British, and other sources drawn from three continents (du Plessis, 1972; Mayson, 1963).

However, the Khoi and the San links are among the largest and most neglected segments of these personal and family histories. Up to 2.5 million 'Coloured' South Africans would identify themselves this way, but until recently the opportunity for these peoples to explore their roots has been compromised and distorted by the horrors of Apartheid (Marais, 1957; Ross, 1976, 1993; Schapera, 1930).

Previous representations of the Khoisan peoples had been saturated with racist colonial discourse, as was noted by Parsons (1988) in his superb study of Khoisan stereotyping in the treatment of Frantz, a southern Kalahari Bushman who was taken to England in the early twentieth century to appear in theaters and circuses. The doctrine of progress ranked peoples on technical achievements and Khoi and San were often presented as exemplars of the bottom of the ladder, as the cast-offs of creation. This pernicious doctrine was used blatantly to justify oppression and dispossession (Gordon, 1992).

For centuries the masses of South African people labelled 'Coloured' have struggled with the problem of identity, situated halfway between the white oppressors with whom they shared language and religion, and the black majority towards whom they felt a mixture of fear, kinship, and ambivalence (Moodie, 1976; Thompson, 1985). But with the heightening of the struggle against Apartheid, a new era opened in Coloured identity politics. One can trace the Khoisan revival ultimately to the Black Consciousness movement of the 1970s, led by the charismatic Steve Biko (1978, 1979).

Black Consciousness had part of its genesis among Coloured students and intellectuals in the Cape Town area. And the anthropological world has been intensely interested in what was and is happening in South Africa in developing an anthropology of liberation. It is of particular interest how people of Khoisan heritage have espoused this powerful set of ideas and re-identified themselves with their ancestors and with the millions of their countrywomen and men who were fighting oppression (Pityana *et al.*, 1992).

Of course, wherever we explore ethnicity and identity politics new complexities emerge. 'Coloured' politics in South Africa has many diverse currents including Islamic fundamentalism, support for the now 'reformed' National Party, commitment to the ideals of the African National Congress, and various left, right, and cultural nationalist tendencies. It is interesting that a prominent 'Coloured' political figure of Trotskyist persuasion, recently had his name legally changed from Benny Alexander to Khoisan X. However, the fact remains that the 'Khoisan roots' question is only one of a number of different cross-currents affecting identity politics today.

For those who do wish to identify with the Khoisan past there are no lack of examples to choose from. The works of Frieda-Nela Williams, John Wright, and Shula Marks, discussed above, show the resilience and pragmatism, the ability to project power and the desire to survive of the Khoisan peoples in the face of overwhelming odds. These stories could form the bases of a popular history of the Khoisan peoples, and in fact such projects are already underway at the University of the Western Cape.

PROBLEMS FOR FURTHER STUDY

The existence of this hidden history, hitherto suppressed by colonial discourse and Apartheid ideology, suggests a number of new directions for anthropologists. An expanded anthropology that celebrates the birth of new ethnicities as well as mourning the passing of the old, embraces new possibilities for research on the politics of identity. The African peoples offer parallels to what is happening in other parts of the world (cf. Schrire and Gordon, 1985; Durning, 1992; Lee, 1992; Hitchcock, 1993, 1994).

In Australia and in North America, perhaps the most significant development of the last decade is indigenous peoples speaking to us in their own voices. In Canada the Innu, the Lubicon, the Teme-Augama and others (as shown in Richardson, 1989) speak to the Canadian public through the medium of plays, novels, and pop music as well as via press conferences. Groups like Yothu Yindi from Arnhem Land in Australia, Kashtin from the Labrador Innu, and Susan Aglukark, the Inuit pop star, have had enormous appeal through their music. Increasingly indigenous peoples are making political alliances with environmentalists, feminists, youth groups, and peoples of color (Burger, 1990;

Durning, 1992; Hitchcock, 1993, 1994). Clearly the cultural renaissance underway in a number of indigenous communities has generated considerable interest in 'traditional' ethos and worldview, governance, subsistence, arts, crafts, ethnobotany, and healing; for these and other spheres of knowledge, the elders and anthropological texts are the main sources of information. If it is happening in Australia and Canada, why not southern Africa?

Although the conditions elsewhere in Africa are quite different from South Africa, similar alliances could be forged between former foragers and activists in, for example, Kenya, Tanzania, Democratic Republic of Congo, and Zambia. However, unlike North America and Australia where there is a clear distinction between natives and newcomers, in most of Africa the category 'indigenous people' is much more problematic. In all but a few countries the majority African populations can rightfully claim that they are no less 'indigenous' than the former hunter-gatherers (Veber et al., 1993; Murumbi, 1994).

In the South African context, there are definitely exciting possibilities for collecting the oral traditions of the old people. Constituting the living history of the nation is a well-established branch of research, for example, in Australia, but it has barely begun in South Africa. There is a need for scholars to walk over the land with rural elders, for studies of placenames; and accounts of sacred sites, battles, and other historical events need to be memorialized. Studies need to be done of Khoi and San words that have remained in the language; their meanings and significance. There is still much to be mined from existing archival sources such as the Bleek and Lloyd collection (1911).

Urban educated people, such as the students at the University of the Western Cape, who feel a sense of kinship with their Khoisan roots, could connect and make field trips to living representatives of that tradition, such as the Ju/'hoansi of Namibia and Botswana. Urban students from the Cape Town area may seek them out to find a sense of *communitas* with others of similar cultural background, but the northern Ju/'hoansi need the skills and strengths of the Cape Town students – in literacy, technical and business skills – at least as much as the Capetonians need them.

CONCLUSION

The hunter-gatherers of Africa are numerically small but in terms of African history and civilization they loom large. In the 1990s foragers are struggling to retain distinct identities while interacting extensively with nonforaging neighbors. They may be found serving in the armed forces or victims of the same armed forces; they may be the beneficiaries of welfare programs or ignored by them (Veber et al., 1993; Hitchcock, 1993; Miller, 1993).

Where sheer survival is not an issue, marginalized peoples can turn their attention to the re-establishment of their historical roots. Recovering history is now a worldwide social movement among encapsulated peoples, not only in South Africa, but in Canada, and Australia, New Zealand, Russia, and elsewhere (Burger, 1990; Durning, 1992). And it is not just an issue for one people or one nation: cultural diversity old and new represented by the hunting and gathering peoples of Africa is part of the heritage of all humanity. It is important that members of these societies themselves be drawn into the task of valorizing and preserving their own cultural heritage. Ultimately it is they who will carry forward this work.

ACKNOWLEDGMENTS

An earlier version of this chapter was presented as a paper at the Humanities Research Centre Conference, 'Africa: precolonial achievement,' held at the Australian National University, in Canberra, Australia on June 10–12, 1995. Graham Connah provided extremely useful recommendations for improvements and Caroline M. Walker went to tremendous lengths to check our references and make corrections. We would like to acknowledge the assistance of members of the various San advocacy groups who provided us with background information, including the Nyae Nyae Farmers Cooperative, Kuru Development Trust, Kgeikani Kweni, the !Xuu and Khwe Trust, and the Working Group of Indigenous Minorities in Southern Africa. We wish to thank the Australian National University, the University of Nebraska, and the University of Toronto for financial support in the research and writing of this paper.

BIBLIOGRAPHY

Amnesty International (1992) *Human rights violations against indigenous peoples of the Americas.* Washington DC and New York, Amnesty International.

Anderson, D. and Grove, R. (eds) (1987) *Conservation in Africa: people, policies, and practice.* Cambridge and New York, Cambridge University Press.

Bahuchet, S. (1988) Food supply uncertainty among the Aka Pygmies (Lobaye, Central African Republic). In de Garine, I. and Harrison, G.A. (eds) *Coping with uncertainty in the food supply.* Oxford, Clarendon Press, pp. 18–49.

Bahuchet, S. (1991) Spatial mobility and access to resources among the African Pygmies. In Casimir, M.J. and Rao, A. (eds) *Mobility and territoriality: social and spatial boundaries among foragers, fishers, pastoralists, and peripatetics* Oxford and New York, Berg Publishers, pp. 205–57.

Bahuchet, S., McKey, D. and de Garine, I. (1991) Wild yams revisited: is independence from agriculture possible for rain forest hunter-gatherers? *Human Ecology.* 19(2): 213–43.

Bailey, R.C. (1991) *The behavioral ecology of Efe Pygmy men in the Ituri Forest, Zaïre.* Ann

Arbor, Michigan, Anthropological Papers, Museum of Anthropology, University of Michigan, No. 86.

Bailey, R.C. and DeVore, I. (1989) Research on the Efe and Lese populations of the Ituri Forest, Zaïre. *American Journal of Physical Anthropology* 78: 459–71.

Bailey, R.C., Head, G., Jenike, M., Owen, B., Rechtman, R. and Zechenter, E. (1989) Hunting and gathering in tropical rain forest? Is it possible? *American Anthropologist* 91(1): 59–82.

Barnard, A. (1992a) *Hunters and herders of Southern Africa: a comparative ethnography of the Khoisan peoples.* Cambridge and New York, Cambridge University Press.

Barnard, A. (1992b) *The Kalahari debate: a bibliographic essay.* Edinburgh, Centre of African Studies, Edinburgh University, Occasional Paper No. 33.

Barrett, C.B. and Arcese, P. (1995) Are integrated conservation-development projects (ICDPs) sustainable? On the conservation of large mammals in Sub-Saharan Africa. *World Development* 23(7): 1073–84.

Biesele, M. (1990) *Shaken roots: the Bushmen of Namibia.* Marshalltown, South Africa, Environmental Development Agency (ENDA).

Biesele, M. (1993) *'Women like meat.' Ju/'hoan Bushmen folklore and foraging ideology.* Johannesburg, Witwatersrand University Press.

Biesele, M. (1994) Human rights and democratization in Namibia: some grassroots political perspectives. *African Rural and Urban Studies* 1(2): 49–72.

Biesele, M., Guenther, M., Hitchcock, R., Lee, R. and MacGregor, J. (1989) Hunters, clients, and squatters: the contemporary socioeconomic status of Botswana Basarwa. *African Study Monographs* 9(3): 109–51.

Biko, S. (1978) *Black consciousness in South Africa.* New York, Random House.

Biko, S. (1979) *I write what I like.* London, Heinemann.

Blackburn, R.H. (1974) The Okiek and their history. *Azania* 9: 139–57.

Blackburn, R.H. (1982) In the land of milk and honey: Okiek adaptations to their forests and neighbors. In Leacock, E. and Lee, R. (eds) *Politics and history in band societies.* Cambridge, Cambridge University Press, pp. 283–305.

Blackburn, R.H. (1996) Fission, fusion, and foragers in East Africa: micro- and macroprocesses of diversity and integration among Okiek groups. In Kent, S. (ed.) *Cultural diversity among twentieth-century foragers: an African perspective.* Cambridge and New York, Cambridge University Press, pp. 88–212.

Bleek, W.H.I. and Lloyd, L.C. (1911) *Specimens of Bushman folklore.* London, G. Allen.

Blurton Jones, N.G., Hawkes, K. and O'Connell, J.F. (1989) Modelling and measuring costs of children in two foraging societies. In Standen, V. and Foley, R.A. (eds) *Comparative socioecology: the behavioral ecology of humans and other animals.* Oxford, Blackwell Scientific Publications, pp. 367–90.

Blurton Jones, N.G., Hawkes, K. and O'Connell, J.F. (n.d.) History and the Hadza. Unpublished manuscript.

Botha, L.J. and Steyn, H.P. (1995) Report on the Bushmen of Kagga Kamma, and their southern Kalahari origins. Stellenbosch, South Africa, University of Stellenbosch.

Brown, M. and Wyckoff-Baird, B. (1992) *Designing integrated conservation and development projects.* Washington DC, Biodiversity Support Program and World Wildlife Fund.

Burger, J. (1987) *Report from the frontier: the state of the world's indigenous peoples.* London, Zed Press.

Burger, J. (1990) *The Gaia atlas of first peoples: a future for the indigenous world.* New York and London, Anchor Books (Doubleday).

Cabral, A. (1974) *Return to the source: selected speeches.* New York, Monthly Review Press.

Cavalli-Sforza, L.L. (ed.) (1986) *African Pygmies*. Orlando, Florida, Academic Press.

Clark, J.D. (1951) Bushmen Hunters of the Barotse Forests. *Northern Rhodesia Journal* 1: 56–65.

Clark, J.D. and Brandt, S.A. (eds) (1984) *From hunters to farmers: causes and consequences of food production in Africa*. Berkeley and Los Angeles, University of California Press.

de Almeida, A. (1965) *Bushmen and other non-Bantu peoples of Angola: three lectures*. Johannesburg, Witwatersrand University Press for the Institute for the Study of Man in Africa.

Dowson, T.A. (1992) *Rock engravings of southern Africa*. Johannesburg, Witwatersrand University Press.

du Plessis, I.D. (1972) *The Cape Malays: history, religion, traditions, folk tales, the Malay Quarter*. Balkema, Cape Town.

Durning, A.B. (1989) *Action at the grassroots: fighting poverty and environmental decline*. Washington DC, Worldwatch Paper 88, Worldwatch Institute.

Durning, A.B. (1992) *Guardians of the land: indigenous peoples and the health of the earth*. Washington DC, Worldwatch Paper 112, Worldwatch Institute.

Elphick, R. (1977) *Kraal and castle: Khoikhoi and the founding of white South Africa*. New Haven, Connecticut, Yale University Press.

Gibbons, A. (1995) Old dates for modern behavior. *Science* 268: 495–6.

Gordon, R.J. (1992) *The Bushman myth: the making of a Namibian underclass*. Boulder, Colorado, Westview Press.

Grinker, R.R. (1990) Images of denigration: structuring inequality between foragers and farmers in the Ituri Forest, Zaïre. *American Ethnologist* 17(1): 111–30.

Grinker, R.R. (1994) *Houses in the rainforest: ethnicity and inequality among farmers and foragers in central Africa*. Berkeley and Los Angeles, University of California Press.

Guenther, M.G. (1986) *The Nharo Bushmen of Botswana: tradition and change*. Hamburg, Helmut Buske Verlag.

Gurr, T.R. (1993) *Minorities at risk: a global view of ethnopolitical conflicts*. Washington DC, The U.S. Institute of Peace Press.

Gurr, T.R. and Harff, B. (1994) *Ethnic conflict in world politics*. Boulder, Colorado, Westview Press.

Hahn, T. (1881) *Tsuni-//goam: the supreme being of the Khoi-Khoi*. London, Trubner and Company.

Hall, M. (1987) *The changing past: farmers, kings, and traders in southern Africa, 200–1860*. Cape Town and Johannesburg, David Philip.

Harako, R. (1981) The cultural ecology of hunting behavior among Mbuti Pygmies in the Ituri Forest, Zaïre. In Harding, R.S.O. and Teleki, G. (eds) *Omnivorous primates: gathering and hunting in human evolution*. New York, Columbia University Press, pp. 499–555.

Hewlett, B.S. (1993) European and African perceptions of Aka and Baka Pygmy development. In Ellanna, L.J. (ed.) *Hunters and gatherers in the modern context, book of presented papers, Volume I (Seventh International Conference on Hunting and Gathering Societies, CHAGS 7)*. Moscow, Institute of Ethnology and Anthropology, Russian Academy of Sciences, pp. 285–97.

Hewlett, B.S. (1996) Cultural diversity among African Pygmies. In Kent, S. (ed.) *Cultural diversity among twentieth-century foragers: an African perspective*. Cambridge and New York, Cambridge University Press, pp. 215–44.

Hitchcock, R.K. (1992) *Communities and consensus: an evaluation of the activities of the Nyae Nyae Farmers Cooperative and the Nyae Nyae Development Foundation in northeastern Namibia*. Ford Foundation, New York, and Nyae Nyae Development Foundation, Windhoek, Namibia.

Hitchcock, R.K. (1993) Africa and discovery: human rights, environment and development. *American Indian Culture and Research Journal* 17(1): 129–52.

Hitchcock, R.K. (1994) International human rights, the environment, and indigenous peoples. *Colorado Journal of International Environmental Law and Policy* 5(1): 1–22.

Hitchcock, R.K. (1995) Centralization, resource depletion, and coercive conservation among the Tyua of the northeastern Kalahari. *Human Ecology* 23(2): 169–98.

Hitchcock, R.K. (1996) *Kalahari communities: Bushmen and the politics of the environment in Southern Africa.* Copenhagen, International Work Group for Indigenous Affairs, Document No. 79.

Hitchcock, R.K. and Holm, J.D. (1993) Bureaucratic domination of hunter-gatherer societies: a study of the San in Botswana. *Development and Change* 24(2): 305–38.

Hitchcock, R.K. and Holm, J.D. (1995) Grassroots political organizing among Kalahari Bushmen. *Indigenous Affairs* 3/95: 4–10.

Human Rights Watch 1996. *Genocide in Rwanda: the planning and execution of mass murder.* Washington DC and New York, Human Rights Watch.

Ichikawa, M. (1978) The residential groups of the Mbuti Pygmies. *Senri Ethnological Studies* 1: 131–88.

Ichikawa, M. (1983) An examination of the hunting-dependent life of the Mbuti Pygmies, Eastern Zaïre. *African Study Monographs* 4: 55–76.

Kaare, B.T.M. (1994) The impact of modernization policies on the hunter-gatherer Hadzabe: the case of education and language policies of postindependence Tanzania. In Burch, E.S. Jr and Ellanna, L.J. (eds) *Key issues in hunter-gatherer research.* Oxford, Berg Publishers, pp. 315–31.

Kelly, R.L. and Poyer, L.A. (1993) Ethnoarchaeology among the Mikea of southwestern Madagascar: report of activities, July–August, 1993. San Francisco, Report to the L.S.B. Leakey Foundation.

Kent, S. (ed.) (1996) *Cultural diversity among twentieth-century foragers: an African perspective.* Cambridge and New York, Cambridge University Press.

Kopytoff, I. (ed.) (1987) *The African frontier: the reproduction of traditional African societies.* Bloomington, Indiana, Indiana University Press.

Kratz, C.A. (1994) *Affecting performance: meaning, movement, and experience in Okiek women's initiation.* Washington DC, Smithsonian Press.

Kretsinger, A. (1993) *Recommendations for further integration of BaAka interests in project policy, Dzanga-Sangha Dense Forest Reserve.* Washington DC, Report to the World Wildlife Fund.

Land Claim Committee, Southern Kalahari Bushmen (1995) *Northern Cape Province: land claim and submission to the Minister of Land Affairs.* Cape Town and Stellenbosch, Land Claim Committee, The Southern Kalahari Bushmen.

Lee, R.B. (1979) *The !Kung San: men, women, and work in a foraging society.* Cambridge, Cambridge University Press.

Lee, R.B. (1992) Art, science or politics? The crisis in hunter-gatherer studies. *American Anthropologist* 94(1): 23–46.

Lee, R.B. (1993) *The Dobe Ju/'hoansi.* 2nd edn, Fort Worth, Texas, Harcourt Brace College Publishers.

Lee, R.B. (1994) Autonomy and dependency: evaluating Ju/'hoan oral histories and ethnohistories. In Vossen, R., Ross, R. and Wilmsen, E. (eds) *Khoisan studies.* Frankfurt, Helmut Buske Verlag.

Lee, R.B. and DeVore, I. (eds) (1976) *Kalahari hunter-gatherers: studies of the !Kung San and their neighbors.* Cambridge, Massachusetts, Harvard University Press.

Lee, R.B. and Guenther, M. (1991) Oxen or onions: the search for trade (and truth) in the Kalahari. *Current Anthropology* 32(5): 592–601.

Lee, R.B. and Guenther, M. (1993) Problems in Kalahari historical ethnography and the tolerance of error. *History in Africa* 20: 185–235.

Lee, R.B. and Guenther, M. (1995) Errors corrected or compounded? A reply to Wilmsen. *Current Anthropology* 36: 298–305.

Lewis-Williams, D.J. (1981) *Believing and seeing: symbolic meanings in southern San rock paintings.* London, Academic Press.

Marais, J.S. (1957) *The Cape Coloured people: 1652–1937.* Johannesburg, Witwatersrand University Press.

MacCalman, H.R. and Grobbelaar, B.J. (1965) Preliminary report of two stone-working OvaTjimba groups in the northern Kaokoveld of South West Africa. *Cimbebasia* 13: 1–39.

McDowell, W. (1981a) *Hadza traditional economy and its prospects for development.* Dar es Salaam, Tanzania, Report to the Rift Valley Project, Ministry of Information and Culture.

McDowell, W. (1981b) *A brief history of Mangola Hadza.* Tanzania, Report to the Rift Valley Project, Ministry of Information and Culture, Division of Research, Government of Tanzania and District Development Directorate, Mbulu District, Arusha Region, Mbulu.

Marks, S. (1972) Khoisan resistance to the Dutch in the seventeenth and eighteenth centuries. *Journal of African History* 8: 55–80.

Marshall, J. (1989) *The constitution and communal lands in Namibia. Land rights and local governments. Helping 33,000 people classified as 'Bushmen': the Ju/wa case.* Namibia, Nyae Nyae Development Foundation, Windhoek.

Marshall, J. and Ritchie, C. (1984) *Where Are the Ju/Wasi of Nyae Nyae? Changes in a Bushman society: 1958–1981.* South Africa, Centre for African Area Studies, University of Cape Town, Communications No. 9, Rondebosch, Cape.

Marshall, L. (1976) *The !Kung of Nyae Nyae.* Cambridge, Massachusetts, Harvard University Press.

Mayson, J.S. (1963) [1861]. *The Malays of Capetown.* Africana Connoisseurs Press.

Miller, M.S. and Cultural Survival (eds) (1993) *State of the peoples: a global human rights report on societies in danger.* Boston, Massachusetts, Beacon Press.

Mogwe, A. (1992) *Who was (t)here first? An assessment of the human rights situation of Basarwa in selected communities in the Gantsi District.* Gaborone, Botswana, Botswana Christian Council (BCC) Occasional Paper No. 10.

Moodie, T.D. (1976) *The Afrikaner civil religion.* New Haven, Connecticut, Yale University Press.

Murdock, G.P. (1959) Part Two: African hunters. In *Africa: its peoples and their culture history.* New York, McGraw-Hill Book Company, pp. 46–63.

Murumbi, D. (1994) The concept of indigenous peoples in Africa. *Indigenous Affairs* 1/94: 51–7.

Ndagala, D.K. (1988) Free or doomed? Images of the Hadzabe hunters and gatherers of Tanzania. In Ingold, T., Riches, D. and Woodburn, J. (eds) *Hunters and gatherers 1: history, evolution, and social change.* Oxford and New York, Berg Publishers, pp. 65–72.

Ndagala, D.K. (1993) State intervention and food dependence among the Hadzabe. In Ellanna, L.J. (ed.) *Hunters and gatherers in the modern context, book of presented papers, Volume II (Seventh International Conference on Hunting and Gathering Societies, CHAGS 7).* Moscow, Institute of Ethnology and Anthropology, Russian Academy of Science, pp. 477–85.

Neitschmann, B. (1994) The Fourth World: nations versus states. In Demko, G.J. and Wood, W.B. (eds) *Reordering the world: geopolitical perspectives on the 21st century.* Boulder, Colorado, Westview Press, pp. 225–42.

Nurse, G.T. and Jenkins, T. (1977) *Health and the hunter-gatherer: biomedical studies on the hunting and gathering populations of southern Africa*. Basel, S. Karger.

Parsons, N. (1988) Frantz or Klikko, the wild dancing Bushman: a case study of Khoisan stereotyping. *Botswana Notes and Records* 20: 71–6.

Passarge, S. (1907) *Die Bushmänner der Kalahari*. Berlin, D. Reimer.

Phillipson, D.W. (1985) *African archaeology*. Cambridge, Cambridge University Press.

Pityana, B., Ramphele, M., Mpumlwana, M. and Wilson, L. (eds) (1992) *Bounds of possibility: the legacy of Steve Biko and black consciousness*. London, Zed Press.

Reynolds, B. (1972a) The Kwandu of southwestern Zamiba: an example of an incidental record. *Ethnohistory* 19(3): 237–47.

Reynolds, B. (1972b) Kwandu settlement: isolation, integration, and mobility among a south-central African people. In Ucko, P.J., Tringham, R. and Dimbleby, G.W. (eds) *Man, settlement, and urbanism*. London, Duckworth.

Richardson, B. (ed) (1989) *Drumbeat: anger and renewal in the Indian Country*. Toronto, Ontario, Summerhill Press/Assembly of First Nations.

Ross, R. (1976) *Adam Kok's Griquas: a study in the development of stratification in South Africa*. Cambridge, Cambridge University Press.

Ross, R. (1993) *Beyond the pale: essays on the history of colonial South Africa*. Middleton, Connecticut, Wesleyan University Press.

Schapera, I. (1930) *The Khoisan peoples of South Africa: Bushmen and Hottentots*. London, Routledge and Kegan Paul.

Schrire, C. (ed.) (1984) *Past and present in hunter-gatherer studies*. Orlando, Florida, Academic Press.

Schrire, C. and Gordon, R. (eds) (1985) *The future of former foragers: Australia and southern Africa*. Cambridge, Massachusetts, Cultural Survival Occasional Papers, No. 18.

Silberbauer, G.B. (1981) *Hunter and habitat in the central Kalahari Desert*. Cambridge and New York, Cambridge University Press.

Smith, A. (1992) *Pastoralism in Africa: origins and development ecology*. London, Hurst and Company.

Smith, K. (1988) *The changing past: trends in South African historical writing*. Athens, Ohio, Ohio University Press.

Solway, J.S. and Lee, R.B. (1990) Foragers, genuine or spurious? Situating the Kalahari San in history. *Current Anthropology* 31(2): 109–46.

Steyn, H.P. (1994) Role and position of elderly !Xu in the Schmidtsdrift Bushman community. *South African Journal of Ethnology* 17(2): 31–7.

Stiles, D. (1981) Hunters of the northern East African Coast: origins and historical processes. *Africa* 51(4): 848–62.

Stiles, D. (1991) Tubers and Tenrecs: the Mikea of Southwestern Madagascar. *Ethnology* 30: 251–63.

Stiles, D. (1993a) Aweer of Kenya and Somalia. In Miller, M.S. and Cultural Survival (eds) *State of the peoples: a global human rights report on societies in danger*. Boston, Massachusetts, Beacon Press, p. 164.

Stiles, D. (1993b) Sustainable development in tropical forests by indigenous peoples. *Swara* 16(5): 24–7.

Szalay, M. (1995) *The San and the colonization of the Cape, 1770–1879: conflict, incorporation, acculturation*. Koln, Research in Khoisan Studies 11. Rudiger Koppe Verlag.

Tanaka, J. (1980) *The San, hunter-gatherers of the Kalahari, a study in ecological anthropology*. Tokyo, University of Tokyo Press.

Thompson, L. (1985) *The political mythology of Apartheid*. New Haven, Connecticut, Yale University Press.

Turnbull, C.M. (1961) *The forest people: a study of the Pygmies of the Congo*. New York, Simon and Schuster.

Turnbull, C.M. (1965) *The Mbuti Pygmies: an ethnographic survey*. New York, Anthropological Papers of the American Museum of Natural History.

Turnbull, C.M. (1983) *The Mbuti Pygmies: change and adaptation*. New York, Holt, Rinehart and Winston.

United States Department of State (1993) *Country reports on human rights practices for 1993*. Washington DC, US Government Printing Office.

Uys, C. (1994) *Schmidtsdrift: where next?* Rondebosch, Cape, South Africa, Diploma in African Studies, University of Cape Town.

Uys, J. (1980) *The gods must be crazy*. Gaborone, Botswana, Mimosa Films.

van der Post, L. (1958) *The lost world of the Kalahari*. London and New York, Hogarth Press.

van der Post, L. (1961) *The heart of the hunter*. London and New York, Hogarth Press.

van Zwandenberg, R.M. (1976) Dorobo hunting and gathering: a way of life or a mode of production? *African Economic History* 2: 12–21.

Veber, H., Dahl, J., Wilson, F. and Waehle, E. (eds) (1993) '... *Never drink from the same cup': Proceedings of the Conference on Indigenous Peoples in Africa. Tune, Denmark, 1993*. Copenhagen, International Working Group for Indigenous Affairs and the Centre for Development Research.

Wells, M., Brandon, K. and Hannah, L. (1992) *People and parks: linking protected area management with local communities*. Washington DC, World Bank, World Wildlife Fund, and U.S. Agency for International Development.

White, H.(1993) The homecoming of the Kagga Kamma Bushmen. *Cultural Survival Quarterly* 17(2): 61–3.

White, H. (1995) *The Kagga Kamma Bushmen*. Rondebosch, Cape, South Africa, University of Cape Town Press.

Williams, F-N. (1991) *Precolonial communities of southwestern Africa: a history of the Owambo kingdoms 1600–1920*. Windhoek, Namibia, National Archives of Namibia.

Wilmsen, E.N. (1988a) The antecedents of contemporary pastoralism in Western Ngamiland. *Botswana Notes and Records* 20: 29–37.

Wilmsen, E.N. (1988b) Comment on Yellen and Brooks, 'The Late Stone Age archaeology of the !Kangwa and /Xai/Xai Valleys.' *Botswana Notes and Records* 20: 37–9.

Wilmsen, E.N. (1989) *Land filled with flies: a political economy of the Kalahari*. Chicago, Illinois, University of Chicago Press.

Wilmsen, E.N. and Denbow, J.R. (1990) Paradigmatic history of San-speaking peoples and current attempts at revision. *Current Anthropology* 31(5): 489–524.

Wilson, M. and Thompson, L. (eds) (1968) *The Oxford history of South Africa, Volume 1*. Oxford, Oxford University Press.

Wily, E.A. (1979) *Official policy towards San (Bushmen) hunter-gatherers in modern Botswana: 1966–1978*. Gaborone, Botswana, National Institute of Development and Cultural Research.

Wily, E.A. (1982) A strategy of self-determination for the Kalahari San (the Botswana Government's programme of action in the Ghanzi Farms). *Development and Change* 13(2): 291–308.

Wily, E.A. (1994) Hunter-gatherers and the land issue in Botswana. *Indigenous Affairs* 2(94): 6–19.

Wolf, E. (1982) *Europe and the people without history*. Berkeley, California, University of California Press.

Woodburn, J. (1964) The social organization of the Hadza of North Tanganyika.

Unpublished PhD thesis, University of Cambridge.

Woodburn, J. (1968) Stability and flexibility in Hadza residential groupings. In Lee, R.B. & De Vore, I. (eds) *Man the Hunter*. Chicago, Aldine, pp. 103–10.

Woodburn, J. (1970), *Hunters and gatherers: the material culture of the nomadic Hadza*. London, British Museum.

Wright, J.B. (1971) *Bushman raiders of the Drakensberg 1840–1870: a study of their conflict with stock-keeping peoples in Natal*. Pietermaritzburg, University of Natal Press.

Yellen, J.E. and Brooks, A.S. (1988) The Late Stone Age archaeology of the !Kangwa-/Xai/Xai valleys, Ngamiland, Botswana. *Botswana Notes and Records* 20: 5–28.

Yellen, J.E., Brooks, A.S., Cornelissen, E., Mehlman, M.J. and Stewart, K. (1995) A Middle Stone Age worked bone industry from Katanda, Upper Semliki Valley, Zaïre. *Science* 268: 553–6.

CHAPTER 3

THE ECOLOGY OF FOOD PRODUCTION IN WEST AFRICA

Joanna Casey

The question of the origins of agriculture is one of the crucial topics in West African archaeology because the commitment to food production appears to have been a prerequisite for many of the cultural events that followed, including the emergence of sedentary occupations in the forest and savanna regions south of the Sahara Desert. Investigations into the origins of agriculture in West Africa have been hampered by the low preservation potential for direct evidence, and by the sheer size of the African continent, with a low number of researchers, few of whom have undertaken projects aimed at illuminating agricultural origins. Of perhaps equal or greater significance, has been a tendency for archaeologists to apply models for the origins of agriculture that are derived from parts of the world that are ecologically different from West Africa. This tendency has impeded investigations by obscuring those aspects of the West African environment that have offered specific limitations and opportunities to human occupants, and which may have conditioned the timing and form of agriculture in this part of Africa.

The West African climate is characterized by wet and dry seasons. It is the dry season that determines the flora of West Africa and its attendant fauna. The dry season is longer and more intense the farther north one moves from the coast, resulting in the zonation of vegetation types. Consequently, farming practices vary dramatically from the rain-forest farms in the south that can be cropped all year, to farms in the extreme north where cultivation is made possible only by the annual flooding of the Niger River. In the Sahelian and dry savanna zones of West Africa, where the wet season is the most attenuated, fishers, farmers, and pastoralists engage in three relatively separate but interrelated subsistence orientations. The labor requirements of these activities conflict with each other to some extent, meaning that under certain circumstances, especially where the dry season is particularly long and harsh, they can most efficiently be undertaken as specialties.

Understanding the conditions that perpetuate this tripartite subsistence regime can help us to understand the circumstances under which the cultivation of plant foods became an important subsistence activity. There is evidence that the arrangement of wet and dry seasons that currently characterizes West Africa only came into being some 7500 years ago. The change from a climate where rain fell throughout the year to one where it was confined to a single season would have had a dramatic impact on all life-forms in the region. The archaeological record from this period appears to corroborate the climatic evidence, first by the settlement of previously mobile hunter-gatherers around permanent bodies of water, and second by the appearance of nomadic pastoralists whose lifestyle is adapted to the extreme changes of wet and dry seasonality. Cultivation does not become visible until much later, but the manipulation of wild plants probably dates to this earlier period, particularly among those peoples whose movements were restricted by their dependence on a permanent and immovable resource such as water.

With the onset of the final desiccation of the Sahara Desert, the hunter-gatherer-fishers and pastoralists intensified their subsistence strategies, but were eventually forced to abandon the central Sahara altogether. It is at this point that the first evidence for cultivation appears, and pastoralists and settled communities appear south of the Sahel.

THE ISSUE OF AGRICULTURAL ORIGINS IN WEST AFRICA

The idea of Africa as an independent center of domestication came relatively late to the archaeological literature. It was first postulated by botanists working in Africa (Chevalier, 1933; Portères, 1950, 1962, 1976; Vavilov, 1951) but was not really taken up by archaeologists until much later. Archaeological theories for the origins of agriculture in Africa have followed popular trends in the discipline (Stahl, 1984), being dominated alternatively by diffusionist models citing movements of ideas or peoples (Balout, 1955; Davies, 1962; Clark, 1962, 1964, 1967), notions of 'nuclear zones' (Munson, 1976: 189) and 'fertile crescents' (Hobler and Hester, 1969) and by models emphasizing population pressure or resource stress (Munson, 1976; Clark, 1976; Coursey and Coursey, 1971; Coursey, 1976; Shaw, 1978). Most recently, the idea of intensification, a process with multiple possible initiatives and outcomes, has started to be investigated as an avenue of inquiry into agricultural origins (Stahl, 1985, 1993; Casey, 1993).

There are many methodological problems with investigating early environments and human activity in the Sahara. The types of conditions that may be expected to yield evidence in the form of sediments, artifacts and organic remains have disappeared in all but a few places due to desiccation and erosion. West Africa is an enormous territory with comparatively few workers in it. Vast expanses of it have received little, if any attention. To further complicate matters, research has been undertaken by scholars working in several different languages. Published works are widely scattered in a variety of sources which are not always available. For the archaeology, research is patchy, dating is rare, and many reports remain unpublished or inaccessible (Shaw, 1984). Much of what appears in the anglophone literature consists of reviews of secondary and tertiary sources. Rarely have the original reports been consulted; rarely has this been possible. Thus the barrier is not so much one of language, as it is of dissemination of information. In the past two decades or so, much has been written on the origins of agriculture in Saharan and sub-Saharan West Africa (Andah, 1993; Harlan, 1989a; A.B. Smith, 1980; Clark and Brandt, 1984; Harlan, deWet and Stemler, 1976). Virtually all these are reviews of the evidence which, sadly, has not had anything new added to it for more than twenty years.

Early work on the origins of African agriculture was primarily undertaken by botanists who were trying to trace the ancestors of modern African cultigens. Centers for African domestication have been postulated in Ethiopia and Somalia (Vavilov, 1951), the inland delta of the Niger River (Portères, 1950, 1962, 1970, 1976; McIntosh and McIntosh, 1984), the headwaters of the Niger River (Murdock, 1959; Stanton, 1962; Anderson, 1960, 1967) and at the edge of the Sahara (Chevalier, 1933). Harlan (1971) has described the origins of African agriculture as being noncentric, indicating that African plants were probably domesticated independently in several places.

Actual evidence for domestic plants has been scarce, and appears late in the archaeological record. The first hard evidence for domestic cultigens comes from Dhar Tichitt in Mauritania (Fig. 3.1), where seed impressions on pottery indicate an increasing reliance on first, wild, and then, cultivated millet (Munson, 1968, 1970, 1976; Holl, 1985; Amblard and Pernès, 1989). Millet does not appear to have been domesticated at Dhar Tichitt, but arrived as a cultigen from elsewhere, implying an even earlier date for the domestication of this plant (Munson, 1976).

Other evidence for cultigens has been indirect and circumstantial. Domesticated sorghum appears in Pakistan at around 2000 BC (Weber, 1991), and may occur as early as the mid fourth to early third millennium BC in the Arabian Peninsula (Potts, 1993). As this plant is indigenous to Africa, researchers have postulated that it must have first been cultivated in Africa considerably earlier than this date (Harlan 1989a: 337), either in Ethiopia (Doggett, 1965, 1970; Harlan and Stemler, 1976; Purseglove, 1976), or across the margins of the Sahara (de Wet, Harlan and Price, 1976). One possible sorghum grain was found at Adrar Bous, Niger (Fig. 3.1), from a context of about 4000 bp (Clark, 1971), but it is difficult to assess the significance of a single grain. Rice cultivation is thought to have developed in the inland delta of the Niger River, where the seasonal floods created a suitable environment. However, the first direct evidence for rice does not occur until about AD 100 at Jenne-Jeno (Fig. 3.1), and there is not sufficient evidence to suggest that it was domesticated there (McIntosh and McIntosh, 1984: 172).

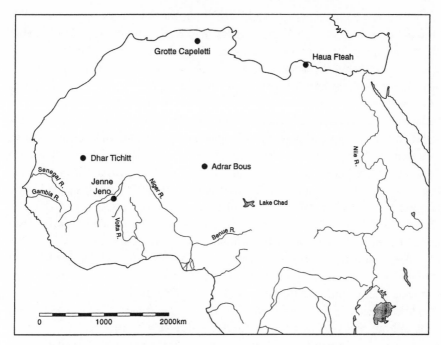

Fig. 3.1 North and West Africa showing the locations of places mentioned.

Vegeculture is thought to have enabled people to settle in the southern, forested parts of West Africa (Posnansky, 1984). The staple cultigen in this zone is the yam, which (it has been assumed) leaves no trace in the archaeological record. The date for the domestication of this plant has been suggested as no later than 6000 bp on the basis of linguistic evidence (Ehret, 1984). The appearance in the archaeological record of specialized tools such as picks and bored stones that may have been digging stick weights has been cited as evidence for early yam cultivation (Davies, 1968), but these artifacts could easily have been used to dig wild yams, and have served other functions as well. Coursey and Coursey (1971; Coursey, 1976) have suggested that the prohibition against using metal tools during the Yam Festivals in West Africa indicates that yam cultivation predates the Iron Age.

The domestication of plants and animals in West Africa appear to have had two entirely different trajectories, and rarely are the two discussed together in the archaeological literature. Hard evidence for domestic animals appears at least 3000 years earlier than does the first good evidence for domestic plants. This separation of domestic plants and animals in the literature on agricultural origins is not unique to West Africa, but the great time lag between the two seems to encourage archaeologists to specialize in investigations of either one or the other. Pastoralism appears to have been established first in the northeast of Africa and to have then spread throughout the Sahara and the Sahel, while the important West African plant foods may have been domesticated *in situ*.

Domestic livestock is said to have come to Africa sometime before 7000 bp (Hassan, 1986) but the actual origins of African cattle are obscure. Controversy surrounds the issue of whether cattle were indigenously domesticated from the African bovid *Bos primigenius* whose bones are found in prepastoral sites, or whether the species and techniques of pastoralism were imported from the Middle East. Sheep and goats, which appear at around the same time as cattle, are definitely imports from elsewhere since their ancestors do not come from the African continent. The earliest dates for domestic animals in Africa are 6800 bp at Haua Fteah (Higgs, 1967; Klein and Scott, 1986), 6600 bp at Grotte Capeletti (Muzzolini, 1993) and 5750 bp at Adrar Bous (Clark, Williams and Smith, 1973) (Fig. 3.1), although herding activity may have started earlier than this (see reviews by Gautier, 1987; Smith, 1992; Muzzolini, 1993). Wendorf *et al.* (1991) suggest that domestic cattle may have been in the Egyptian Western Desert as early as 9000 bp, but the domestic status of most of the very early remains is in dispute (Clutton-Brock, 1993). Wild bovids appear to have been exploited for a long time before domestic cattle appear. Gautier (1987) has pointed out that researchers have taken considerable liberties with the data for domestic cattle in Africa. This strong desire to find domestic cattle all over the Sahara, and to label every site with cattle bones a 'pastoral' one, has led to an overrepresentation of this particular lifeway in the archaeological literature. That domestic cattle appeared throughout the Sahara after about 6500 bp is clear, but what this represents in terms of human adaptation and interaction is another question entirely.

The desiccation of the Sahara Desert after about 4000 bp has provided an almost irresistible cataclysmic event which has been cited in virtually all models as having had the power to force people into agriculture. Such 'prime mover' explanations have been heavily criticized as being too simplistic, too deterministic, and as not being either sufficient or necessary causes for the shift to agriculture (Harris, 1977; Price and Brown, 1985). Much of the criticism has been aimed at parts of the world such as the Middle East where there is little evidence for a major climatic change at the time when agriculture arises (see review in Henry, 1989). The climatic changes in West Africa, however, are too dramatic to be overlooked. There is ample geological, botanical, and archaeological evidence for at least three major climatic shifts during the Holocene, when agriculture developed and took hold. But these climatic events were not deterministic. Agriculture was never the only option open to people living in the Sahel and dry savanna, but at some point it became an optimal subsistence strategy for some of the people living there.

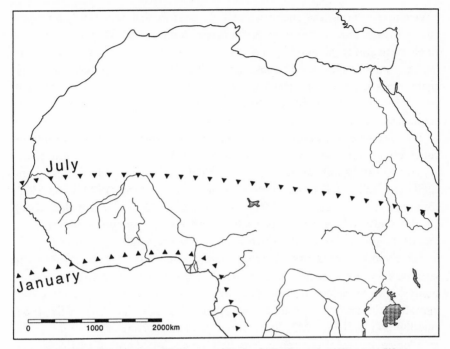

Fig. 3.2 The position of the Inter-Tropical Convergence Zone in West Africa in January and July.

THE CLIMATE OF WEST AFRICA

Rainfall regimes in the tropics occur in zones running parallel to the equator. They are a response to low pressure troughs which occur when the sun heats the air, causing it to rise and creating a zone of low pressure. Trade Winds from the northern and southern tropics meet in this equatorial area which is called the Inter-Tropical Convergence Zone (ITCZ). When two wind systems converge, both airstreams are forced upward, and the consequent rapid cooling of the moisture laden air causes heavy rains to fall in storms (Gill, 1991). As the sun moves north and south with the seasons, variations in temperature also cause the conditions that create the ITCZ to shift seasonally, and the ITCZ migrates correspondingly, though lagging behind the position of the sun (Fig. 3.2). In West Africa, the ITCZ reaches its northernmost extent, near the Tropic of Cancer (23° 27′ N), in July, when warm, moist monsoonal air extends over West Africa to the southern margin of the Sahara. The ITCZ reaches its southernmost position at approximately 4°N in January when most of West Africa is under the influence of the dry, continental trade winds, resulting in dry conditions (Leroux, 1988; Lézine and Vergnaud-Grazzini, 1993). As the ITCZ travels north during the summer, not only does rainfall decrease in intensity, but its distribution changes. At the northern limits of the ITCZ, rain falls in a single peak and is followed by a dry season of up to eleven months. Closer to the equator, rain falls in two peaks, first as the ITCZ starts to move, and then again when it returns. Between the two peaks is a long, humid season. The actual dry season may be less than three months long, and even then, not completely dry (Gill, 1991; Whyte, 1968).

The decreasing intensity of rainfall inland from the coast results in vegetational zones which appear as broad east-west bands. The form of the vegetation can be influenced locally by a number of other factors including soil conditions, relief, and more recently, human activity (Ahn, 1970; Cole, 1986; Lawson, 1986; Morton, 1986; Moss and Morgan, 1970; Swaine and Hall, 1986). To the south, where rainfall is heaviest and the dry season is shortest, the climate supports rain forests which exhibit little seasonality. North of the rain forest, there are savannas of progressively drier types. Definitions of the savanna vary, but virtually all researchers agree that the extremes of seasonally available water define the savanna and heavily influence its structure and formation (Beard, 1967; Bourlier and Hadley, 1983; Cole, 1986; Hills, 1965; Huntley and Walker, 1982; Sarmiento, 1984). A characteristic feature of the savanna environment is a continuous grass cover dotted with trees that do not grow in sufficient density to create a closed canopy. The Sahel was formerly classified as a type of savanna, but recent research regards it as an eco-climatically autonomous region (Gritzner, 1988: 3). The Sahel receives 100–500 millimeters of rainfall per year in a single wet season, and has a dry season that can be up to eleven months long (Gritzner, 1988; Maley, 1977, 1980). The vegetation in this zone is primarily low, discontinuous grass cover, thorn scrub and hardy trees. Rainfall in the Sahel and the dry savannas is not only low, but it is also highly variable. The amount and timing of rainfall can vary dramatically between years and locations.

THE NATURE OF TROPICAL SEASONALITY

Seasonality in temperate environments is determined by changes in temperature and day length. In most temperate regions, rainfall can be fairly regular year round, although if there is a peak, it normally occurs during the winter. In tropical environments, seasonality is determined by wet and dry phases. At the equator, day length does not vary throughout the year and at the edge of the tropics, the difference between maximum and minimum day length is only around three hours (as compared to eight hours at 50° N or S) (Gill, 1991: 39).

In tropical environments, a dry month is one in which less than 100 millimeters (about 4 inches) of rain falls. Below 100 millimeters rainfall is considered to be insufficient to meet the needs of plants as measured by potential evapotranspiration. In tropical climates, high temperatures and insolation can result in water deficits at rainfalls less than 100 millimeters (Walsh, 1981). Often, climates are described purely by the amount of rainfall they receive, but in seasonal environments this is not particularly informative. A more recent, and considerably more useful classification of tropical climates, has concentrated on the degree of contrast between wet and dry months and the total number of dry months per year (Walsh, 1981). An area which receives 100 millimeters of precipitation in a year, distributed throughout the year, would be an arid wasteland, whereas one that receives all 100 millimeters in one month would be a seasonal environment with a short growing season.

Savanna and Sahelian plants are well adapted to surviving water stress during the season when there is no available water. Tree species are deep rooting to ensure access to all available water. Barks and seed cases tend to be extremely thick to conserve the moisture of the important parts of the plants. Many plants store moisture and nutrients in underground storage organs, and can produce regrowth from adventitious buds on roots and branches, lignotubers and xylopodia (Cole, 1986: 50). Most importantly, most species in the savanna undergo a dormant period that coincides with the dry season. Many savanna tree species lose their leaves, and grasses and shrubs die back. Species that produce tubers protect themselves from predation by producing thorns and toxins, or by burying themselves very deeply underground. Species above ground that do not shed their leaves are often thorny to discourage browsing by animals. During the wet season, savanna plants must be able to react to the first rains by maturing and setting seed as fast as possible. This is most efficiently accomplished by growing in clumps or colonies of the same species, which all come into flower at the same time to enhance the chances of being pollinated.

Dry savanna animals adapt by having low requirements for water, living in small groups and by being active only in the cooler mornings and evenings or at night. During the dry season some migrate to lakes and river sides where gallery forests thrive in the perennially available moisture (Dorst and Dandelot, 1976; Estes, 1991).

HUMAN ADAPTATION TO SEASONAL ENVIRONMENTS

The secret to the effective exploitation of seasonal resources for human populations living in seasonally dry environments is scheduling and storage. Human beings living in seasonal environments need specialized subsistence systems that can take maximum advantage of the ripening schedules of plants, while at the same time maintaining access to water. Nomadic hunter-gatherers do not appear to exist in areas with such long dry seasons as the West African Sahel; however, sedentary or semisedentary hunter-gatherers do, especially if they rely heavily on riverine or lacustrine resources. Today, in the arid regions of West Africa, fishers, cultivators, and pastoralists are three kinds of subsistence systems which all maximize the potential of the seasonal environment. Each system can, and in some instances does, function independently, but in modern West Africa the three rely to some extent upon each other in a sort of tripartite subsistence regime. While fish, crops, and cattle form the basis of these three systems, all three also rely upon wild plants and animals.

The annual cycle of cultivation, harvest, and storage in farming societies is an outgrowth of the natural cycles of seasonal plants. In seasonal tropical environments the farming schedule revolves around the coming of the rains. The farming season begins with clearing the land of last year's stubble and burning the refuse. Tilling starts after the first good, soaking rains. If the ground is broken before the soil is well soaked, there is a risk that the topsoil will be eroded by wind or by the action of the first rains. Protecting the topsoil and the seeds and seedlings therein is an important part of tropical farming. Plants are intercropped to mimic the natural vegetation in the area. Millet and sorghum are usually interplanted with a fast-growing vine such as beans, which quickly produces ground cover that protects the other crops until they take hold. The broken soil is also an excellent environment for opportunistic 'weedy' plants which are encouraged both because they protect the young plants from the hard rain, and also as a source of food. As the crops mature, two or more sessions of weeding are necessary to thin the field. At the end of the rains a few weeks of sunshine are necessary to ripen and dry the grains before they are harvested. Other crops are harvested in sequence as they become ripe, usually ending with the big grain crop in December.

Storage is an essential component of the subsistence agricultural economy in seasonal environments because it enables harvesters to avail themselves of the resource long after its season has passed. In arid West Africa, storage is particularly easy to accomplish because, unlike temperate environments where the winter is both the season of the most inclement weather and the season over which agricultural products must be stored, in tropical West Africa the season during which food must be stored coincides with the driest time of the year, when there is absolutely no fear of rain. Dry season storage facilities can be of the most ephemeral kind. Storage need only be aimed at insuring air circulation and protection from predators. Therefore, temporary facilities such as baskets and sacks are perfectly adequate. With the arrival of the wet season, even food stored in relatively substantial structures suffers from destruction and loss through bacterial action, moulds, and fungus (Burnham, 1980: 154; Forsyth,

1962; Irvine, 1969). It is perhaps for this reason that the West African tradition of feasting following the harvest has arisen. The dry season is the time for festivals and funerals when people entertain lavishly and travel widely to visit relatives. At this time of the year, larders are full, and farming activity has ceased until the next season. Feasting stores food within the body as reserves of fat, resulting in wide seasonal weight fluctuations among West African agriculturalists (Hunter, 1967). In addition to fat, the body can store a variety of nutrients such as vitamins A and C, thiamine, niacin, folic acid, and calcium. By the time the wet season returns the stores of food are low, the labor involved in farming makes increased physical demands on the body and diseases such as malaria and dysentery which are related to the wet conditions are also taking their toll (Wheeler, 1980). Because nutrients and fats can be stored in the body for long periods of time, many months of deficient diets are necessary to produce symptoms of malnutrition in previously well-nourished individuals (Longhurst and Payne, 1981: 47). Storage within the body moderates seasonal abundances and deficiencies in food supply, and also acts as insurance against the potential destruction of stored foods with the coming of the rains.

In dry savanna and Sahelian environments, the annual rainfall and therefore the harvest can vary dramatically over not very great distances. An area with a particularly bad crop can be bordered by one that has had a good harvest. Agricultural households can be large, but if the harvest has not been very productive, a common method of conserving it is by migration (Longhurst, 1986; Toumin, 1986; Watts, 1981; White, 1986). Household members may travel to visit relatives who have been more fortunate, and stay for extended lengths of time, sometimes evoking even the most tenuous claims to kinship. Such arrangements are always reciprocal. Although additional members impose a burden on the household that receives them, doing so strengthens ties that may need to be called upon at some future time. No farmer can be sure that he will never need to call upon his relatives when his crops fail. This web of obligations and rights provides a safety net in times of trouble, but also gives others inalienable rights to a good harvest.

Pastoralists are people whose primary subsistence focus is herds of animals. Pastoralism takes many forms depending upon the types of animals that are herded, and the degree to which other resources, particularly cultivated grain are relied upon. Common to virtually all pastoralists, however, is a primary dependence upon herd animals and a pattern of seasonal movement (Bernus, 1979; Goldschmidt, 1979). According to Swift:

> Seasonality is at the very heart of nomadic pastoralism which has its origins in the opportunistic effort to exploit through the use of domestic animals, the huge potential offered by the rich plant growth caused by the rains each year. (Swift, 1981: 80)

Nomadic pastoralists migrate to distant pastures during the wet season in order to make use of ephemeral sources of water and protein-rich pasture. Cattle produce their young at this time, and milk for humans and calves is plentiful and protein-rich. With the coming of the dry season, surface water dries up, ephemeral sources of forage disappear and the pastoralists must return to well-known water holes. Unfortunately, forage in the immediate vicinity of the water sources is quickly depleted and every few weeks the pastoralists must move to find more food for their cattle (White, 1986). Forage becomes the most important resource, and women and children may be sent to fetch water from sources that are a half-day's walk from the camp. During the dry season, milk production drops, and the milk that is produced is lower in protein. Animals as well as people are under stress. At this time of the year, the sick, weak, and old animals may be killed and eaten because they are likely to die anyway, and this way the forage and water is saved for the rest of the herd. Today, pastoralists consume more grains and wild foods in the dry season. Grains are either collected in the wild (S.E. Smith, 1980), or purchased from cultivators. However, work on the Wo Daa Be in the 1950s and 60s found that household herds were large enough for year-round subsistence. Then, there was sufficient milk for consumption as well as for trade. During the dry season reduced milk production was offset by the larger herds (White, 1986: 24). There is a particular threshold below which a household's herd cannot fall if they are to maintain a nomadic pastoral lifestyle. The majority of the diet comes from milk, milk products, and from blood. Among the Kel Adrar Twareg in northern Mali, for instance, the key to successful subsistence is mixed herds of cattle, camels, sheep, and goats which have different breeding and hence lactation schedules (Swift, 1981: 81).

Along the banks of the Niger River are several groups of people such as the Bozo, Sorko, Somono, and Sorkawa who make their living primarily by fishing. Most of Niger River flows through the Sahel where the rainy season is limited to one to three months per year, with precipitation amounting to only a few hundred millimeters. However, the river gets its water from the highlands in the south. There the rainy season is much longer and more bountiful and the flooding schedule of the river coincides with conditions much further south. Most of the fishing peoples along the river also grow crops or engage in trading relationships with farmers and herders, but some of the more remote peoples get their subsistence entirely from the river. Their lives revolve around the rise and fall of the river and the breeding and mobility schedule of the fish (Sundström, 1972).

The seasonal harvest of wild grass seeds is an important part of many economies in West Africa (Harlan, 1989b; S.E. Smith, 1980). Harlan (1989b) estimates that there are some 60 species of wild grass that are harvested for their grains in Africa. While most are famine or occasional foods, he names eleven species that are extremely important in the Sahara, Sahel, and savanna zones of West Africa. Some of these species are collected by peoples who also cultivate domestic grains, but the primary users of wild grass seeds are the nomadic pastoralists who protect the wild stands from their herds, and return to productive areas to harvest the grain. Some of the wild grass seed harvests are so plentiful that the grain is sold in local markets (Harlan, 1989b).

INTERACTION BETWEEN SUBSISTENCE SPECIALISTS

Today in West Africa interrelationships between fishers, pastoralists, and agriculturalists are common. All these subsistence activities cycle on different schedules according opportunities for mutually beneficial exchanges. Conversely, the obligations attached to each speciality keep the activities quite separate. Under the 'pristine' conditions that archaeologists are so fond of imagining prehistoric peoples as living in, each subsistence strategy could probably function on its own. However, contact may have provided a buffer against disaster, and probably, too, a certain amount of conflict.

The heaviest labor requirements for fishing, herding, and farming often occur at different times of the year. Farmers put in their most intensive work during the wet season when fields have to be cultivated, planted, and tended. This is the season of the greatest stress, when labor requirements are high and food supplies are low. At this time of the year, mobile pastoralists can move to distant pastures to graze their herds on protein-rich forage, at ephemeral water sources far from the permanent water sources and locations of reliable but protein-poor fodder. The wet season is also the time of year when it is imperative that herds be kept away from any wild or domestic grains that are to be a human food source during the dry season (Harlan, 1989b). For riverine fishers, the wet season is the time when water sources swell and fish move from the pools and shallows, out into the main river channels, enabling intensive net fishing. Fishers on the Niger River stay out for weeks at a stretch, fishing and selling their catches to the farmers along the shore. During the dry season, farmers can enjoy the benefits of their full larders while pastoralists undergo their most stressful season, constantly on the move searching for forage and water for their depleted animals.

At certain times of the year, a sort of symbiosis is possible between cultivators and pastoralists. Among the Bambara of central Mali, for example, cultivators will share their wells with pastoralists. In return the pastoralists keep their herds on the farmers' fields, where they eat the stubble and fertilize the thin soils with their droppings (Toumin, 1986). Even so, within a relatively short time the forage for the cattle is finished and the pastoralists must move on.

In the savanna zones of West Africa, specialized pastoralists are a feature of every farming village. Farmers may own cattle, but they are rarely cattle keepers. Cattle keeping is generally done by families of Fulani herders who have settled in these places and receive the animal biproducts in exchange for taking care of the cattle. Caring for cattle is a full-time job, and not one that can be done part-time in a village surrounded by fields of crops. The cattle keepers are responsible for finding food and water for the cows and most importantly, for keeping them away from the crops. During the farming season, conflicts over the destruction of crops by domestic animals are exceedingly frequent. Small stock are more easily controlled and can do less damage than can cattle. After the crops have been harvested the cattle are released into the fields, where they eat the stubble and fertilize the soil.

In the more arid parts of West Africa, settled cattle keeping is much more difficult. There is a distinct disadvantage to owning herds of cattle when one is settled around a permanent water source in an area of thin forage. Ethnographically, the Sahelian environment cannot support herds of cattle around water holes for longer than a few weeks. Thus, even during the driest time of the year, nomadic pastoralists in the Sahel are forced to seek other sources of pasture for their animals.

Fishers on the Niger River vary in their degree of dependence on land-based economies (Sundström, 1972). Those that are the most highly specialized fishers are the ones who are most closely associated with farming communities. Highly specialized fishers, such as the Bozo, and some of the Songay, fish year round, exchanging fish for grain with farmers along the banks of the river. Others either return to the land in June and December in order to help with field preparation and harvest, or organize labor in such a way that some of the community fishes full-time, while the rest of the community farms. Culturally, the fishers on the Niger River vary from the ethnically and linguistically distinct and endogamous Bozo who have an ancient tradition of full-time fishing, to the Sonomo who appear to be more of a caste or professional community with the language and customs of the larger communities in which they live. The coresidence of agriculturalists, pastoralists, and fishers along the Niger is engendered by interlocking seasonal cycles of the occupational groups (Sundström, 1972: 100).

THE CLIMATIC AND CULTURAL PREHISTORY OF THE SAHARA DESERT

The last glacial maximum in Europe at around 18,000 bp was a time of hyperaridity in Africa. Deserts expanded, and the vegetational bands contracted toward the coasts. Today, active sand dunes in the Sahara are present above 20°N, but during the glacial maximum they extended south of Lake Chad (Sarnthein, 1978; Talbot, 1980). As the glaciers receded, the African continent underwent a humid phase which was well underway by 12,500 bp. This period of climatic amelioration continued until about 4000 bp, broken by the occasional dry period, the most significant of which lasted from approximately 8000 to 6500 bp. Dry periods were felt differently in different parts of the Sahara. Where high water tables fed large, open lakes, the effects of a drying trend were considerably reduced, while those areas which rely on precipitation and more ephemeral sources of water suffered much more immediate and dramatic effects of climate change. Pollen cores from the western Sudan indicate that a major pluvial event between 9500 and 4500 bp pushed vegetational zones 4° to 5° north of their present positions, bringing wooded steppe and wooded savanna vegetation to the now hyperarid Eastern Sahara (Ritchie, Eyles and Haynes, 1985; Ritchie and Haynes, 1987). The Taoudenni Basin in Northern Mali records a widespread lacustrine episode between 9500 and 3500 bp. At this time lake and swamp deposits became extensive and were associated with large fish (including *Lates niloticus*) and freshwater mollusc species that indicate large, deep, and permanent bodies of water (Petit-Maire and Riser, 1981; Petit-Maire, 1988, 1991) that were evidently surrounded by Sahelian and savanna vegetation (Neumann and Schultz, 1987; Schultz, 1991). Pollen cores taken off the coast of Senegal, indicate that forests and wooded savanna vegetation had expanded into the land that now supports a Sahelian flora. The Sahelian zone appears to have been much reduced and was probably confined to the margin of the Sahara (Lézine, 1987).

The earliest evidence for post-Pleistocene human reoccupation of the Sahara is prior to 10,000 bp. Significantly, pottery and grinding stones appear at some of the earliest post-Pleistocene sites in the Egyptian Western Desert (Wendorf, Schild and Close, 1984) and in the massifs of the central Sahara (Roset, 1987; Barich, 1984); however, not all the sites in this time range have produced these artifacts. These early post-Pleistocene occupants supported themselves by hunting, gathering, and fishing the local resources, and sites of this time period display regional diversity of animal exploitation. The first post-Pleistocene climatic optimum came between 9500 and 8000 bp. Near the end of this phase, the lakes became occupied by groups of apparently settled hunter-gatherer-fishers. Holocene lacustrine sites appear to share a fishing technology and pottery style, and superficial similarities at sites from this period stretch from Khartoum to Cape Verde (Sutton, 1974, 1977). More recent research shows that the lakeside fishers from this period share an adaptation rather than a culture complex, because differences between these sites are more substantial than are the similarities (Muzzolini, 1993). At around 8000 bp, the Sahara went through a drying phase. Aridity was so severe in the Eastern Sahara, that it appears to have been completely abandoned. In the western part of the Sahara, lakes underwent a phase of shallowing, but did not actually dry up (Petit-Maire and Riser, 1981).

After about 6500 bp, the Sahara became repopulated and there is the first evidence for pastoralism. Domestic animal bones appear at sites throughout the central Sahara and sites start to show much more regional diversity in terms of artifact styles.

The climatic optimum appears to have been at around 5500 bp. At this time, lake levels were high all over West Africa. This was followed by the sudden onset of aridity at around 4500 bp. The central Saharan sites are abandoned around this time, and pastoralists appear in more southerly locales (Connah, 1976; Smith, 1974, 1975, 1978, 1979). It is at this point that the first evidence for domestic plants becomes apparent at Dhar Tichitt in Mauritania. A brief period of humidity is recorded at around 3500 bp, but after that the environment appears to have dried out completely, and present day conditions prevailed.

THE ORIGIN OF SEASONALITY

The final desiccation of the Sahara was preceded some 3500 years before by a climatic event that would have had an equally dramatic impact on the inhabitants. That event is the emplacement of the seasonal wet and dry regime. Prior to the mid-Holocene dry phase, the annual rainfall appears to have been consistent throughout the year (Lézine, 1987: 10; Lézine and Cassanova, 1989; Maley, 1977; Rognon, 1976a, b; Roset, 1987; Servant, 1974; Servant and Servant-Vildary, 1980; Schultz, 1991; Talbot, 1980; Talbot et al., 1984). It is not known why the early Holocene rainfall pattern was different from the present pattern. Rognon (1976a, 1976b) has postulated that a change in the structure of the ITCZ resulted in conditions under which the monsoonal air was forced over the continental air, creating a warm front. This is in opposition to the current situation. Servant (1974) and Maley (1977) have suggested that winter rains of northern origin extended down into the desert, creating year-round precipitation as the area was under the influence of rainfall from both north and south.

After 7500 bp a shift to a wet and dry seasonal regime is noted at several places in the Sahara. In the Lake Chad Basin, geological deposits dating to around 7500 bp show sorting of sediments into layers of coarse and fine particles, a feature that would seem to indicate periods of intense fluviatile activity interspersed with periods of low activity such as are found where wet and dry seasonal patterning prevails (Maley, 1980; Lauer and Frankenberg, 1980). In the Tibesti, pollen samples indicate a change to a Sahelian flora dating to 6500–5500 bp. Such vegetation is prevalent within the 100–500-millimeter isohyet; however, the sudden, massive appearance of cobbles and pebbles indicates that the rain fell in storms of monsoonal origin (Maley, 1977: 577). Off the coast of Senegal–Mauritania pollen cores chart a degradation of flora in the Sahelian zone at around 6000 bp which has been interpreted as being due to a reduction in rainfall, and the lengthening of the dry season (Lézine, 1989: 187; Rognon, 1980; Williams, 1984).

THE ARCHAEOLOGICAL RECORD RECONSIDERED

Many of the large-scale changes in the human occupation of the Sahara during the mid-Holocene can be interpreted as responses to a change in climate. Localized changes in the predictability or the amount of rainfall were probably making themselves felt by the resident populations long before the large-scale drying trend we can recognize geologically at 8000 bp was under way. One way for plants and animals to mitigate the effects of water stress is to relocate near to permanent sources of water. Mobile hunter-gatherers in the central Sahara appear to have abandoned their nomadic lifeway in favor of the permanent water sources prior to the mid-Holocene dry phase, possibly as a response to an alteration in the distribution of rainfall. From the relative security of the lakes they could intensify their use of fish and the seasonal plants in the immediate vicinity.

It is at this point that storage became an important consideration. Prior to the onset of seasonality, gathering wild foods and storing them may not have been such an attractive option. Constant precipitation year round would have required a substantial form of waterproof storage. Furthermore, storage may not have been necessary before the onset of seasonality if resources were available year round. However, in regions under the influence of the monsoonal climatic regime, rain occurs during the productive season, and the dry season coincides with the period when most food must be stored. It is likely that with the onset of seasonality, hunter-gatherers were presented not only with the necessity for storing seasonally available plant foods, but also with the means for accomplishing it. Under these circumstances, as long as there were sufficient stands of wild grains or other storable plant foods, actual cultivation may not have been necessary. For peoples living around Saharan lakes, stored grains were probably only one of a spectrum of available resources, but their abundance and the relative ease with which they could be collected and stored may have increased their value over time.

Perhaps an even more dramatic response to a seasonal environment was pastoralism. As mentioned previously, pastoralism is a subsistence strategy that is particularly amenable to extreme seasonal variations in rainfall. Cattle pastoralism appears at the end of the mid-Holocene dry period during which the harsh climate forced people out of the desert. Smith (1992: 65) describes the environmental conditions that would have greeted the pastoralists upon their return:

> This arid phase lasted long enough for an open ecological niche to be available for occupancy by the time the climate had improved. This niche seems to have been an open grassland environment, not unlike that which existed during the previous wetter period. The timing was excellent for the spread of the idea of domestication of animals throughout the Sahara. (Smith, 1992: 65)

But the new environment was vastly different from the Sahara prior to the mid-Holocene dry phase, because the new environment was seasonal. The herders poised on the edge of the Sahara were not gazing at newly vacated fields of waving grass just waiting to be converted into milk and muscle by their animals, they were looking at a relatively sparsely vegetated, highly seasonal environment that their herds would enable them to exploit.

Once the pastoralists have appeared in the Sahara, archaeologists tend to ignore any other lifestyle that may have been coexisting at the time. Any site that contains the bones of domestic cattle or caprids is automatically designated a pastoral site. But then, any site not containing the bones of domestic animals is also designated a pastoral site, because specialized nomadic pastoralists rarely kill their animals for meat (Gabriel, 1987). Most researchers acknowledge that hunter-gatherers continued to live in the Sahara (Clark, 1976: 78; Smith, 1984: 91), but little is made of the type of lifestyle that they pursued, or of the relationship that they may have had with the pastoralists. The presence of animal bones is necessary to help us chart the movement of herders, but naming every site where animal bones occur a 'pastoral' site is not reasonable. This desire to classify virtually every site a pastoral site is also strange in light of the fact that, according to Robertshaw (1990), pastoral sites are extremely difficult to recognize archaeologically. In semiarid areas they are primarily short-term occupations and, as pastoralists characteristically keep material possessions to a minimum, sites can be expected to contain very few material remains (Gabriel, 1987; Aumassip, 1984; Robertshaw, 1990).

The bones of domestic animals do sometimes appear in mid-Holocene lakeside sites but it is difficult to assess their importance. Often the mere presence of domestic animal bone is sufficient to label the site a pastoral one, even though this may not be a prudent assumption. If settled cultivators or fisherfolk were in a regular trading relationship with nomadic pastoralists, it can be expected that over time bone accumulations would resemble the cull patterns of stock keepers who regularly eat their animals. Young males and old animals of both sexes would be expected to occur more frequently than would female cattle which are needed for breeding and milk production. At least some bone would stand a better chance of survival at a settlement than it would on the surface of the desert in a temporary campsite.

Pastoralism is unlikely to have been taken up automatically by the mid-Holocene peoples settled around the lakesides. Cattle need constant attention in order to find them food and water, to keep them from straying, and most importantly, to keep them away from food plants. Settled hunter-gatherer-fishers who rely on the collection and storage of wild plants would be in direct competition with cattle for those resources, unless some vigorous management was employed to restrain the cattle (Harlan, 1989b). This requires the allotment of labor and resources to keep the cattle under control. A few small livestock may not pose such a serious problem, but a large herd of any sort of animal will require management. Evidence from the margins of the Inland Niger Delta seem to demonstrate that fishers, who had been living there since 4000 bp, were little affected by the appearance of pastoralists at around 2300 bp (MacDonald and Van Neer, 1994).

CONCLUSIONS

Clark (1976, 1980) has suggested that it was the symbiotic relationship between pastoralists and fishers at the margins of the Sahara that was one of the factors that may have led to the development of agriculture. He suggests that as the Sahara dried out, the settled gatherer fishers turned to domestic plants as a means of both replacing their diminishing aquatic food sources and maintaining their trading relationships with pastoralists.

Seasonality is perhaps the key to the development and maintenance of this relationship in the first place. Because both subsistence regimes rely on the schedules of seasonal products, and because the seasons for pastoral movement and the gathering and storing of seasonal resources cycle at different intervals, relationships between these two peoples were probably of a very long standing nature. During the mid- Holocene climatic optimum, protein was probably not a problem for either party, because the lakes were stocked with fish, and herds were able to thrive on the rich seasonal forage. Trading relationships between fishers and herders may have been asymmetrical, with the herders requiring the grain products of the settled peoples more urgently than the fishers required pastoral products. The pastoralists, in turn, may have traded not only their animals and animal biproducts, but also exotic items from distant sources.

With the final desiccation of the Sahara, the nature of the relationship would have changed. The lakeside fishers would have found their primary source of protein disappearing, and may therefore have found the products of the herders to be more crucial to their survival. It is also likely that, with the shrinking of the lakes and the disappearance of the lakeside resources, seasonal grains likewise became a more critical resource. These two considerations were probably the primary impetus for an intensified effort to enhance and manipulate stands of wild grains, perhaps first by concentrating them onto the lake beds newly exposed by the retreating water levels. It was this manipulation that brought about the genetic changes that render cultigens visible archaeologically. We should expect to see them first where the effects of the final desiccation were earliest felt. Not in the low-lying lake basins of the central Sahara, which are fed by underground aquifers and were therefore relatively slow to reflect changes in rainfall, and not in the highest points of the massifs where altitude moderates the effects of evapotranspiration. The effects of the desiccation would be most likely to have had the earliest and most dramatic impact on those areas that were most dependent on rainfall in the immediate vicinity to replenish lake levels.

With the increasing desiccation, there was undoubtedly a reorganization of subsistence activities. Full-time specialization in the cultivation of grains arose as one subsistence option which was embraced by both fishers who had lost their primary source of food and trade, and also by herders for whom the aridity would have resulted in the loss of stock. Eventually, people would have been forced to abandon the hyperarid reaches of the Sahara and move to regions where their lifestyles could be maintained.

To summarize, the circumstances under which the cultivation of domestic plants arose in West Africa as a subsistence speciality need to be sought in conditions that are unique to West Africa. The relatively late appearance of the wet and dry seasonal regime, with a dry season which both necessitates and makes possible the storage of seasonal products, and the occurrence of a tripartite subsistence system that relies on the interlocking seasonal imperatives of herding, harvesting, and fishing, contribute to a scenario for the commitment to farming that is unlike those developed for other environments.

BIBLIOGRAPHY

Ahn, P. (1970) West African soils. Oxford, Oxford University Press.
Amblard, S. and Pernès, J. (1989) The identification of cultivated pearl millet (Pennisetum) amongst plant impressions on pottery from Oued Chebbi (Dhar Oualata, Mauritania). African Archaeological Review 7: 117–26.
Andah, B.W. (1993) Identifying early farming traditions of West Africa. In Shaw, T., Sinclair, P., Andah, B. and Okpoko, A. (eds) The archaeology of Africa: food, metals and towns. London, Routledge, pp. 240–54.
Anderson, E. (1960) The evolution of domestication. In Tax, S. (ed.) Evolution after Darwin, Volume 2. Chicago, University of Chicago Press, pp. 67–84.

Anderson, E. (1967) The bearings of botanical evidence on African culture history. In Gabel, C. and Bennett, N.R. (eds) *Reconstructing African culture history*. Boston, Boston University Press, pp. 167–80.

Aumassip, G. (1984) Ti-n-Hanakaten, Tassili-n-Ajjer, Algérie, Bilan de 6 campagnes de fouilles. *Libyca* 29/9: 115–27.

Balout, L. (1955) *Préhistoire de l'Afrique du Nord*. Paris, Arts et Métiers Graphiques.

Barich, B. (1984) Fieldwork in the Tadrart Acacus and the 'Neolithic' of the Sahara. *Current Anthropology* 25(5): 683–86.

Beard, J.S. (1967) Some vegetation types of tropical Australia in relation to those of Africa and America. *Journal of Ecology* 55: 271–90.

Bernus, E. (1979) Le contrôle du milieu naturel et du troupeau par les éleveurs touaregs sahéliens. In L'Equipe écologie et anthropologie des sociétés pastorales (eds) *Pastoral production and society*. Cambridge, Cambridge University Press, pp. 67–74.

Bourlier, F. and Hadley, M. (eds) (1983) *Tropical savannas*. Ecosystems of the World 13. Amsterdam, Elsevier.

Burnham, P. (1980) Changing agricultural and pastoral economies in the West African savanna region. In Harris, D.R. (ed.) *Human ecology in savanna environments*. New York, Academic Press, pp. 147–70.

Casey, J. (1993) The Kintampo Complex in northern Ghana: late Holocene human ecology on the Gambaga Escarpment. Unpublished PhD thesis, University of Toronto.

Chevalier, A. (1933) Le territoire géo-botanique de l'Afrique tropicale nord-occidentale et ses subdivisions. *Bulletin de la Societé Botanique de France* 80: 4–26.

Clark, J.D. (1962) The spread of food production in sub-Saharan Africa. *Journal of African History* 3(2): 211–28.

Clark, J.D. (1964) The prehistoric origins of African culture. *Journal of African History* 5(2): 161–83.

Clark, J.D. (1967) The problem of Neolithic culture in subsaharan Africa. In Bishop, W.W. and Clark, J.D. (eds) *Background to evolution in Africa*. Chicago, University of Chicago Press, pp. 601–27.

Clark, J.D. (1971) An archaeological survey of northern Aïr and Ténéré. *Geographical Journal* 137(4): 445–7.

Clark, J.D. (1976) Prehistoric populations and pressures favoring plant domestication in Africa. In Harlan, J.R., de Wet, J.M.J. and Stemler, A.B.L. (eds) *Origins of African plant domestication*. The Hague: Mouton, pp. 67–105.

Clark, J.D. (1980) Human populations and cultural adaptations in the Sahara and the Nile during prehistoric times. In Williams, M.A.J. and Faure, H. (eds) *The Sahara and the Nile*. Rotterdam, Balkema, pp. 527–82.

Clark, J.D. and Brandt, S.A. eds (1984) *From hunters to farmers*. Berkeley, University of California Press.

Clark, J.D., Williams, M.A.J. and Smith, A.B. (1973) The geomorphology and archaeology of Adrar Bous, central Sahara: a preliminary report. *Quaternaria* 18: 245–97.

Clutton-Brock, J. (1993) The spread of domestic animals in Africa. In Shaw, T., Sinclair, P., Andah, B. and Okpoko, A. *The archaeology of Africa: food, metals and towns*. London, Routledge, pp. 61–70.

Cole, M. (1986) *The savannas*. New York, Academic Press.

Connah, G. (1976) The Daima sequence and the prehistoric chronology of the Lake Chad region of Nigeria. *Journal of African History* 17(3): 321–52.

Coursey, D.G. (1976) The origins and domestication of yams in Africa. In Harlan, J.R., de Wet, J.M.J. and Stemler, A.B.L. (eds) *Origins of African plant domestication*. The Hague: Mouton, pp. 383–408.

Coursey, D.G. and Coursey, C.K. (1971) The new yam festivals of West Africa. *Anthropos* 66: 444–84.

Davies, O. (1962) Neolithic cultures of Ghana. In Mortelmans, G. and Nenquin, J. (eds) *Actes du IVe Congrès Panafricain de Préhistoire et de l'étude du Quaternaire, Séction III: Pré- et Protohistoire*. Tervuren, Belgium, Musée Royal de l'Afrique Céntrale, pp. 291–302.

Davies, O. (1968) The origins of agriculture in West Africa. *Current Anthropology* 9(5): 479–82.

de Wet, J.M.J., Harlan, J.R. and Price, E.G. (1976) Variability in *Sorghum bicolor*. In Harlan, J.R., de Wet, J.M.J. and Stemler, A.B.L. (eds) *Origins of African plant domestication*. The Hague, Mouton, pp. 453–63.

Doggett, H. (1965) The development of the cultivated sorghums. In Hutchinson, J. (ed.) *Essays on crop plant evolution*. Cambridge, Cambridge University Press, pp. 50–9.

Doggett, H. (1970) *Sorghum*. London, Longmans.

Dorst, J. and Dandelot, P. (1976) *A field guide to the larger mammals of Africa*. London, Collins.

Ehret, C. (1984) Historical/linguistic evidence for early African food production. In Clark, J.D. and Brandt, S.A. (eds) *From hunters to farmers*. University of California Press, pp. 26–35.

Estes, R.D. (1991) *The behaviour guide to African mammals*. Berkeley, University of California Press.

Forsyth, J. (1962) Major food storage problems. In Wills, J.B. (ed.) *Agriculture and land-use in Ghana*. London, Oxford University Press, pp. 394–401.

Gabriel, B. (1987) Palaeoecological evidence from neolithic fireplaces in the Sahara. *African Archaeological Review* 5: 93–103.

Gautier, A. (1987) Prehistoric men and cattle in North Africa: a dearth of data and a surfeit of models. In Close, A. (ed.) *Prehistory of arid North Africa*. Dallas, Southern Methodist University Press, pp. 163–87.

Gill, G.J. (1991) *Seasonality and agriculture in the developing world*. Cambridge, Cambridge University Press.

Goldschmidt, W. (1979) A general model for pastoral social systems. In L'Equipe écologie et anthropologie des sociétés pastorales (eds) *Pastoral production and society*. Cambridge, Cambridge University Press, pp. 15–27.

Gritzner, J.A. (1988) *The West African Sahel*. University of Chicago Geography Research Paper No. 226. Chicago, University of Chicago Press.

Harlan, J.R. (1971) Agricultural origins: centers and non-centers. *Science* 174: 468–74.

Harlan, J.R. (1989a) The tropical African cereals. In Harris, D.R. and Hillman, G.C. (eds) *Foraging and farming*. London, Unwin Hyman, pp. 335–43.

Harlan, J.R. (1989b) Wild grass seed harvesting in the Sahara and Sub-Sahara of Africa. In Harris, D.R. and Hillman, G.C. (eds) *Foraging and farming*. London, Unwin Hyman, pp. 79–98.

Harlan, J.R., de Wet, J.M.J. and Stemler, A.B.L. (eds) (1976) *Origins of African plant domestication*. The Hague, Mouton.

Harlan, J.R. and Stemler, A.B.L. (1976) The races of sorghum. In Harlan, J.R., de Wet, J.M.J. and Stemler, A.B.L. (eds) *Origins of African plant domestication*. The Hague, Mouton, pp. 465–78.

Harris, D.R. (1977) Alternative pathways toward agriculture. In Reed, C.A. (ed.) *Origins of agriculture*. The Hague, Mouton, pp. 179–243.

Hassan, F. (1986) Desert environment and origins of agriculture in Egypt. *Norwegian Archaeological Review* 19: 63–76.

Henry, D.O. (1989) *From foraging to agriculture*. Philadelphia, University of Pennsylvania Press.

Higgs, E.S. (1967) Environment and chronology: evidence from the mammalian fauna. In McBurney, C. (ed.) *The Haua Fteah (Cyrenaica) and the Stone Age of the South-East Mediterranean.* Cambridge, Cambridge University Press, pp. 16–44.

Hills, T.L. (1965) Savannas: a review of a major research problem in tropical geography. *Canadian Geographer* 9: 220–32.

Hobler, P.M. and Hester, J.J. (1969) Prehistory and environment in the Libyan Desert. *South African Archaeological Bulletin* 23: 120–30.

Holl, A. (1985) Subsistence patterns of the Dhar Tichitt Neolithic, Mauritania. *African Archaeological Review* 3: 151–62.

Hunter, J. M. (1967) Seasonal hunger in a part of the West African savanna: a survey of body weights in Nangodi, northeastern Ghana. *Transactions of the Institute of British Geographers* 41: 167–85.

Huntley, B.J. and Walker, B.H. (1982) *Ecology of tropical savannas.* Berlin, Springer-Verlag.

Irvine, F.R. (1969) *West African crops.* London, Oxford University Press.

Klein, R.G. and Scott, K. (1986) Re-analysis of faunal assemblages from the Haua Fteah and other Quaternary archaeological sites in Cyrenaica, Libya. *Journal of Archaeological Science* 13: 515–42.

Lauer, W. and Frankenberg, P. (1980) Modelling of climate and plant cover in the Sahara for 5500 BP and 18,000 BP. *Palaeoecology of Africa and the Surrounding Islands* 12: 307–14.

Lawson, G.W. (1986) Vegetation and environment in West Africa. In Lawson, G.W. (ed.) *Plant ecology in West Africa.* London, J. Wiley and Sons, pp. 1–11.

Leroux, M. (1988) La variabilité des précipitations en Afrique occidentale: les composantes aérologiques du problème. *Vielle Climatique Satellitaire* 22: 26–46.

Lézine, A-M. (1987) Paléoenvironnements végétaux d'Afrique nord-tropicale depuis 12,000 BP: analyse pollinique de séries sédimentaires continentales (Sénégal-Mauritanie). Thèse d'Etat, L'Université d'Aix, Marseille II.

Lézine, A-M. (1989) Vegetational palaeoenvironments of northwest tropical Africa since 12,000 BP: pollen analysis of continental sedimentary sequences (Sénégal-Mauritania). *Palaeoecology of Africa and the Surrounding Islands* 20: 187–8.

Lézine, A-M. and Cassanova, J. (1989) Pollen and hydrological evidence for the interpretation of past climates in tropical West Africa during the Holocene. *Quaternary Science Reviews* 8: 45–55.

Lézine, A-M. and Vergnaud-Grazzini, C. (1993) Evidence of forest extension in West Africa since 22,000 BP: a pollen record from the eastern tropical Atlantic. *Quaternary Science Reviews* 12(3): 203–10.

Longhurst, R. (1986) Household food shortages in response to seasonality. *Institute of Development Studies (Sussex) Bulletin* 17(3): 27–35.

Longhurst, R. and Payne, P. (1981) Seasonal aspects of nutrition. In Chambers, R., Longhurst, R. and Pacey, A. (eds) *Seasonal dimensions to rural poverty.* London, Francis Pinter, pp. 45–52.

MacDonald, K.C. and Van Neer, W. (1994) Specialized fishing peoples in the later Holocene of the Méma region (Mali). In Van Neer, W. (ed.) *Fish exploitation in the past.* Tervuren, Belgium, Annales du Musée Royal de l'Afrique Céntrale, Sciences Zoologiques, No. 274, pp. 243–51.

McIntosh, R.J. and McIntosh, S.K. (1984) Early Iron Age economy in the Inland Niger Delta (Mali). In Clark, J.D. and Brandt, S.A. (eds) *From hunters to farmers.* Berkeley, University of California Press, pp. 158–72.

Maley, J. (1977) Paleoclimates of central Sahara during the early Holocene. *Nature* 269: 573–7.

Maley, J. (1980) Les changements climatiques de la fin du Tertiaire en Afrique: leur conséquence sur l'apparition du Sahara et de sa végétation. In Williams, M.A.J. and Faure, H. (eds) *The Sahara and the Nile*. Rotterdam, Balkema, pp. 63–84.

Morton, J.K. (1986) Montane vegetation. In Lawson, G.W. (ed.) *Plant ecology in West Africa*. New York, J. Wiley and Sons, pp.247–71.

Moss, R.P. and Morgan, W.P. (1970) Soils, plants and farmers in West Africa. In Garlick, J.P. and Keay, R.W.J. (eds) *Human ecology in the tropics*. Oxford, Pergamon Press, pp. 1–31.

Munson, P.J. (1968) Recent archaeological research in the Dhar Tichitt region of south-central Mauritania. *West African Archaeological Newsletter* 10: 6–13.

Munson, P.J. (1970) Corrections and additional comments concerning the 'Tichitt Tradition.' *West African Archaeological Newsletter* 12: 47–8.

Munson, P.J. (1976) Archaeological data on the origins of cultivation in the southwestern Sahara and their implications for West Africa. In Harlan, J.R., de Wet, J.M.J. and Stemler, A.B.L. (eds) *Origins of African plant domestication*. The Hague: Mouton, pp. 187–209.

Murdock, G.P. (1959) *Africa: its peoples and their culture history*. New York, McGraw Hill.

Muzzolini, A. (1993) The emergence of a food-producing economy in the Sahara. In Shaw, T., Sinclair, P., Andah, B. and Okpoko, A. (eds) *The archaeology of Africa: food, metals and towns*. London, Routledge, pp. 227–39.

Neumann, K. and Schultz, E. (1987) Middle Holocene savanna vegetation in the central Sahara—preliminary report. *Palaeoecology of Africa and the Surrounding Islands* 18: 163–6.

Petit-Maire, N. (1988) Climatic change and man in the Sahara. In Bower, J. and Lubell, D. (eds) *Prehistoric cultures and environments in the Late Quaternary of Africa*. Oxford, BAR, International Series 405, pp. 19–42.

Petit-Maire, N. (1991) Recent Quaternary climatic change and man in the Sahara. *Journal of African Earth Sciences* 12(1–2): 125–32.

Petit-Maire, N. and Riser, J. (1981) Holocene lake deposits and paleoenvironments in central Sahara, northeastern Mali. *Paleogeography, Paleoclimatology, Paleoecology* 35: 45–61.

Portères, R. (1950) Vieilles agricultures Africaines avant le XVIème siècle. Berceaux d'agriculture et centres de variation. *L'Agronomie Tropicale* 5(9–10): 489–507.

Portères, R. (1962) Berceaux agricoles primaires sur le continent africain. *Journal of African History* 3(2): 195–210.

Portères, R. (1970) Primary cradles of agriculture in the African continent. In Fage, J.D. and Oliver, R.A. (eds) *Papers in African prehistory*. Cambridge, Cambridge University Press, pp. 43–58.

Portères, R. (1976) African cereals: eleusine, fonio, black fonio, teff, *Brachiaria, Paspalum, Pennisetum*, and African rice. In Harlan, J.R., de Wet, J.M.J. and Stemler, A.B.L. (eds) *Origins of African plant domestication*. The Hague, Mouton, pp. 409–52.

Posnansky, M. (1984) Early agricultural societies in Ghana. In Clark, J.D. and Brandt, S.A. (eds) *From hunters to farmers*. Berkeley, University of California Press, pp. 147–51.

Potts, D.T. (1993) The late prehistoric, protohistoric and early historic periods in Eastern Arabia (c 5000–1200 BC). *Journal of World Prehistory* 7(2): 163–212.

Price, T.D. and Brown, J.A. (1985) Aspects of hunter-gatherer complexity. In Price, T.D. and Brown, J.A. (eds) *Prehistoric hunter-gatherers*. New York, Academic Press, pp. 3–20.

Purseglove, J.W. (1976) The origins and migrations of crops in tropical Africa. In

Harlan, J.R., de Wet, J.M.J. and Stemler, A.B.L. (eds) *Origins of African plant domestication*. The Hague, Mouton, pp. 291–310.

Ritchie, J.C., Eyles, C.H. and Haynes, C.V. (1985) Sediment and pollen evidence from an early to mid-Holocene humid period in the eastern Sahara. *Nature* 314: 352–5.

Ritchie, J.C. and Haynes, C.V. (1987) Holocene vegetation zonation in the eastern Sahara. *Nature* 330: 645–7.

Robertshaw, P. (1990) *Early pastoralists of south-western Kenya*. Nairobi, Memoirs of the British Institute in Eastern Africa, No. 11.

Rognon, P. (1976a) Essai d'interprétation des variations climatiques au Sahara depuis 40,000 ans. *Revue de Géographie Physique et de Géomorphologie Dynamique* 18: 251–82.

Rognon, P. (1976b) Constructions alluviales holocenes et oscillations climatiques du Sahara meridional. *Bulletin de l'Association des Géographes Français* 433: 77–84.

Rognon, P. (1980) Pluvial and arid phases in the Sahara: the role of non-climatic factors. *Palaeoecology of Africa and the Surrounding Islands* 12: 45–62.

Roset, J.P. (1987) Paleoclimatic and cultural conditions of neolithic development in the early Holocene of northern Niger (Aïr and Ténéré). In Close, A. (ed.) *Prehistory of arid North Africa*. Dallas, Southern Methodist University Press, pp. 211–34.

Sarmiento, G. (1984) *The ecology of neotropical savannas*. Cambridge, Mass, Harvard University Press.

Sarnthein, M. (1978) Sand deserts during glacial maximum and climatic optimum. *Nature* 272: 43–6.

Schultz, E. (1991) Paléoenvironment dans le Sahara central pendant l'Holocène. *Palaeoecology of Africa and the Surrounding Islands* 22: 191–201.

Servant, M. (1974) Les variations climatiques des régions intertropicales du continent africain depuis la fin du Pléistocène. *Société Hydrotechnique de France, Journée de l'Hydrolique* 8: 1–10.

Servant, M. and Servant-Vildary, S. (1980) L'environment quaternaire du bassin du Tchad. In Williams, M.A.J. and Faure, H. (eds) *The Sahara and the Nile*. Rotterdam, Balkema, pp. 133–62.

Shaw, C.T. (1978) *Nigeria: its archaeology and early history*. London, Thames and Hudson.

Shaw, C.T. (1984) Archaeological evidence and effects of food-producing in Nigeria. In Clark, J.D. and Brandt, S.A. (eds) *From hunters to farmers*. Berkeley, University of California Press, pp. 152–7.

Smith, A.B. (1974) Preliminary report on excavations at Karkarichinkat Nord and Karkarichinkat Sud, Tilemsi Valley, Republic of Mali, Spring 1972. *West African Journal of Archaeology* 4: 33–55.

Smith, A.B. (1975) A note on the flora and fauna from Karkarichinkat Nord and Sud. *West African Journal of Archaeology* 5: 201–4.

Smith, A.B. (1978) Terracottas from the Tilemsi Valley, Mali. *Bulletin de l'Institut Fondamental d'Afrique Noire* 40, sér. B(2): 223–8.

Smith, A.B. (1979) Biogeographical considerations of colonisation of the Lower Tilemsi Valley in the 2nd millennium BC. *Journal of Arid Environments* 2: 355–61.

Smith, A.B. (1980) Domesticated cattle in the Sahara and their introduction into West Africa. In Williams, M.A.J. and Faure, H. (eds) *The Sahara and the Nile*. Rotterdam, Balkema, pp. 489–501.

Smith, A.B. (1984) Origins of the Neolithic in the Sahara. In Clark, J.D. and Brandt, S.A. (eds) *From hunters to farmers*. Berkeley, University of California Press, pp. 84–92.

Smith, A.B. (1992) *Pastoralism in Africa*. London, Hurst.

Smith, S.E. (1980) The environmental adaptation of nomads in the West African Sahel: a key to understanding prehistoric pastoralists. In Williams, M.A.J. and Faure, H. (eds) *The Sahara and the Nile*. Rotterdam, Balkema, pp. 467–87.

Stahl, A.B. (1985) Reinvestigation of Kintampo 6 rockshelter, Ghana: implications for the nature of culture change. *African Archaeological Review* 3: 117–50.

Stahl, A.B. (1993) Intensification in the West African Late Stone Age: a view from central Ghana. In Shaw, T., Sinclair, P., Andah, B. and Okpoko, A. (eds) *The archaeology of Africa: food, metals and towns*. London, Routledge, pp. 261–73.

Sundström, L. (1972) *Ecology and symbiosis: Niger water folk*. Uppsala, Studia Ethnographica.

Sutton, J.E.G. (1974) The aquatic civilization of Middle Africa. *Journal of African History* 15(4): 527–46.

Sutton, J.E.G. (1977) The African Aqualithic. *Antiquity* 51: 25–34.

Swaine, M.D and Hall, J.B. (1986) Forest structure and dynamics. In Lawson, G.W. (ed.) *Plant ecology in Africa*. New York, John Wiley and Sons, pp. 47–93.

Swift, J. (1981) Labour and subsistence in a pastoral economy. In Chambers, R., Longhurst, R. and Pacey, A. (eds) *Seasonal dimensions to rural poverty*. London, Francis Pinter, pp. 80–7.

Talbot, M.R. (1980) Environmental responses to climatic change in the West African Sahel over the past 20,000 years. In Williams, M.A.J. and Faure, H. (eds) *The Sahara and the Nile*. Rotterdam, Balkema, pp. 37–62.

Talbot, M.R., Livingstone, D.A., Parker, P.G., Maley, J., Melack, J.M., Delibrias, G. and Gullik-Sen, S. (1984) Preliminary results from sediment cores from Lake Bosumtwi, Ghana. *Palaeoecology of Africa and the Surrounding Islands* 16: 172–92.

Toumin, C. (1986) Access to food, dry season strategies and household size amongst the Bambara of central Mali. *Institute of Development Studies (Sussex) Bulletin* 17(3): 58–66.

Vavilov, N.I. (1951) *Phytogenetic basis of plant breeding of cultivated plants*. New York, Ronald Press.

Walsh, R.P.D. (1981) The nature of climatic seasonality. In Chambers, R., Longhurst, R. and Pacey, A. (eds) *Seasonal dimensions to rural poverty*. London, Francis Pinter, pp. 11–29.

Watts, M. (1981) The sociology of seasonal food shortage in Hausaland. In Chambers, R., Longhurst, R. and Pacey, A. (eds) *Seasonal dimensions to rural poverty*. London, Francis Pinter, pp. 201–6.

Weber, S.A. (1991) *Plants and Harappan subsistence*. Bombay, American Institute of Indian Studies.

Wendorf, F., Close, A., Schild, R. and Wasylikowa, K. (1991) The combined prehistoric expedition: results of the 1990 and 1991 seasons. *Newsletter of the American Research Centre in Egypt* 154: 1–8.

Wendorf, F., Schild, R. and Close, A. (1984) *Cattle keepers of the Eastern Sahara: the Neolithic of Bir Kiseiba*. Dallas, Southern Methodist University.

Wheeler, E.F. (1980) Nutritional status of savanna peoples. In Harris, D.R. (ed.) *Human ecology in savanna environments*. New York, Academic Press, pp. 439–55.

White, C. (1986) Food shortages and seasonality in Wo Daa Be communities in Niger. *Institute of Development Studies (Sussex) Bulletin* 17(3): 19–26.

Whyte, R.O. (1968) *Grasslands of the monsoon*. London, Faber and Faber.

Williams, M.A.J. (1984) Late Quaternary prehistoric environments in the Sahara. In Clark, J.D. and Brandt, S.A. (eds) *From hunters to farmers*. Berkeley, University of California Press, pp. 74–83.

CHAPTER 4

BEFORE THE EMPIRE OF GHANA: PASTORALISM AND THE ORIGINS OF CULTURAL COMPLEXITY IN THE SAHEL

K. C. MacDonald

The Empire of Ghana is the earliest textually recorded state in West Africa, yet the ethnic identity of its founders, the time of its foundation, and its socioeconomic basis have remained subjects for conjecture. In this chapter, past arguments which posit a postmetallurgical origin for complex societies in West Africa are reexamined and challenged in the light of recent research. In particular, it is advanced that the first complex societies of semiarid West Africa should be sought not in the Empire of Ghana, but in what are termed 'Mobile Elites' — transitory peaks of pastoral wealth and power accumulation which occurred in the Sahara and Sahel from 4000 BC.

A case for the existence of Saharan complex societies by the late Holocene pluvial is supported by the presence of three phenomena: cattle accumulation, valued objects in polished stone, and monuments. A plethora of pastoral or agro-pastoral traditions lacking substantial settlement sites, but possessing burial monuments, are known to have existed across the Sahara from 4000 BC. Associated with these cultures were common assemblages of polished stone axes, hachettes, bracelets, and beads, made of raw materials whose sources are scattered across the continent. Despite this, their ceramic and lithic traditions are distinctive, indicating diverse traditions sharing a common set of valued items and practices.

A form of social stratification within these societies is evidenced by contemporary tumulus and open burial strategies in the Central Sahara, and by the uneven distribution of grave goods at better excavated sites such as Jebel Moya (Sudan). It is asserted that despite their highly mobile nature, often taken as being prohibitive for the formation of complex society in the absence of preexisting states, these pastoral traditions independently developed prestige-goods economies leading to individual and lineage wealth accumulation. It is further suggested that where these usually transitory Mobile Elites encountered additional climatic or cultural stimuli, semisedentary 'Chiefdoms' or 'Medium Scale Societies' developed (for example Dhar Tichitt-Walata and Kerma).

The Empire of Ghana stands as the earliest textually recorded state in West Africa. Al-Fazari, a geographer in the court of the Abbasid Caliph in Baghdad, first made note of Ghana late in the eighth century AD both as a state and as a 'land of gold.' Another Arab geographer, al-Ya'kubi, would write of Ghana in AD 872, stating that it possessed a powerful king and mines of gold, and further, that this king had beneath him in authority many other lesser kings and their kingdoms (Levtzion and Hopkins, 1981).

It was not until the tenth and eleventh centuries AD that travelers and compilers of travelers' tales began to assemble a more complete written record of Ghana – an Empire reaching the end of its existence at that time. Most notable among them are ibn Hawkal, a late tenth-century traveler and al-Bakri, the great geographical synthesist whose masterwork was completed in AD 1068. Only eight years after this, the Almoravid Berbers completed their invasion of the Empire of Ghana which had begun in AD 1054 and captured its then current capital, Kumbi Saleh. It would appear this act effectively laid waste to the power structure of this state and marked its effective dissolution.

Because of these writings the existence of Ghana as a state has never been in doubt. But the ethnic identity of its founders, the time of its foundation, and its socioeconomic basis have remained subjects for conjecture. In this chapter, I will examine how arguments for the origins of complex society in West Africa have developed and how recent research has impacted upon them. In particular, it will be advanced that the origins of complex society in semiarid West Africa should not be sought in the Empire of Ghana itself, nor even in a proto-Ghana, but in what I will term 'Mobile Elites:' transitory peaks of pastoral wealth and power accumulation which occurred in the West African Sahel between 4000 and 1000 BC.

COMPLEX SOCIETY IN THE WEST AFRICAN SAHEL: INDIGENOUS OR IMPORTED?

In 1977, the excavations of Roderick and Susan McIntosh at Jenne-Jeno profoundly changed the way historians and archaeologists viewed the formation of states and urban centers in precolonial West Africa (McIntosh and McIntosh, 1980). Their work from this season, and a subsequent one in 1981, established the existence of a distinctively African urban civilization along the Middle Niger by AD 400 (McIntosh, 1995). The substantiation of the sociopolitical complexity of this civilization has rested upon concepts such as Central Place Theory and the rank-size distribution of sites (cf. Crumley, 1976). In essence, it was demonstrated that Jenne-Jeno was in the midst of burgeoning site clusters from its initial occupation in the last few centuries BC, and that it became the center of a regional site hierarchy during the period AD 400 to 800: at which time there was also significant evidence from the site for interregional exchange in raw materials, agricultural produce and prestige goods (both in glass and metal) (McIntosh, 1995). Evidence for steady local growth at Jenne-Jeno, both in area and sophistication, challenged long-held assumptions concerning the foundation of contemporary polities such as the Empire of Ghana, which were long seen as the product of Berber or Arabic invasion (Delafosse, 1912; Urvoy, 1949; Mauny, 1954; Bovill, 1968).

Such views of external stimulus or outright invasion as rationales for the evolution of complex societies in West Africa have never been totally laid to rest. The colonial-era writings of Delafosse and Urvoy were no doubt the most extreme, being overtly racist in tone. They asserted that Semitic or other white races, being warlike, ambitious, and possessing the mental template of Mediterranean civilization, diffused civilization to an otherwise inert mass of black peasantry (Delafosse, 1912; Urvoy, 1949: 21–6). Mauny (1954) and Bovill (1968) later moderated these views, admitting the potential existence of 'white' founder figures or immigrant groups in some cases, but stressing the centrality of indigenous Mande populations in the evolution of Sudanic states. More recently, the very notion of direct Berber intervention or the presence of 'white elites' in the heart of the Middle Niger has been abandoned for the same reason already outlined by Mauny in 1954: after widespread conversion to Islam in the early second millennium AD, many Mande lineages would have been favorably disposed to invent Berber or Arab ancestral figures. Still, no one would doubt that the medieval cities of Tegdaoust and Kumbi Saleh were substantially Berber in population by the end of the first millennium AD; although the marginality of these desert sites to the activities of urban clusters situated on the banks of the Niger cannot be overemphasized.

Indeed, by the 1970s, it was Arab/Berber stimulus more than Arab/Berber invasion which had to be overcome for the acceptance of an indigenous West African state development model. Levtzion, in his standard work *Ancient Ghana and Mali* (1973), cited trans-Saharan trade as the prime mover in the formation of Ghana. Thus Ghana was seen at its origin as a small-scale indigenous polity whose connection with the trans-Saharan trade and stimulation by northern ideas resulted in the eventual Empire of Ghana. The subsequent findings of the McIntoshes at Jenne-Jeno radically altered these ideas by demonstrating a gradual local evolution of settlement hierarchy, ostensibly based on expanding local trade webs (McIntosh and McIntosh, 1980, 1988, 1993).

However, the issue has not rested there. In 1982, Timothy Garrard's provocative article 'Myth and metrology ...' highlighted for the first time another intriguing possibility: a pre-Arab gold trade between the Roman world and early Ghana carried out by Berber intermediaries. Garrard (1982) suggested, largely on the basis of numismatic evidence, that increases in production at the Carthage mint (which had no local gold source) corresponded exactly with the floruit of Jenne-Jeno (the period beginning around AD 400). Garrard's evidence has not yet been countered and such a trade, with its consequent economic effects on polities near the West African goldfields, cannot be discounted.

Still, as this controversy has evolved most researchers have marginalized evidence from earlier periods which may be relevant to the evolution of complex societies in the region. Some have even gone so far as to write that 'prior to the introduction of iron into West Africa, archaeological evidence for social stratification and hierarchical political structures is rare to nonexistent' (McIntosh and McIntosh, 1988: 110). The current state of evidence for social stratification before metallurgy, however, is not so poor as scholars have imagined. Such data, when carefully examined, provides a long-term narrative of socioeconomic development in Sahelo–Sudanic West Africa which makes debates of an indigenous or external origin for complexity largely redundant.

AN ALTERNATIVE ORIGIN FOR CULTURAL COMPLEXITY: MOBILE ELITES

BACKGROUND

At the beginning of our present decade the outlook for finding complex societies in West Africa before the advent of metallurgy was mixed. Munson (1980) and Holl (1985b) had both ascribed chiefdom status to the settlement sites of Dhar Tichitt, but this polity appeared to be an isolated one, and furthermore was not universally accepted as representative of a 'medium scale' of social organization. The McIntoshes downplayed the importance of Tichitt in their 1988 synthesis 'From stone to metal ...,' and stated regarding the possibility of social complexity before metallurgy:

> We might expect ... that pastoralism would have affected social organization in the LSA [Late Stone Age] Sahara, resulting in the development of hierarchies where livestock constitute wealth and served as a medium of exchange ... Again, such changes are far from evident in the archaeological record ... Burial practices, for example, remain extraordinarily constant through time and space ... there is little in the distribution of exotic goods in the Saharan LSA to suggest increasing wealth differentials ... In summary, the Saharan LSA groups into which metals were introduced after 3000 BP were apparently small-scale herding/hunting/collecting/cultivating societies with a variable component of seasonal mobility, kin-based networks of exchange and interaction, and few archaeologically evident signs of status differentiation. (McIntosh and McIntosh, 1988: 101–2)

Complexity, it would seem, is in the eye of the beholder. Only a decade on from this publication an alternative case can be made, assisted only partly by recent findings. Such an abrupt about-face is due in part both to the vagueness of the archaeological record left by nomadic or seminomadic peoples and to commonly held assumptions regarding sedentism as a prerequisite for complex society.

There are three phenomena which may constitute a case for the existence of 'Mobile Elites' in the Sahara before the Empire of Ghana: valued objects, cattle, and monuments. It will be argued that these represented the means for individuals, families or clans to gain or maintain privileged access to resources. These transitory accumulations could have led under ideal conditions to fundamental changes in social structure, the advent of hereditary rankings, and the formation of pristine chiefdoms. Such entities are exemplified by semisedentary nodes of complexity in an otherwise highly mobile Sahelo–Sudanic landscape, such as Dhar Tichitt.

VALUED OBJECTS AND CATTLE

To begin, let us consider an isochronic diagram of the spread of domestic cattle in Africa, based on Shaw (1977, 1981: Fig. 3) and modified by recent developments (Fig. 4.1). Coupled with this diagram is a plot of sites possessing signature artifacts of a central importance to the present argument. These are what I term stone rings and hachettes. Unfortunately, these artifacts were to the *Néolithique de Tradition Saharo-Sudanais (Récent)* (Camps, 1974) what the bone harpoon and 'wavy-line' pottery were to the African 'Aqualithic' (Sutton, 1977), and it is important to distance them from this monolithic notion.

In definition, hachettes are the smallest class of axes, as defined by their length. Researchers have placed the upper limit for this classification at 3 centimeters (Amblard, 1983; Vernet, 1993a), 4 centimeters (Gaussen, 1990), 6 centimeters (Mauny, 1955; MacDonald, 1994) and 9.5 centimeters (Smith, 1974a). The 6-centimeter limit is based on the measurement of 'votive' or 'gris-gris' (magical charm) axes of modern manufacture, and is the definition utilized here (cf. MacDonald, 1994: 50–1).

Bored stone rings, presumably arm rings, may be differentiated from maceheads and *kwés* (digging-stick weights) (which are rare or nonexistent in the Sahel in any case) by their internal diameter and overall morphology. Stone arm rings on inhumations at Jebel Moya had internal diameters ranging between 5 and 6 centimeters on adults and down to 4 centimeters on children (Addison, 1949). These would seem to be in accord with arm rings from other cemeteries and modern contexts (MacDonald, 1994: 52). A lower internal diameter limit of 4 centimeters is thus proposed.

As can be seen in Fig. 4.1, these distinctive artifacts first began to appear in

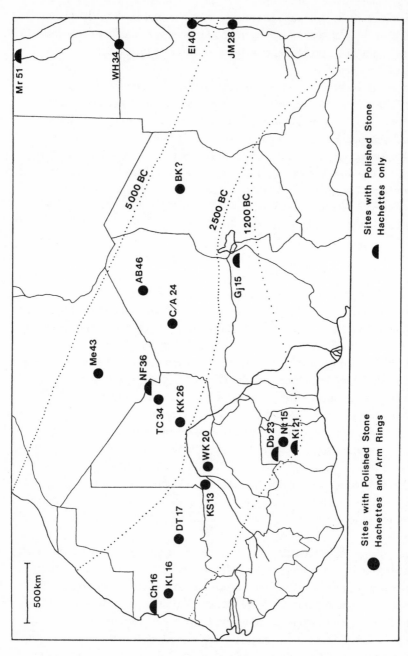

Fig. 4.1 Location of early sites possessing hachettes and stone arm rings with their corresponding median date in hundreds of years cal BC (based on calibrated radiocarbon dates), superimposed on an isochronic diagram (dotted lines) of the spread of domestic cattle in Africa (an update of that presented in Shaw, 1981: Fig. 3). See Table 4.1 for details.

Legend (within figure):

● Sites with Polished Stone Hachettes and Arm Rings

◖ Sites with Polished Stone Hachettes only

Site labels: Mr 51, WH 34, EI 40, JM 28, BK?, 5000 BC, 2500 BC, 1200 BC, AB 46, C/A 24, Gj 15, Me 43, NF 36, KK 26, TC 34, WK 20, Db 23, Nt 15, Ki 21, KS 13, DT 17, KL 16, Ch 16, 500 km tandem in the Central Sahara at sites such as Meniet and Adrar Bous around 4500 BC, although hachettes alone are first known from the agricultural settlement of Merimda (near Cairo) by 5100 BC (see Table 4.1 for references). Subsequently their spread seems to follow the expansion of the pastoral way of life, arriving throughout Sahelo–Sudanic Africa by c. 1200 BC. The greatest floruit of these artifacts appears to occur during the period of 2000–700 BC when they are known to occur in large numbers at many sites, and when their penetration into the forest zone is recorded at sites such as Ntereso (Davies, 1966, 1984). How may we explain their ubiquitous nature? Are they linked with an acculturating pastoral tradition, with a single expanding pastoral people, or have they simply passed between widely different groups from hand to hand? Archaeological history has shown us that we must not begin to invent culture groups solely on the basis of one or two uniform artifacts. Indeed, we may find similar examples of small axes in the Neolithic of France or Anatolia. One may even claim that axes and stone rings, like microliths, occur everywhere because of convergent functional evolution: with constrained raw materials and similar needs, different groups of people will develop broadly similar tools. Polished stone hachettes, stone rings and *objets de parure* (beads, labrets, etc.) are of interest, however, because an argument can be made against their being purely functional, and because of their chronologically patterned distribution. What exactly are they, how did they spread from their source, and what was their purpose?

1. PURELY FUNCTIONAL?

Over the past few decades researchers have taken opposing positions on the significance of these objects. For some they are purely functional: axes for shaping wood, stone rings for adornment (or as digging-stick weights or as armaments). For others they are highly symbolic or commercial artifacts. The debate centers around how to interpret the formal properties of the tools in relation to ethnographic analogies. Smith (1974a: Ch. 6, unnumbered MS) states concerning the hachettes of Karkarichinkat:

> In more than half the cases step-flaking is to be found at both ends, therefore a more likely explanation might be that they were indeed used as axe or adze-heads, since the Eskimos use adze-heads in Nefrite which are the same size and which are double hafted, or it is possible that they were used as wedges for splitting wood. In all cases but two where the cutting edge was damaged so was the butt end … The stone itself would have been ideal for the preparation of wood. If this was the case, the reason for placing a high emphasis on finishing the tools so well can possibly be answered by the place of the modern wood and iron worker

Table 4.1 Key to sites shown on Figure 4.1

Key	Sites(s)	Phase	Earliest R.C. date for finds	Notes	Sources
AB	Adrar Bous	Tenerian Neolithic	5760 ± 500bp (cattle bone) 5430–3800 (4600) cal BC	–	Clarke et al., 1973
BK	Borkou	Néolithique Final	None available	believed on typology to date to 1500–1000 BC	Treinen-Claustre, 1982
C/A	Chin Tafidet & Afunfun	–	3910 ± 150bp (human bone) 2850–2040 (2400) cal BC	mortuary finds from Afunfun dated by ceramic association with Chin Tafidet occupation	Paris, 1984
Ch	Chami	–	3310 ± 240bp (human bone) 2020–1130 (1600) cal BC	–	Petit-Maire, 1979
Db	Daboya	Kintampo Phase	3870 ± 60bp (charcoal) 2460–2140 (2300) cal BC	earlier date from site rejected as spurious (i.e. not dating Kintampo phase)	Shinnie and Kense, 1989
DT	Dhar Tichitt	Khimiya/ Goungou Phase	3465 ± 160bp (animal bone) 2080–1515 (1700) cal BC	these objects continue in subsequent phases	Munson, 1971, 1989
El	El Kadada	–	5170 ± 110bp (shell) 4220–3800 (4000) cal BC	includes mortuary finds	Geus, 1983
Gj	Gajiganna B	–	1700–1200 (1500) cal BC	only the calibrated date available	Breunig et al., 1993

Code	Site	Phase/Period	Date	Notes	References
JM	Jebel Moya	—	4200 ± 80bp (charcoal) 2910–2580 (2870, 2800, 2780) cal BC	early date from western perimeter of site, thought to represent beginning of Jebel Moya tradition (all finds mortuary contexts)	Clark and Stemler, 1975; Addison, 1949
Ki	Kintampo	Kintampo Phase	3700 ± 90bp (palm kernel) 2280–1890 (2080) cal BC	—	Stahl, 1985
KK	Karkarichinkat Nord (& Sud)	—	4070 ± 90bp (charcoal) 2870–2400 (2580) cal BC	—	Smith, 1974 a and b; Mauny, 1955
KL	Khatt Lemaiteg	—	3350 ± 130bp (plant remains) 1990–1380 (1620) cal BC	dated on organic temper from within ceramics	Vernet, 1993b
KS	Kolima Sud	Period II	3084 ± 73bp (cattle tooth) 1430–1170 (1380, 1330) cal BC	—	MacDonald and Van Neer, 1994; MacDonald, 1996
Me	Meniet	—	5400 ± 150bp (charcoal) 4810–3660 (4300, 4250) cal BC	—	Hugot, 1963
Mr	Merimda	—	6130 ± 110bp (charcoal) 5250–4840 (5060) cal BC	—	Hawass et al., 1988
NF	Nécropole de la Frontière	—	4750 ± 80bp (charcoal) 3650–3370 (3620, 3590, 3530) cal BC	charcoal associated with burial possessing numerous hachettes	Mauny, Gaussen and Gaussen, 1968

Table 4.1 continued

Key	Sites(s)	Phase	Earliest R.C. date for finds	Notes	Sources
Nt	Ntereso	Neolithic	3270 ± 100bp (charcoal) 1740–1400 (1520) cal BC	an earlier date from the site was a stratigraphic inversion which Davies rejected as 'old wood'	Davies, 1966, 1973
TC	Tagnout Chaggeret (Site MK 42)	–	4710 ± 120bp (charcoal) 3670–3140 (3500, 3410, 3380) cal BC	–	Petit-Maire and Riser, 1983
WH	Wadi Halfa	A-Group	4700 ± 110bp (cattle skin) 3650–3340 (3500, 3420, 3380) cal BC	mortuary finds	Nordstrom, 1972
WK	Windé Koroji Ouest	–	3635 ± 90bp (charcoal) 2180–1780 (2010) cal BC	bracelets are in terracotta	MacDonald *et al.*, 1994

Note regarding r.c. dates: Calibration was carried out using the CALIB programme. Dates in brackets represent curve intersection points of mean dates (Stuiver, M. and Reimer, P., 1993. CALIB rev 3.0.3. *Radiocarbon* 35: 215–30).

among West African societies today ... It is possible that the small hornfels axes were specific to the caste and therefore given special attention.

Working upon an assemblage from this very same site, however, Raymond Mauny (1955: 622, translated by the author) came to an entirely different conclusion:

Their excellent state of preservation and fine finish lead me to think that they must be 'votive axes' ('gris-gris' against lightning strikes and other dangers, or fertility talismans ... and perhaps even, in the case of the smallest examples, carried in a leather pouch?). A good number have absolutely intact cutting edges, which leads one to suppose that this essential portion was not used.

Having had a chance to study the Karkarichinkat assemblages still housed in Bamako and Dakar, as well as the countless other hachettes from other sites and my own field studies, I must agree with Mauny that the generally pristine condition of these artifacts is striking. One factor which may have affected Smith's analysis was the relatively broad size-range he gave to his small axes which would include much of what other authors include as axes. Additionally, we are not without experimental studies investigating the effects of woodworking on polished stone axes. Van Noten (1968: 13–16), noted after several experiments using different types of wood and axes, that step-flaking on the blade only occurred when already damaged implements were used. Continued use of polished axes on hard woods only resulted in an eventual blunting followed by resharpening. Thus Smith's (1974a) criteria for a functional use of small axes are not convincing for two reasons: 1) his size-range for small axes is twice as wide as that of other researchers, and 2) in the light of experimental evidence it is not clear that the damage he observed was due to woodworking.

Some researchers have suggested alternative functional explanations such as the use of hachettes as leather-working tools (Vernet, 1993a: 93), or for fine work on bone (Amblard, 1983: 277), but the majority of modern researchers have chosen to invoke more esoteric possibilities. There remains, however, one further functional possibility.

2. PASTORAL ASSOCIATIONS

In all dated instances where hachettes and stone arm rings have occurred together in a suite of artifacts, evidence for pastoralism has been securely associated (see Table 4.1). Indeed, they would seem to follow along hand-in-hand with the spread of domestic animals throughout Sahelo–Sudanic Africa. This evidence for association is particularly striking in the large mortuary contexts of Jebel Moya in Sudan (Addison, 1949) and Afunfun in Niger (3300 bp, Paris, 1984), where hachettes, stone rings, cattle, ovicaprines and domestic dogs are all present in the sites' cemeteries. This may simply imply their use as status objects, a possibility considered below, but is there another explanation?

In 1990, Jean Brown gave an entirely new twist to the use of both small and large ground stone axes in her article 'Horn-shaping ground-stone axe-hammers' (Brown, 1990). During fieldwork with the Pokot of Kenya, Brown found that these modern pastoralists still manufacture and use ground stone axes for the shaping of livestock horns. These objects, axe sized for bulls and small axe/hachette sized for goats, are used to perform delicate operations on living animals: smashing the skull of livestock around the base of the horns until the horn cores are loosened allowing them to be repositioned. The Pokot recognize 25 cattle horn styles, many with a special significance only allowed to one bull of a herd at a time. The horn-shaping is compared to an initiation ritual with only reshaped animals being regarded as 'mature' (Brown, 1990: 61).

Furthermore, the tools used to effect these operations have a great value, Brown (1990: 57) notes:

> They are regarded as their most prized possessions after the cattle themselves and are spoken of as 'the foundation of all property,' meaning livestock. They are owned by individual families but are considered communal property which can be borrowed when required without payment. Usually only two to three such axe-hammers are to be found in any sub-location. They are looked after very carefully and are never given away. The loss of two when Pokot were fleeing from a Turkana raid was regarded as a very serious matter.

Brown goes on to speculate about the antiquity of the use of these objects in this role, and would associate them with earlier southern Nilotic peoples (i.e. groups ancestral to the Pokot and Turkana). Indeed, she cites several probable prehistoric examples from the 'neolithic' of Kenya.

The idea that many of our ubiquitous polished stone axes, both small and large, could have nothing at all to do with woodworking is a provocative one. In any event, a strong pastoral association for these objects cannot be denied.

3. 'PRIMITIVE CURRENCIES'

At the turn of the century, R.C. Temple wrote that, 'Barter is the exchange of one article for another; currency implies exchange through a medium; money that the medium is a token' (Temple, 1899: 100), and further that '... currency

implies that the medium of exchange is a domestically usable article ...'
(Temple, 1899: 112). Whatever the social or physical function of stone rings,
hachettes and *objets de parure*, it is evident that they were valued objects. As a
precondition for an object becoming a currency, Eyo (1979) has cited three
factors: (1) scarcity, (2) provenance from an external source, and (3) durability.
In most cases our suite of objects, often derived from difficult-to-find rock/
mineral deposits in remote regions, would suit Eyo's requirements very well.
Gaussen (1990) and Milburn (1988) are both advocates of a 'currency'
hypothesis for the polished stone objects of the Sahara. Gaussen (1990: 567;
trans. by the author) writes:

> To be valid as currency, objects must respect certain rules. They must
> have an intrinsic functional value, or be rare in material or necessitate a
> deal of human labour for their manufacture. They must be acceptable as
> valuable over a wide area and must not be too heavy or cumbersome.
> Our small objects correspond well with all of these conditions.

The idea that there is more to African stone hachettes than meets the eye is
quite an old one, and stems from early twentieth-century finds of hachettes at
Merimda in Egypt (Junker, 1930). Hoffman (1991: 177) noted that 'the
possibility of [their] being at least partially ceremonial was suggested by the
occasional use of an attractive but utterly useless material like hematite.'
Meanwhile, at Jebel Moya, hachettes, bracelets, and strings of carnelian and
amazonite beads were turning up in their thousands associated with 'rich'
graves (Addison, 1949). In at least one grave at Afunfun, Niger, a hachette was
placed upon the forehead of the deceased (Paris, 1984, Sép. No. 2), and at the
Nécropole de Frontier Mali/Algeria (Mauny, Gaussen and Gaussen, 1968) the
single tumulus excavated was found to contain one individual, five hachettes,
three 'flat axes,' and two bone tools. Such items could have served equally as a
form of early currency or a prestige marker.

As to stone rings, Jeffreys (1954) draws parallels between the prehistoric
stone rings of Africa and similarly shaped metal rings still in use as currency in
southern Africa at the beginning of the colonial era. He notes in particular that
brass rings and collars were in use as currency, but not money, in Zululand
before the eighteenth century, and that their value was a one-to-one equivalent
with slaves or wives. Such rings were also given as tribute to notables by the
Zulu king. Jeffreys (1954: 408) notes, 'The payment of *lobolo* by one such ring is
clear evidence that one is not dealing with money, but with wealth.' Thus it
would appear that even limited quantities would not have precluded the use of
stone rings as a valuable currency.

Our next question should be, what would necessitate the existence of a
currency in these early economies? In hunter-gatherer societies the accumulation

of wealth is made difficult by a lack of capital. True, such capital could exist in the form of arrowheads or digging sticks, but unless stone or wood sources are distant and rare almost anyone with knowledge could have access to any number of these 'commodity-producing' artifacts. One could argue that dried fish or game meat could result in individual wealth, but such accumulations would be extremely transient, differing in size from one year to the next. With the advent of agriculture, and particularly pastoralism, wealth could be stockpiled from one season to another. Cattle are prominently visible, often live longer than one decade, are highly mobile and can be accumulated. Certainly there is ethnohistoric evidence for the use of cattle as 'currency' in West Africa, particularly in the case of the Fulani/Peulh who do not cull their herds but use them as a sort of 'bank on the hoof.' These cattle are used for bride price, to trade for agricultural goods and to trade for durable valued objects (today radios, motorcycles, and western clothing take on this role) (Frantz, 1978; Konczacki, 1978; Grayzel, 1990). There is also archaeozoological evidence for the existence of such accumulatory practices in the prehistory of the region by at least as early as 100 BC (MacDonald and MacDonald, in press).

Even in Euroasian prehistory, cattle probably had a more focal role in the development of complex economies than has been previously admitted. Sherratt (1982: 14) writes:

> The movement of livestock is likely to be of major importance in explaining regional exchange systems in prehistory. One site which may be illuminated by being considered in this light is Catal Hüyük in Central Anatolia ... Cattle formed over 90 per cent of the faunal remains recovered from the site ... The site also had a key role in relation to its surrounding region, since it is notable for the extraordinary quantity and variety of imported materials: some thirty-five different foreign materials have been identified, including rocks for axes, grinding stones, pigments and beads, as well as several varieties of flint and very large quantities of obsidian.

This of course brings us back to hachettes, stone rings and *objets de parure*. What could have served as a magnet for the catalog of rare imported materials into early agro-pastoral sites such as Dhar Tichitt (Amblard, 1983), Jebel Moya (Addison, 1949), Windé Koroji Ouest (MacDonald *et al.*, 1994), if not the wealth of cattle? Each of these sites features axes in imported rock types, and carnelian and amazonite beads often from a distance of more than 1000 kilometers. Such items are lacking at earlier hunter-gatherer sites in the same regions. Why did such items become desirable or necessary in pastoral societies?

I would argue that they served a role not only as a type of alternative currency to cattle for trade with neighboring pastoral and non-pastoral groups, but also as a form of durable insurance against natural disaster. Even the wealthiest pastoralist can be laid low by a drought or a plague affecting his livestock. To ensure against financial ruin (and perhaps starvation) why not accumulate durable value objects for use in exchange or the invocation of ritual aid agreements for regeneration of lost stock? Indeed, such objects may have begun as a means for the latter and gradually become the former as they became universally recognized outside the bounds of a single pastoral culture.

The broad distribution of hachettes and stone rings in Africa is thus best explained not by the wide spread of a specific group of people, but by their use as a widely accepted medium of exchange. This should not be surprising in light of the long-standing contention of Neolithic trade in comparable stone objects throughout Eurasia (Clark, 1965; Bradley and Edmonds, 1993). In Africa, there is little doubt that these items were linked with pastoralism in the earlier stages of their development. During the second millennium BC in the Sahel, there is evidence to the effect that they were recognized as valuables by many diverse cultures. There are three reasons for claiming this: (1) they are widespread among widely differing ceramic/lithic traditions, (2) they are made of raw materials whose nearest sources are often at great distances from their find-spots, and (3) they appear in excavated mortuary contexts to the near exclusion of other nonorganic objects except pots (MacDonald, 1994). It is not difficult to understand how such objects could have long proved a smokescreen to the inherent socioeconomic diversity of what has traditionally been termed the recent Saharo–Sudanese Neolithic.

MONUMENTS

Monuments of stone and earthen mounds, serving as both as tombs and ritual centers, have long been associated with pastoral peoples. From the Scythians of Western Asia to the modern Tuareg of the Sahara, tombs have remained the one enduring testament to great nomadic peoples. In the Sahara, stone burial monuments seem to have a great antiquity, directly dated examples from Chad to the west giving a temporal range of almost 4000 BC to AD 500, with the greatest temporal concentration falling between 3000 and 500 BC (21 out of 35 dates; Mauny, Gaussen and Gaussen, 1968; Maitre, 1971; Roset, 1974; Paris, 1984, 1990; Saliège, Person and Paris, 1995) (Fig. 4.2). For the most part, these tumuli lack substantial grave goods, although their construction is often both sophisticated and elaborate.

South of the Sahara *sensu stricto* evidence for monuments dating to before the last two millennia is scarce. Unfortunately, the countless stone tumuli associated with the Tichitt-Oualata complex in Mauritania have never been excavated (Holl, 1986). In Senegal the monuments of the northern 'tumulus zone' have been shown to be comparatively recent, probably all dating to the second

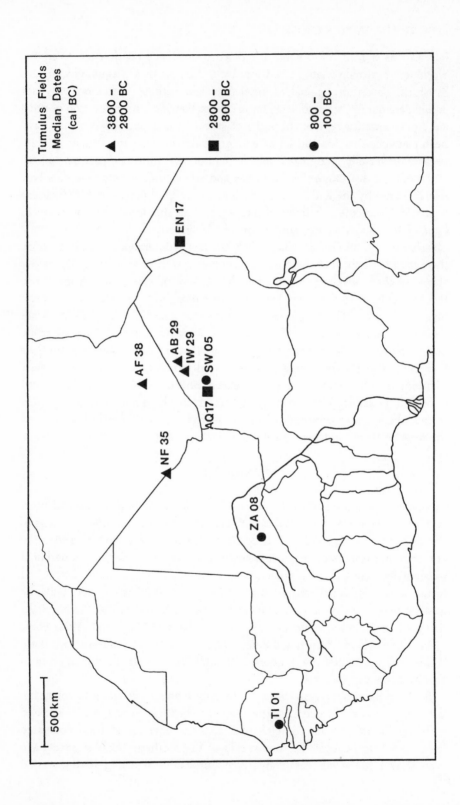

Tumulus Fields
Median Dates
(cal BC)

▲ 3800 –
2800 BC

■ 2800 –
800 BC

● 800 –
100 BC

NF 35

AF 38

AB 29
IW 29
AQ17 ■● SW 05

EN 17

ZA 08

TI 01

500 km

millennium AD (McIntosh and McIntosh, 1993). However, those from the southern 'megalith zone' are a bit earlier and have a well-established radiocarbon chronology which places their earliest phases of construction between c. 200 BC and AD 100 (Thilmans, Descamps and Khayat, 1980).

More recently, my own research has discovered substantial tumulus fields nearer to the Middle Niger – in the Southern Gourma region (MacDonald et al., 1994). In particular two major fields have been found, those of Windé Koroji and Zampia. Nine structures make up the larger Zampia group, which extends in a geographic north-south alignment across an open plain at the western tip of the Dyoundé escarpment (Fig. 4.3). These structures are all clay mounds, capped with local sandstone cobbles. The mounds themselves vary between 14 and 40 meters in diameter. With the exceptions of Tumulus No. 1 which is a two-layer affair rising c. 2 meters above the plain and Tumulus No. 6 which is an overlapping 'twin' tumulus, all are simple structures, semi-circular in cross-section, with a relief of 80 to 100 centimeters.

One of these structures was excavated in 1993, but an inhumation was not located. Instead a plethora of 'grave goods,' if they may be termed such, were found in the superficial layers of the mound. The finds included a minimum number of 120 broken vessels, one sandstone hachette, three grinding platforms, ten upper grindstones and large quantities of calcined animal bone. Of the animal bone, only tooth rows and the distal ends of metapodials and, in two cases, radii remained identifiable. All of these remains were clearly identifiable to cattle (Bos cf. taurus) and ovicaprines (Ovis/Capra). When reconstructed, the tooth rows show a minimum number of three individuals from each of the taxa. Significantly, in both groups we are dealing with two fully adult, and one immature individual. This symmetry suggests some sort of ritual organization, as does the placement of objects on the mound's surface (Fig. 4.4). To begin with, the burned remains of the cattle and ovicaprines seem to have been placed on opposite sides of the mound. Additionally, the

Fig. 4.2 (see opposite page) Location of directly-dated dry-stone and/or clay tumuli with their corresponding median date in hundreds of years cal BC. Key (from left to right):
TI: Tiékène-Boussoura (3 dates); Thilmans, Descamps and Khayat, 1980
ZA: Zampia (1 date); MacDonald, 1994; MacDonald et al., 1994
NF: Nécropole de la Frontière Mali/Algérie (1 date); Mauny, Gaussen and Gaussen, 1968
AQ: Asaqqaru (1 date); Paris, 1984
SW: Shin Wasadan (1 date); Paris, 1984
AF: Afilal (1 date); Maitre 1971; Roset, 1974
IW: Iwelen (13 dates on 10 tumuli); Paris, 1990; Saliège, Person and Paris, 1995
AB: Adrar Bous (13 dates on 10 tumuli); Saliège, Person and Paris, 1995
EN: Enneri Nodi (1 date); Roset, 1974

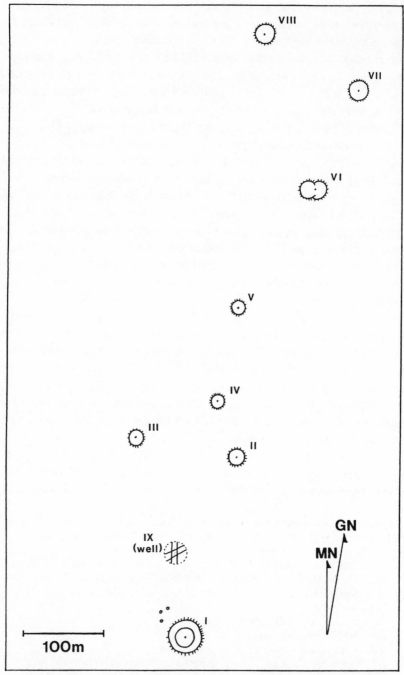

Fig. 4.3 Plan of Zampia Tumulus Field. The small dots to the northwest of Tumulus I are concentrations of stone cobbles and potsherds. Tumulus IX was used as a 'platform' for a well dug in the 1980s.

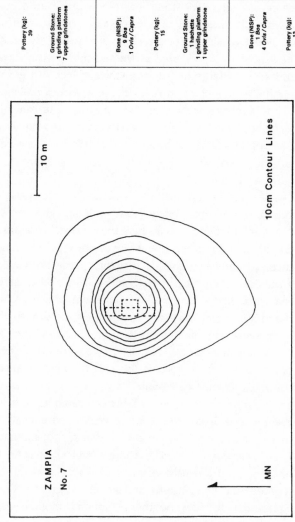

Distribution of Bone and
Artifacts
by Excavation Unit

Bone (NISP):
11 *Bos*

Pottery (kg):
39

Ground Stone:
1 grinding platform
7 upper grindstones

Bone (NISP):
12 *Bos*
5 *Ovis / Capra*

Pottery (kg):
12

Ground Stone:
1 upper grindstone

Bone (NISP):
9 *Bos*
1 *Ovis / Capra*

Pottery (kg):
15

Ground Stone:
1 hachette
1 grinding platform
1 upper grindstone

Bone (NISP):
1 *Bos*
4 *Ovis / Capra*

Pottery (kg):
12

Ground Stone:
1 grinding platform
1 upper grindstone

ZAMPIA
No. 7

10 m

10cm Contour Lines

MN

Fig. 4.4 Zampia Tumulus No. VII: location of excavation units and distribution of finds.

ceramics show a marked tendency for placement on the northern portion of the mound, as do upper grindstones. The hachette's placement was in the central zone. However, it is probable that all of these objects were originally only naturally or shallowly buried, so some post-depositional shifting is to be anticipated. A date of 900–540 cal BC (2607 ± 86 bp, GX–19232–AMS) has been obtained on flecks of wood charcoal from an ash lens within the structure.

A further tumulus, or 'pseudotumulus,' was excavated at the nearby Windé Koroji tumulus field. Again, no inhumation was encountered, but instead almost a cubic meter of rough sandstone was recovered from a quadrantic excavation, along with 108 kilograms of pottery, two grinding platforms, 37 upper grindstones, and two sandstone pestles. Of the pottery, although a minimum of 44 vessels were represented in the assemblage, only two were found intact. Additionally, a large hollow terracotta object, in the form of a pipe, was found at the center of the structure along with a polished stone hammer/phallus. Thus, approximately four cubic meters of broken rock, 450 kilograms of pottery and a number of polished stone objects were used in the construction of this mound. All of the broken rock could have been gathered from the base of the Dyoundé escarpment, which is approximately 1 kilometer to the southeast.

Interpretations of the nature and role of these curious structures must at present be tentative, since their incomplete excavation has not ruled out their use as tumuli. Still, one is tempted to invoke here the modern Senoufou ritual of Yavvatyègi (meaning literally: the place where one disposes of the things of the dead). In this practice each time an individual dies their possessions are taken to a designated spot outside the village, broken, and laid in a pile. For instance, when an old woman dies, her pots, grinding equipment, and even the rocks from her fireplace and any metal tools she used are disposed of in this way. Over time family mounds may gain some height if not washed away or scattered by the rains. Inhumations are all placed away from this sacred 'cult' zone where no one is allowed to walk or loiter (N. Coulibaly, Institut des Sciences Humaines, Mali, personal communication).

In the Southern Gourma the presence of broken ceramics and domestic objects within these mounds, if not the stone phalluses and animal sacrifices, argues for a practice more allied to a 'pseudotumulus phenomenon' (cf. Szumowski, 1957) or Yavvatyègi than of the more 'typical' Saharan tumulus. Indeed, typical tumuli generally consist of piled circles of stones (sometimes dressed), bare except for their inhumation(s) and associated grave goods within. A Yavvatyègi explanation for the Southern Gourma monuments would certainly help to justify the vast numbers of broken vessels on the mounds' surfaces and the plethora of other ground stone objects within – numbers which seem excessive for a single individual. But the clay or stone constructions themselves, and the labor necessary to raise them, add a slightly different twist to our 'pseudotumulus phenomenon.' What was the social function of these mounds, and does it have any bearing on issues of cultural complexity?

Although the Southern Gourma 'tumuli' lack the grandiose and rather personalized aspect of many of their Saharan and Senegalese counterparts, they are at c. 900–540 BC the earliest monuments known from the Middle Niger, if not from the whole of Sub-Saharan West Africa.

A striking parallel which exists between all of these monuments, both tumuli and pseudotumuli, is their inevitable association with pastoral or agro-pastoral peoples (Paris, 1984; Vernet, 1993a). It is significant that pastoralists have the capacity to accumulate and pass on wealth, be it in grazing territories or livestock. Thus, the identity of one's ancestors becomes highly important (cf. Meillassoux, 1972). You may be the descendant of rich 'clan' x, who can expect ritual assistance from 'clans' y and z for past generosity. Or you may need to demonstrate visually the boundaries of your group's principal territory to interlopers. Finally, as 'clan leader,' certain privileges may be usefully legitimated through the ritual construction of monuments to the honored ancestral dead.

The situation in the Gourma is, however, slightly confused by the ambiguous nature of the monuments: were they 'cult localities,' 'ancestral shrines,' 'cenotaphs' or something outside the bounds of our expectations? Whatever their purpose they required effort and material sacrifice to build, as well as some form of central coordination: the alignment of the Zampia 'Tumulus' Field implies a degree of long-term planning. Additionally, they would appear to stem from a need to impress: someone had to sacrifice, perhaps as a form of *fait social total*, livestock, pots, and ground stone objects. Even if they represent the possessions of a certain dead individual, his or her descendants have shown that they are big enough not to have need of them. Indeed, in modern agro-pastoral Hausa society, as in most other Sahelian societies, it is the 'chief' who must be shown to be doing the sacrificing for the good of all (Nicolas, 1986). Thus, we may see here the hand of some limited social hierarchy.

Both tumuli (*sensu stricto*) and the putative pseudotumuli indicate aspects of social organization which would not be out of place in Neolithic Europe. In other words, it is curious that these monuments have not yet elicited the interpretations for complexity bestowed upon Neolithic cairns and barrows in Britain (e.g. Renfrew, 1973; Edmonds, 1995). Renfrew used the distribution of such features across the British landscape to argue the territorial boundaries for early 'Chiefdoms.' It seems not unreasonable to suggest that such monuments in Africa, their nonuniversality, and their systematic placement in the landscape, may indicate comparable levels of social organization.

SEMISEDENTARY FOCI IN A MOBILE CONTINUUM

KERMA

On at least two occasions during the third and second millennia BC, sedentary or semisedentary complex societies arose in the African Sahelo–Sudanic zone. The first of these was Kerma, which although situated firmly in an Egyptian sphere of influence, was in its early stages a distinctively Sahelian polity (Bonnet, 1990, 1992). Known from between the second and fourth cataracts of the Nile, the Kerma tradition grew out of an agro-pastoral economy with certain affinities to the more mobile A-Group. Its first structures were circular, sunken huts (Pre-Kerma 3500–2500 BC). From 2500 BC rectilinear dwellings in mudbrick become more common at the principal site of Kerma, although a very large circular structure ('the large hut') remained a principal, probably elite, dwelling in the mid-second millennium BC. Tumuli, particularly of the Early Kerma (2500–2050 BC) and Middle Kerma (2050–1750 BC) periods, have apparent affinities in size, shape and construction with typical Saharan tumuli (see, for example, Paris, 1984). They differ, however, in the scale and type of their grave goods. In Early Kerma these included sheep-sacrifices, adorned with faience beads, and human sacrifices, along with more mundane pottery and polished stone items. Burials were also covered with leather blankets, a practice also evident in Central Niger at this time (Paris, 1990). By the Middle Kerma period entire cattle and sheep herds were sacrificed and buried around the perimeter of some tumuli. From the Classic Kerma period (1750–1580 BC) grandiose tumuli with vast super-structures and associated temples appeared, and the last vestiges of Sahelian characteristics gave way to an increasing influence from Egypt.

DARFUR

Between the Nile and Lake Chad there is an additional, if putative, early sedentary focus point. Within northern Darfur, there exist several large dry-stone-masonry settlements associated with round, stone and earthen tumuli. Some of these sites which displayed evidence of iron-working were test-excavated during the 1980s and dated to between AD 300 and 1000 (Jabal Mao, Ain Farah and Jabal Bora, cf. Musa Mohammed, 1986 and Musa, 1993). More recently, Dumont and El Moghraby (1993) have asserted that some unexcavated architectural sites in the area (e.g. Abu Garan, Malha, and Seringeti) may be much older than those tested by Musa Mohammed.

It should be noted that of the ten architectural sites surveyed by Musa Mohammed (1986) in the Darfur region, iron objects were recovered only from three, and that of the four first millennium AD radiocarbon dates presented by Musa Mohammed (1986: 253–5) three came from these 'metallurgical' sites with the fourth being from a cave site. Dumont and El Moghraby (1993), by survey of additional architectural sites, have presented a chronological argument based upon population estimates from site size and climate. They assert that some of these sites, with populations of up to 6000 people, could not have existed in the region after the recent hyperarid phase began at c. 3000 bp (as derived from the Lake Melha climatic sequence). Dumont and El Moghraby (1993:.385) note the presence of stone axes and arrowheads at the sites, as well as more modern trade artifacts ('bronze' objects and cowries). Despite such seemingly contradictory elements of material culture, a second to first millennium BC age-range for the founding of these sites would not seem far-fetched. As such, they would fit in well with similar manifestations at Kerma and Dhar Tichitt.

DHAR TICHITT

Unlike Kerma, whose floruit could be attributed to Egyptian stimulus, Dhar Tichitt stands alone as a manifestly 'pristine' complex society, far removed from any contemporary civilizations. The Dhar Tichitt tradition stretches along the southern escarpments of Mauritania, from Dhar Tichitt east to Dhar Oualata and Dhar Néma, eventually crossing the modern Malian frontier into the Méma region (Munson, 1971, 1980; MacDonald and Van Neer, 1994; MacDonald, 1996). The chronology of the Dhar Tichitt complex has long remained a matter for debate, with radiocarbon dates providing the basis for sequences of eight phases (Munson, 1971, 1980), four phases (Vernet, 1993a; MacDonald, 1996), two phases (Holl, 1993) and one phase (Amblard, 1983). The basic reasons for retaining a measure of developmental chronology are well outlined in Munson (1989). The view to be presented here follows the four-phase chronology.

After a pre-2000 BC hunter-gatherer occupation of the region, pastoralists without domesticated cereals entered the Dhar Tichitt region. From 2000 to 1400 BC there would appear to have been no permanent dry-stone constructions. Sites would have been temporary, serving as grain-gathering, fishing and pastoral encampments. But from 1400 BC substantial changes occurred at Dhar Tichitt on a regional scale. Between 1400 and 800 BC evidence for the local domestication of millet appears, along with the full expression of the Tichitt architectural tradition on Dhars Tichitt and Oualata, and the spread of Tichitt tradition sites from the principal escarpment to the Méma region (e.g. the site of Kolima Sud, see Fig. 4.1) (Munson, 1971, 1976; Amblard and Pernès 1989; MacDonald, 1996). Settlement hierarchies which have been documented by Holl (1985, 1993) were also in place at this time. It has been posited that these dramatic changes were the result of general environmental deterioration in the Sahel at this time, reducing stands of wild grain and pasture land; resulting in agricultural innovations and increased territoriality (Munson, 1980; personal communication). However, the Tichitt civilization was short-lived. Between 800 and 200 BC it declined rapidly due to continuing environmental degradation and the raiding of Berber people from the north. During this period most sites were abandoned, and those which remained were of reduced size in easily defendable locations.

The case for Tichitt at its height as a 'chiefdom,' or medium-level complex society has already been well-presented by Munson (1980) and Holl (1985, 1993). Essentially arguments have been based upon evidence for sedentism, coupled with site size, and definite evidence for settlement hierarchy among its numerous dry-stone masonry villages. Arguments could also be advanced on the basis of evidence for broad exchange networks, with a wide array of imported polished and chipped stone artifacts being recovered from Dhar Tichitt tradition sites (cf. Amblard, 1983). Holl (1993) has identified four levels of site hierarchy among sites recorded on the main Tichitt escarpment: Regional Centers (number: 1, area: 80.5 hectares, excluding a nearby satellite site), District Centers (number: 5, area: c. 15 hectares), Small Villages (number: 12, area: c. 10 hectares), and Hamlets (number: 72, area: c. 1–2 hectares). The regional center, Dakhlet el Atrous (Fig. 4.5) is particularly impressive, being of a scale comparable to the largest Middle Niger urban sites of the first millennium AD. Within its compound walls are the foundations of granaries, and dotted around the site's perimeter are both numerous stone tumuli, and what have long been assumed to be cattle corrals. None of the tumuli have been excavated, perhaps because the region's researchers were long convinced they were only recent Berber constructions (Munson, personal communication). Evidence from adjoining regions would, however, suggest that many, if not most, of these were likely to be contemporaneous with Dhar Tichitt's 'Neolithic' occupation.

Undoubtedly the continued study of the Tichitt tradition will add further points and refinements of detail to its developmental sequence and to its social structure. But certain facts will remain: a nonagricultural, mobile pastoral society developed in the space of a few hundred years into a sedentary or semisedentary agro-pastoral society with elaborate settlement structures. In this, Tichitt provides the best case for the crystallization of Mobile Elites into a durable and expansive ranked society.

DISCUSSION: WHY MOBILE ELITES?

The social organization of Sahelo–Sudanic pastoralists has relentlessly been depicted as one of minimal social hierarchy (e.g. Bonte, 1977; Burnham, 1979; Johnson and Earle, 1987). Priorities of freedom of family movement, self-determination and socioeconomic fluidity have been emphasized: tendencies

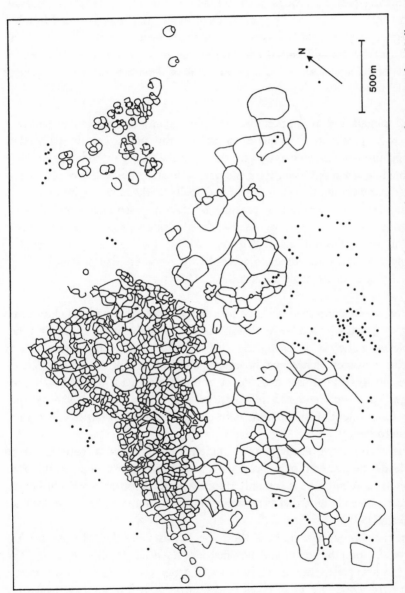

Fig. 4.5 Plan of Dakhlet el Atrous, the largest Dhar Tichitt 'village' site, being 80 hectares in surface area (after Holl, 1993). The dots represent tumuli. Note that the enclosures represent stone compound and 'corral' walls, not houses.

which leave little room for the development of durable hierarchies and central authority. Exceptions, such as nomadic Tuareg 'chiefdoms,' have been viewed as arising from the preexistence of states or sedentary communities to which such raiding pastoral groups could be parasitic (Burnham, 1979). In contrast, Sàenz (1991) has presented a very different model for the derivation of ranked Tuareg society, which is based around the breeding control of surviving animals after a drought period, and only secondarily on parasitism. His case for the eastern Tuaregs serves as a good point of departure for a more general model. He writes:

> As animals perish in periodic droughts (under conditions in which average profits are adequate to supply the needs of the pastoral population, but breeding stock for restoring the slowly reproducing herds would be lacking) the warrior aristocrats controlling the source of revenue used in rebuilding the herds would eventually (in the long run) become an elite class ... If through ... prestige or charisma associated with ritual, managerial effectiveness, or some such – an elite gains control over the rights to surplus animals, that group, like the Twareg *imajaghan*, would eventually come to dominate access to the resources that sustain life at the expense of its rivals. (Sàenz, 1991: 118)

Here, we are concerned with the possibility that African pastoral elites came about in 'pristine' conditions; that is, before the advent of states or other complex sedentary societies in their vicinity. Unfortunately, the preexistence of an external source of revenue, however peripheral, is still inherent in Sàenz's model. But his hypothesis provides a good core idea for a 'pristine' model: drought conditions and a fragile pastoral economy can crystallize existing elites. How might such transient elite elements, Sàenz's 'warrior aristocrats,' come into being?

Even in the most 'egalitarian' of modern Sahelian pastoral societies, there exist leader figures who may direct the activities of larger groups on the basis of popular consent. This is certainly the case for the Wodaabe or Peulh Bororo of Niger, generally regarded as an exemplar of nonstratified African pastoralists (Burnham, 1979).

The social organization of the Wodaabe, at least since the 19th century, has been based upon the common denominator of the *dudal* (Bonfiglioli, 1988). The *dudal* is, in simplest terms, a family or social group economically reliant upon a single herd. *Dudal* are themselves fluidly incorporated into *kinnal*, which are voluntary sociopastoral federations. However, within the *kinnal* there is no common property in terms of herds or water sources, only loose territorial affiliations derived from common pastures (Bonfiglioli, 1988: 47).

At the level of *dudal* there is always a headman, both of the herd and the family (*jom wuro* and *jom n'ai*), and significantly at the level of the *kinnal* there is also a leader. This 'federation' or 'clan' leader-figure is the *ardo*. An *ardo* only governs through the trust of the *kinnal* in his competence in the management of herds and his justice in the arbitration of disputes. The *ardo* directs the movements of herds, negotiates with external groups on the behalf of the *kinnal*, and is a source of local judgment. The position of *ardo* is of course not an hereditary one, but one of merit (Bonfiglioli, 1988: 51–2).

It would be a mistake, however, to assume that this historical 'snapshot' of pastoral social organization is indicative of a never-changing type of society. Indeed, one of the roles of archaeology should be the provision of time-depth for the temporally impoverished study of ethnography. Archaeology must anticipate social situations and developmental sequences for which there is no modern nor historical analog. It is not difficult to imagine how social arrangements like those of the Wodaabe might have thrown up short-lived elite structures in prehistory, which under certain optimal conditions might have become fixed.

From 4000 BC, the pastoral societies of the Sahara probably possessed relatively egalitarian social structures comparable to those of the modern Wodaabe (Bonfiglioli, 1988) or the Turkana (Johnson and Earle, 1987). 'Clan' leaders could have coordinated a trade in valued objects to cement cooperative alliances both within and without their sociopastoral groups. On occasion the most successful of these leaders might have merited special graves within their group's pasture areas. However in the event of climatic crises or cattle epidemics, such leaders may have found themselves in the possession of power which was no longer fully consensual. 'Bottlenecks' in cattle wealth caused by such tragedies would have placed certain clan leaders and federations in positions superior to that of their fellows. Whilst in more minor crises an essentially egalitarian social structure could be maintained through ritual aid agreements and the 'cashing-in' of valued objects, in major crises this might not have been possible due to a lack of sufficient remaining cattle capital. Master-client relationships might have been formed between clans who had successfully preserved their herds, and those who had lost them completely. Droughts may have also caused greater competition for pasture areas, leading to conflicts, an increased sense of territoriality, and a greater importance of long-term loyalty to a centralized authority. For the most part such concentrations of power or wealth would soon have been dissipated, with a subsequent return to more egalitarian organization. But as the tempo of environmental deterioration increased after 2000 BC, such disequilibria would have become more and more commonplace: ever-increasing sparks onto the awaiting tinder of durable stratified society. In certain regions, such as at Dhar Tichitt, these sparks caught. Then, sedentary chiefdoms, aided by the emergence of cereal agriculture, came into being.

CONCLUSIONS

The model which I would advocate for the origin of complex societies in semiarid West Africa stresses two factors: primarily cattle wealth, and secondarily environmental change. Without an ability to control the means of production there can be no emergence of an elite. In our area cattle initially provide this means, and gradual desiccation provides an added stimulus by making the control of dwindling herds and decreasing supplies of arable land crucial as well. Hachettes, stone rings and *objets de parure* have been put forward as the durable expression of livestock wealth. Such objects could be accumulated as insurance against disaster, displayed as a sign of wealth or power, and used as a medium of exchange against commodities on a small scale. Their manipulation, and the manipulation of herds, would have created a power base for the first 'elites' in the later prehistory of West Africa. Eventually, with the advent of metallurgy, these commodities would become less central in the maintenance of localized power bases. Metals would become, by the time of the Empire of Ghana, the economic prime mover.

Thus, in summary, I propose that Middle Niger complex societies may have evolved in the following manner. From about 4000 BC the accumulation of cattle wealth and a limited array of prestige goods, coupled with natural irregularities in climate and resources, would occasionally have allowed certain 'clans' or 'clan leaders' to operate from a trade position superior to that of their fellows. These accumulations would have been transitory, and normally wiped away within the course of one generation. From about 2000 BC continued population concentration around dwindling waterways, would have led to a scarcity of land. The effective protection of territories would have encouraged the formation of federations of 'clans' under the leadership of the elites of the moment. Initially these elite-led groups would have been largely mobile, revolving around ritual centers placed in regions of annual concentration (e.g. 'Big Man Collectivities,' Johnson and Earle, 1987). However, in certain favorable regions, more archaeologically prominent semisedentary 'chiefdoms' or 'medium-scale societies' could have formed (such as at Dhar Tichitt in the west, or Kerma to the east).

These Mobile Elites, and subsequent 'chiefdoms' (from about 1500 BC), would have monopolized and redistributed long-distance trade goods (particularly objects in semiprecious stone) and cattle. The authority of elites could have been maintained through ritual display involving the construction of monuments or through threat of violence and raiding of those operating outside of their authority. By the time of metallurgy's introduction to the area by 800 BC, these elites would have been in the position to gain initial control over this new technology. Iron goods, it may be supposed, allowed an increase in agricultural production which rapidly resulted in the growth of large sedentary villages throughout the Middle Niger. Groups of these villages, led by the successors of the original mobile elites, would thus represent the foundations of the Empire of Ghana. From this basis, a neophyte state would emerge, and through its already existing trade connections and regional authority, be in a position to thrive on trans-Saharan trade offered on equal terms by the Berbers in the early first millennium AD.

ACKNOWLEDGMENTS

I would like to thank my wife and colleague Rachel Hutton MacDonald for her aid in the assembly of this chapter. Also, I acknowledge gratefully several useful comments of my friend and colleague Cyprian Broodbank concerning nomenclature. The personal research discussed here was funded by grants from the Swan Fund (Oxford) and the Anthony Wilkin Fund (Cambridge), and was performed in cooperation with the Malian Institut des Sciences Humaines.

This chapter is dedicated to my many Peulh friends and acquaintances in Mali, particularly the Sidibés and Bas of Nampala, and the Cissés of Douentza.

BIBLIOGRAPHY

Addison, F. (1949) *Wellcome excavations in the Sudan: I, Jebel Moya, 1910–1914.* Oxford, Oxford University Press.

Amblard, S. (1983) *Tichitt-Walata (R.I. Mauritanie): Civilisation et industrie lithique.* Paris, Editions Recherches sur les Civilisations.

Amblard, S. and Pernès, J. (1989) The identification of cultivated pearl millet (*Pennisetum*) amongst plant impressions on pottery from Oued Chebbi (Dhar Oualata, Mauritania). *African Archaeological Review* 7: 117–26.

Bonfiglioli, A.M. (1988) *Dudal: histoire de famille et histoire de troupeau chez un groupe de Wodaabe du Niger.* Cambridge, Cambridge University Press.

Bonnet, C. (ed.) (1990) *Kerma, royaume de Nubie.* Geneva, Mission Archéologique de l'Université de Genève au Soudan.

Bonnet, C. (1992) Excavations at the Nubian royal town of Kerma: 1975–91. *Antiquity* 66: 611–25.

Bonte, P. (1977) Non-stratified social formations among pastoral nomads. In Friedman J. and Rowlands, M. (eds) *The evolution of social systems.* London, Duckworth, pp. 173–200.

Bovill, E.W. (1968) *The golden trade of the Moors.* Oxford, Oxford University Press.

Bradley, R. and Edmonds, M. (1993) *Interpreting the axe trade: production and exchange in Neolithic Britain.* Cambridge, Cambridge University Press.

Breunig, P., Ballouche, A., Neumann, K., Rosing, F., Thiemeyer, H., Wendt, P. and Van Neer, W. (1993) Gajiganna: new data on early settlement and environment in the Chad Basin. *Berichte des Sonderforschungsbereichs.* 268(2): 51–74.

Brown, J. (1990) Horn-shaping ground-stone axe-hammers. *Azania* 25: 57–67.

Burnham, P. (1979) Spatial mobility and political centralization in pastoral societies. In

L'Equipe écologie et anthropologie des sociétés pastorales (eds) *Pastoral production and society*. Cambridge, Cambridge University Press, pp. 349–60.

Camps, G. (1974) *Les civilisations préhistoriques de l'Afrique du Nord et du Sahara*. Paris, Doin.

Clark, J.D. and Stemler, A. (1975) Early domesticated sorghum from central Sudan. *Nature* 254: 588–91.

Clark, J.D., Williams, M.A.J. and Smith, A.B. (1973) The geomorphology and archaeology of Adrar Bous, central Sahara: a preliminary report. *Quaternaria* 12: 245–67.

Clark, J.G.D. (1965) Traffic in stone axe and adze blades. *Economic History Review (2nd Series)* 18: 1–28.

Crumley, C. (1976) Towards a locational definition of state systems of settlement. *American Anthropologist* 78: 59–73.

Davies, O. (1966) The invasion of Ghana from the Sahara in the Early Iron Age. In *Actas del V Congreso Panafricano de Prehistoria, Tenerife 1963*. Tenerife, Museo Arquelogico, pp. 27–42.

Davies, O. (1973) *Excavations at Ntereso, Gonja, northern Ghana. Final Report*. Pietermaritzburg, Natal Museum.

Davies, O. (1984) The Ntereso Culture in Ghana. In Schwartz, B. and Dumett, R. (eds) *West African culture dynamics: archaeological and historical perspectives*. The Hague, Mouton, pp. 205–25.

Delafosse, M. (1912) *Haut-Sénégal-Niger*. Paris, Larose.

Dumont, H.J. and El Moghraby, A.I. (1993) Holocene evolution of climate, and stone 'city' ruins in northern Darfur, Sudan: is there a relationship? In Krzyzaniak, L., Kobusiewiz, M. and Alexander, J. (eds) *Environmental change and human culture in the Nile basin and northern Africa until the second millennium BC*. Poznan, Poznan Archaeological Museum, pp. 381–97.

Edmonds, M. (1995) *Stone tools and society: working stone in Neolithic and Bronze Age Britain*. London, Batsford.

Eyo, E. (1979) *Nigeria and the evolution of money*. Lagos, Central Bank of Nigeria and the Federal Department of Antiquities.

Frantz, C. (1978) Ecology and social organization among the Nigerian Fulbe (Fulani). In Weissleder, W. (ed.) *The nomadic alternative*. The Hague, Mouton, pp. 97–118.

Garrard, T. (1982) Myth and metrology: the early trans-Saharan gold trade. *Journal of African History* 23: 443–61.

Gaussen, M. (1990) Petits instruments en pierre polie du Sahara méridional (Oued Tilemsi et ses abords). *l'Anthropologie* 94: 559–68.

Geus, F. (1983) *Direction Generale des Anitiquités et des Musées Nationaux du Soudan, Section Française de Recherche Archéologique: rapport annuel d'activité 1980–1982*. Lille, Presses de l'Université de Lille III.

Grayzel, J. (1990) Markets and migration: a Fulbe pastoral system in Mali. In Galaty, J. and Johnson, G. (eds) *The world of pastoralism: herding systems in comparative perspective*. London, Guilford, pp. 35–67.

Hawass, Z., Hassan, F. and Gautier, A. (1988) Chronology, sediments, and subsistence at Merimda Beni Salama. *Journal of Egyptian Archaeology* 74: 31–8.

Hoffman, M. (1991) *Egypt before the Pharaohs*. 2nd edn, Austin, University of Texas Press.

Holl, A. (1985) Background to the Ghana Empire: archaeological investigations on the transition to statehood in the Dhar Tichitt region (Mauritania). *Journal of Anthropological Archaeology* 4: 73–115.

Holl, A. (1986) *Economie et société Néolithique du Dhar Tichitt (Mauritanie)*. Paris, Editions Recherche sur les Civilisations, Mémoire No. 69.

Holl, A. (1993) Late Neolithic cultural landscape in southeastern Mauritania: an essay in spatiometrics. In Holl, A. and Levy, T.E. (eds) *Spatial boundaries and social dynamics: case studies from food-producing societies*. Ann Arbor, International Monographs in Prehistory, pp. 95–133.

Hugot, H-J. (1963) *Recherches préhistoriques dans l'Ahaggar nord-occidental, 1950–1957*. Paris: Arts et Métiers Graphiques (Mémoires du CRAPE, No. 1).

Jeffreys, M. (1954) Some Negro currencies in Nigeria. *South African Museums Association Bulletin* 5: 405–16.

Johnson, A.W. and Earle, T. (1987) *The evolution of human societies: from foraging group to agrarian state*. Stanford, Stanford University Press.

Junker, H. (1930) Vorläufiger Bericht über die zweite Grabung der Akademie der Wissenschaften in Wien auf der vorgeschichtlichen Siedlung Merimde-Benisalâme vom 7.Februar bis 8.April 1930. *Anzeiger der Akadamie der Wissenschaften in Wien, Philosophische-historische Klasse* 5–13: 21–83.

Konczacki, Z.A. (1978) *The economics of pastoralism: a case study of Sub-Saharan Africa*. London, Frank Cass.

Levtzion, N. (1973) *Ancient Ghana and Mali*. London, Methuen.

Levtzion, N. and Hopkins, J. (1981) *Corpus of early Arabic sources for West African history*. Cambridge, Cambridge University Press.

MacDonald, K.C. (1994) Socio-economic diversity and the origins of cultural complexity along the Middle Niger (2000 BC to AD 300). Unpublished PhD thesis, University of Cambridge.

MacDonald, K.C. (1996) Tichitt-Walata and the Middle Niger: evidence for cultural contact in the second millennium BC. In Soper, R. and Pwiti, G. (eds) *Aspects of African archaeology: papers from the 10th Congress of the PanAfrican Association for Prehistory and Related Studies*. Harare, University of Zimbabwe Publications, pp. 429–40.

MacDonald, K.C. and MacDonald, R.H. (in press) The origins and development of domesticated animals in arid West Africa. In Blench, R. and MacDonald, K.C. (eds) *The origins and development of African Livestock*. London, University College London.

MacDonald, K.C., Togola, T., MacDonald, R.H. and Capezza, C. (1994) International news: Douentza, Mali. *Past: The Newsletter of the Prehistoric Society* 17: 12–4.

MacDonald, K.C. and Van Neer, W. (1994) Specialised fishing peoples along the middle Niger: evidence from the Later Holocene of the Méma region (Mali). In Van Neer, W. (ed.) *Fish exploitation in the past*. Tervuren, Musée Royale de l'Afrique Centrale, pp. 243–51.

McIntosh, S.K. (ed.) (1995) *Excavations at Jenné-Jeno, Hambarketolo, and Kaniana (Inland Niger Delta, Mali), the 1981 Season*. Berkeley, University of California.

McIntosh, S.K. and McIntosh, R.J. (1980) *Prehistoric investigations in the region of Jenne, Mali*. Oxford, 2 vols, BAR, International Series 89(i) & (ii).

McIntosh, S.K. and McIntosh, R.J. (1988) From stone to metal: new perspectives on the later prehistory of West Africa. *Journal of World Prehistory* 2: 89–133.

McIntosh, S.K. and McIntosh, R.J. (1993) Field survey in the tumulus zone of Senegal. *African Archaeological Review* 11: 73–107.

Maitre, J.P. (1971) *Contribution à la préhistoire de l'Ahaggar (Tedefest Centrale)*. Paris, Arts et Métiers Graphiques (Mémoires du CRAPE, No. 17).

Mauny, R. (1954) The question of Ghana. *Africa*. 24: 200–13.

Mauny, R. (1955) Les gisements Néolithiques de Karkarichinkat (Tilemsi, Soudan Français). In Balout, L. (ed.) *Actes de 2e Congrès Panafricain de Préhistoire, Alger 1952*. Paris, Arts et Métiers Graphiques, pp. 617–29.

Mauny, R., Gaussen, J. and Gaussen, M. (1968) Commentaires sur la datation carbone

14 de deux villages néolithiques du Sahara malien. *Bulletin de l'Institut Fondamental d'Afrique Noire* 30, sér. B: 1317–21.

Meillassoux, C. (1972) From reproduction to production: a Marxist approach to economic anthropology. *Economy and Society* 1: 93–105.

Milburn, M. (1988) Primitive money in Saharan prehistory. In Nowak, H. (ed.) *Sahara Studien*. Berlin, Hallein, pp. 25–6.

Munson, P.J. (1971) The Tichitt Tradition: a late prehistoric occupation of the southwestern Sahara. Unpublished PhD thesis, University of Illinois at Urbana-Champaign.

Munson, P.J. (1976) Archaeological data on the origins of cultivation in the southwestern Sahara and their implications for West Africa. In Harlan, J.R., de Wet, J.M.J. and Stemmler, A.B.L. (eds) *Origins of African plant domestication*. The Hague, Mouton, pp. 187–209.

Munson, P.J. (1980) Archaeology and the prehistoric origins of the Ghana Empire. *Journal of African History* 21: 457–66.

Munson, P.J. (1989) About *Economie et société Néolithique du Dhar Tichitt* (Augustin Holl). *Sahara* 2: 107–9.

Musa, I. (1993) Traditional iron technology and settlement patterns in central Darfur. In Holl, A. and Levy, T.E. (eds) *Spatial boundaries and social dynamics: case studies from food-producing societies*. Ann Arbor, International Monographs in Prehistory, pp. 83–93.

Musa Mohammed, I. (1986) *The archaeology of central Darfur (Sudan) in the 1st millennium AD* Oxford, BAR, International Series 285.

Nicolas, G. (1986) *Don rituel et échange marchand dans une société Sahélienne*. Paris, Institut de l'Ethnologie (Mémoires de l'Institut d'Ethnologie No. 25).

Nordstrom, H. (1972) *Neolithic and A-Group sites: the Scandanavian Joint Expedition to Sudanese Nubia, III*. Stockholm, Scandinavian University Books.

Paris, F. (1984) *La région d'In Gall – Tegidda N Tesemt (Niger): programme archéologique d'urgence 1977–1981. III. Les sépultures du Néolithique Final à l'Islam*. Niamey, Institut de Recherches en Sciences Humaines (Études Nigériennes No. 50).

Paris, F. (1990) Les sépultures monumentales d'Iwelen (Niger). *Journal des Africanistes* 60: 42–74.

Petit-Maire, N. (ed.) (1979) *La Sahara Atlantique à l'Holocene, peuplement et ecologie*. Algiers, CRAPE (Mémoires du CRAPE No. 28).

Petit-Maire, N. and Riser, J. (eds) (1983) *Sahara ou Sahel? Quaternaire récent du Bassin de Taoudenni (Mali)*. Paris, CNRS.

Renfrew, C. (1973) Monuments, mobilisation and social organisation in Neolithic Wessex. In Renfrew, C. (ed.) *The explanation of culture change: models in prehistory*. London, Duckworth, pp. 539–58.

Roset, J-P. (1974) Contribution à la connaissance des populations Néolithiques et protohistoriques du Tibesti (Nord Tchad). *Cahiers de l'ORSTOM, séries Sciences Humaines* 11: 47–84.

Sàenz, C. (1991) Lords of the waste: predation, pastoral production, and the process of stratification among the Eastern Twaregs. In Earle, T. (ed.) *Chiefdoms: power, economy and ideology*. Cambridge, Cambridge University Press, pp. 100–18.

Saliège, J-F., Person, A. and Paris, F. (1995) Preservation of 13C/12C original ratio and 14C dating of mineral fraction of human bones from Saharan tombs, Niger. *Journal of Archaeological Science* 22: 301–12.

Shaw, T. (1977) Hunters, gatherers and first farmers in West Africa. In Megaw, J.V.S. (ed.) *Hunters, gatherers and first farmers beyond Europe*. Old Woking, Leicester University Press, pp. 69–125.

Shaw, T. (1981) The Late Stone Age in West Africa and the beginnings of African food production. In Roubet, C., Hugot, H-J. and Souville, G. (eds) *Préhistoire Africaine: melanges offerts au Doyen Lionel Balout*. Paris, Editions ADPF, pp. 213–35.

Sherratt, A. (1982) Mobile resources: settlement and exchange in early agricultural Europe. In Renfrew, C. and Shennan, S.J. (eds) *Ranking, resource and exchange: aspects of the archaeology of early European society*. Cambridge, Cambridge University Press, pp. 13–26.

Shinnie, P.L. and Kense, F.J. (1989) *Archaeology of Gonja, Ghana: excavations at Daboya*. Calgary, University of Calgary Press.

Smith, A.B. (1974a) Adrar Bous and Karkarichinkat: examples of post-Paleolithic human adaptation in the Sahara and Sahel zones of West Africa. Berkeley, Unpublished PhD thesis, University of California.

Smith, A.B. (1974b) Preliminary report of excavations at Karkarichinkat Nord and Karkarichinkat Sud, Tilemsi Valley, Republic of Mali, Spring 1972. *West African Journal of Archaeology* 4: 33–55.

Stahl, A. (1985) Reinvestigation of Kintampo 6 rock shelter, Ghana: implications for the nature of culture change. *African Archaeological Review* 3: 117–50.

Sutton, J.E.G. (1977) The African Aqualithic. *Antiquity* 51: 25–34.

Szumowski, G. (1957) Pseudotumulus des environs de Bamako. *Notes Africaines* 75: 66–73.

Temple, R.C. (1899) Beginnings of currency. *Journal of the Anthropological Institute of Great Britain and Ireland* 29: 99–122.

Thilmans, G., Descamps, C. and Khayat, B. (1980) *Protohistoire de Sénégal, recherches archéologiques. Tome I: Les sites mégalithiques*. Dakar: IFAN (Mémoires de l'IFAN No. 91a).

Treinen-Claustre, F. (1982) *Sahara et Sahel à l'Age du Fer, Borkou, Tchad*. Paris, Memoires de la Société des Africanistes.

Urvoy, Y. (1949) *Histoire de l'Empire du Bornou*. Dakar, IFAN (Mémoires de l'IFAN No. 7).

Van Noten, F.L. (1968) The Uelian: A culture with a Neolithic aspect, Uele-Basin (NE Congo Republic), an archaeological study. *Annales du Musée Royal de l'Afrique Centrale Série IN-8°*. No. 64.

Vernet, R. (1993a) *Préhistoire de la Mauritanie*. Nouakchott, Centre Culturel Français A. de Saint Exupéry–Sepia.

Vernet, R. (1993b) *Les sites Néolithiques de Khatt Lemaiteg (Amatlich) en Mauritanie occidentale*. Paris, CNRS.

CHAPTER 5

AFRICAN URBANISM: SCALE, MOBILITY AND TRANSFORMATIONS

Roland Fletcher

Indigenous precolonial African urban settlements displayed considerable diversity. They ranged from small, compact settlements, only tens of hectares in extent, to massive, dispersed settlements covering between 30 and 60 square kilometers such as Kampala and Old Oyo. Some were managed using literacy, as in the Islamic north of Nigeria, yet most of the very extensive ones were not. Mobility played a significant role in their social life. In some cases, as in Ethiopia, the entire community moved seasonally. In the West African forest regions there are indications that a substantial part of a residential community may have moved in and out of its main settlement episodically and seasonally. Residential relocation seems to have played a significant role in the scale and transformations of large African urban communities.

The diversity of African indigenous urban settlements suggests that conventional, universalistic models will not suffice to explain their remarkable characteristics. Instead we need to combine an appreciation of culturally unique social transformations with a recognition of the behavioral constraints with which those communities had to cope. Together these otherwise divergent approaches may help to explain the specific outcomes of a myriad alternative ways in which communities of many thousands of people were organized.

INTRODUCTION

Africa is notable for its dispersed, low-density, extensive urban settlements, almost as if some *habitus* of African communities was tending to spread people out as community size increased. The story is not, however, a simple one of social convention, nor would contextualist perspectives lead one to expect a continent-wide social consistency of practice. The Baganda on the northern shores of Lake Victoria in the nineteenth century (Gutkind, 1963) and the Yoruba of Nigeria in the eighteenth and nineteenth centuries (Bascom, 1955) each have to be understood in terms of their own unique styles of human action, yet both produced extensive urban settlements which contained large amounts of open space. Chance might be involved but the literate administrations of medieval and nineteenth-century Ethiopia also created similar residential patterns, as apparently did early Benin City and the Ashanti at Kumasi in the nineteenth century AD (Fig. 5.1). One might incline to seek some deterministic explanation. But the nineteenth century growth of the Yoruba towns, with tens of thousand of people living in walled enclosures under the stress of chronic warfare and massive social upheaval, removes that option. Steep increases in residential density occurred well above those which were previously usual for large West African settlements. We should avoid opting for either specific, unique social explanation or for generalized causes. Instead we might usefully envisage that communities were behaving as if each, in its own unique way, was trying, quite unaware, to cope with behavioral constraints which limited the possible, viable outcomes of whatever the communities sought to do. Such an approach helps to make otherwise opposed theoretical postures complementary at different scales of analysis. The contextually unique will help to explain why people sought to act in some specific way. No behavioral model can do that. What a behavioral approach can do is to specify the operational constraints which limited, complicated, or confounded their efforts. From a knowledge of the behavioral constraints we might then gauge the magnitude of the achievement of the communities which created such extensive aggregates of people. What I will seek to do in this chapter is to review the evidence on the areal extent and overall residential density of the major African communities with populations of over 4000 people approximately. I have excluded from this chapter the Islamic urban communities of Africa which had literate administrations. Their reported population sizes, settlement areas, and residential densities are not in themselves problematic. They fall well within the range of other such communities. The only case of a city with a literate administration which I have included is Addis Ababa as a representative of the *ketema*, the great mobile capitals of medieval and nineteenth-century Ethiopia. It is of critical importance for a discussion of what kinds of residential patterns are or are not sustainable in communities of up to 100,000 people using various forms of residential mobility.

Current use of the term urban is ambiguous and unresolvable. As Robert McC. Adams pointed out more than a decade ago (1981) there is no cross-culturally consistent definition of 'urban' (Fletcher, 1995: 188). I am not making a case about causal or directive factors in the formation of such communities nor am I seeking to offer a universal explanation of their origins, since I do not think they have one. Their size and spatial organization is my concern not the issue of how to define urbanism. I wish to look at the relationship between such communities and the behavioral constraints on the way their populations interacted and communicated. To do this I will compare the available evidence

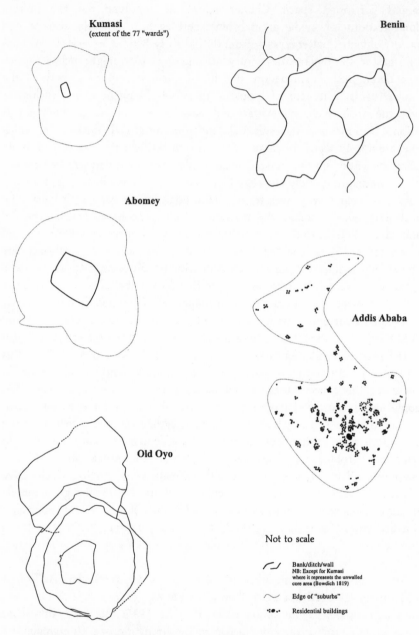

Fig. 5.1 Comparative, schematic urban plans: Kumasi, Abomey, Old Oyo, Benin, Addis Ababa. (Abomey after Houseman *et al* 1986; Addis Ababa after Gleichen, 1898; Benin after Connah, 1975; Kumasi after Bowdich, 1819, Coomasie Survey Plan 1910, and Lewin, 1978; Old Oyo after Soper and Darling, 1980.) Note: Kumasi shown with the center according to Bowdich and the perimeter of the 77 traditional wards.

with the implications of a model of the behavioral limits on tolerable interaction and communication which appear to constrain community life (Fletcher, 1981, 1986, 1991, 1992, 1995). The comparison has two purposes. First to see whether examples can be identified which might lead to a refutation of the proposed limits model, and secondly to see whether the matrix is informative about what was going on in the great African urban settlements. A result of the analysis will also be a discussion of the significance of the African experience for our general understanding of the trajectories of urban growth and decline.

There are three major issues concerning the operation of African urban communities. First, how did the ones which do not appear to have made much use of literacy function, and, secondly, what role did mobility play in the workings of these communities? The third related issue is the role and impact of externally induced economic, operational, and political change.

INTERACTION-COMMUNICATION STRESS MATRIX

The main concerns of this chapter are the relationship between the areal extent and the residential density of the settlements, the way in which they managed information and the relative mobility of their residence pattern. These relationships can be mapped on to a matrix of residential density and community size. The Interaction-Communication Stress Matrix (Fig. 5.2) is constructed from three elementary propositions. The actual values for the proposed limits derive from empirical evidence.

(1) Human beings have a finite tolerance of interaction. There will therefore be limits on the degree to which they can be packed together. Such a limit should be apparent as a range of residential densities above which human communities do not appear to function (Fletcher, 1981). There should be a ceiling – an interaction limit (I-limit) – to the operable, average aggregate residential densities for entire settlements. Empirical evidence indicates that there is more than one such limit. One appears to constrain 'mobile' communities, which use substantial residential relocation, and the other constrains permanently sedentary communities (Fletcher, 1991). The precise relationship between these two I-limits and the way in which communities might shift from one to the other are still to be decided. For instance, the extreme alternatives for a shift from mobile to sedentary residence are either that the limit is very 'hard' and therefore can only be crossed under very specific conditions (Fletcher, 1991, 1995: 176–87) or that the mobile I-limit is highly permeable and can be crossed whenever a community happens to become more sedentary. Shifts from sedentism to any form of mobility seem to be quite unconstrained (Fletcher, 1991). I will discuss this issue briefly toward the end of the chapter. However, it cannot be resolved by the urban evidence alone and is beyond the scope of this chapter.

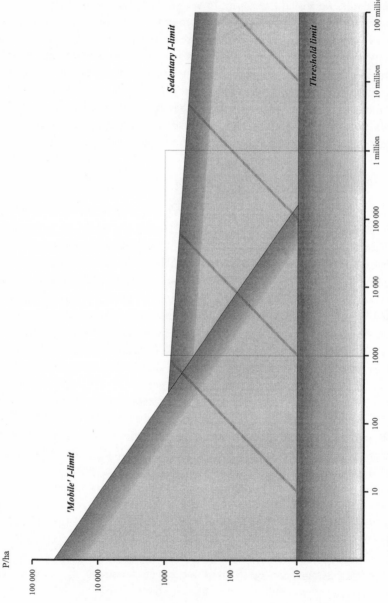

Fig. 5.2 The Interaction-Communication Stress Matrix. Diagonal dashed line equals C-limits. Note: square represents the portion of the matrix shown on Figures 5.3, 5.5, and 5.8.

(2) A communication system only functions adequately over a finite range or settlement area. There should therefore be maximum settlement sizes beyond which a given mode of communication will not function. These maximum areas are a communication limit (C-limit). This kind of limit only applies to compact settlements as I will outline in (3) below. Empirical evidence suggests that there are at least three such C-limits. I have given them conventionalized rounded figures as labels to simplify the presentation. The largest known is near 100 square kilometers and limited the size of literate agrarian-based urban communities in compact settlements. Another limit near 100 hectares (1 square kilometer) apparently constrained settlements which did not have a material means of storing and transmitting information (Fletcher, 1986). There is some indication of a third limit at 1–2 hectares which was involved in the great transitions toward permanent sedentary communities (Fletcher, 1986, 1995: 172–6). In very broad terms there is a roughly hundredfold increase in the maximum operable areal extent of compact settlements after a transition across a C-limit due to a quantum change in communication capacity. This chapter is primarily concerned with the range between the 1 square kilometer (100 ha) and the 100 square kilometer C-limits.

(3) There is also a threshold (T-limit) below which the communication constraint on the extent of a settlement does not apply. The presence of this limit follows from the occurrence of entire rural regions of immense extent, e.g. over the past century in Java, India and China (Fletcher, 1995: 92–5), which function at average regional densities as high as five and ten persons per hectare (Clark, 1989). These regions indicate that for all practical purposes, when considering preindustrial cities, there can be no communication limit on the extent of occupation at such densities. This does not mean that the maximum area of a low-density settlement can and will be infinitely large, merely that the constraint is not one of social communication. We should therefore expect to find, for instance, that at low densities communities without literacy can exceed 100 hectares in extent and communities without industrial modes of communication can exceed 100 square kilometers. For instance the great, dispersed, Khmer city of Angkor in the thirteenth and fourteenth century AD (Jacques, 1990) had only a literate information system yet the city is spread over several hundred square kilometers at the very least.

CONSEQUENCES

All human communities have to manage interaction and communication in order to function adequately. The former requires some control over the amount of engagement between people and the degree to which they are affected by material obstacles to their daily lives. For instance, dispersal cuts down the amount of noise pollution but increases the inertia of the traffic distances required to get services, supplies, or people. Communication involves mechanisms or practices which transmit information in such a way that it can be received and used in a timely fashion. Writing is the classic example of a material means of storing and transmitting information which can assist communication.

The degree of residential mobility practiced by a community also affects interaction and communication. High mobility continually alters both the membership of a residential locality and the continuity and complexity of information dispersal through that locality. Mobility should make interaction more problematic by confronting people either with unfamiliar neighbors or with repeated changes to the activity patterns of their locale. In principle, varying degrees of mobility should reduce the level of detailed familiarity with idiosyncratic local social practice, as new actors episodically enter the residential group. A high communication load would be required to bring into necessary coherence the behavior of the participants who are close together. We might, therefore, expect that a larger community which happened to minimize this load by shifting to residential dispersal and less specified modes of interaction will more readily persist. The further people are apart, the less the need for precise consistency in interaction. At very low residential densities communication may be effectively minimized.

We should, therefore, find that the degree of mobility of the members of a community and the modes of communication available to them will relate quite closely to the overall density at which a residential community can function and the possible extent of the settlement which contains that community. This suggests that viable mobile communities will tend to operate at progressively lower densities as community size increases. Such large, low-density communities would be less likely to generate internal conflict due to inconsistencies in communication. We should also find that large communities which do not use a concrete communication mechanism, like writing, must necessarily function at densities below ten persons per hectare for settlement areas in excess of 1 square kilometer. These could in principle use either a 'mobile' or a permanent sedentary pattern of residence. The T-limit merely specifies that they could not be permanently sedentary and operate above the T-limit without a change in their communication system. What the model does allow is that permanently sedentary communities, which do go beyond a C-limit at densities below ten persons per hectare, may also begin to make more use of residential mobility, because dispersal reduces the demands for behavioral consistency. There would be less constraint on what people do and where they might go, allowing much more episodic and opportunistic mobility in the residential pattern.

IMPLICATIONS

The key implication is that communities which use mobility as a habitual part of their residential pattern may be subject to different behavioral constraints from those which affect permanently sedentary communities. To assess the implications requires further propositions about the interaction and communication demands in the two hypothetical extremes. From these propositions we may then derive statements which can be tested empirically. In a permanently sedentary community, where most people stay in one place most of the time, interaction can be more predictable but, conversely, problems also accumulate from persistent associations. Departure cannot be readily used as a means to resolve disputes or social contradictions and ambiguities. While word of mouth will apparently suffice to deal with the aggregate effects of these demands in compact settlements of up to 1 square kilometer, beyond that areal extent different strategies are required. Quantum change is necessary: either a new communication system or a drop to very low residential densities at which interaction is so reduced that the community can function without undue friction. According to the Interaction-Communication model, a C-limit can only be crossed at higher densities after a new communication system has been adopted. It follows that in the absence of such a communication change, permanently sedentary communities will not have viable, intermediate density options beyond a C-limit. They would only be able to keep going by dropping below the T-limit.

By contrast, in a mobile community, though interaction is more unpredictable because of the fluid composition of the residential group, mobility is in itself a means to relieve interaction stress by allowing the problematic individuals or activities to be disengaged. Most important, mobility is a graduated option. Varying degrees of mobility can be initiated quite readily. In effect, the members of a mobile community should be able to adjust their mobility to deal with varying degrees of interaction stresses. Instead of the quantum divergence of possibilities across the 1 square kilometer C-limit, which is predicted for 'non-literate' permanent sedentism, we might therefore find that mobile communities can operate across a continuum of lower densities as community size increases, without using new communication systems. They would, of course, have to function at lower and lower densities compared to literate permanently sedentary communities because the degree of unpredictable interaction would always be increasing as group size increased. Ultimately, the group size would be so large that the community could only function below the T-limit. This proposition helps to explain the slope of the 'Mobile' I-limit (Fig. 5.2) and has an interesting and initially counterintuitive implication which can be assessed empirically.

The critical implication is that unlike a permanently sedentary community, communities with a consistent practice of residential mobility should be able to function at densities above the T-limit for settlement areas in excess of 1 square kilometer without the need for a material information management system. We should, therefore, find that literacy is not required in the mobile communities, as is indeed indicated by the large North American Plains Indian communities, such as the Indian confederacy camp in the valley of the Little Big Horn in June 1876 (Fletcher, 1991: 404–5). The implication is that without literacy, mobile communities may be able to sustain higher residential densities than some permanently sedentary communities in settlements which are larger than 1 square kilometer. What can now be done is to identify the degree of mobility which will suffice to allow this graduated option, and by corollary, what degree of mobility also traps a community under the mobile I-limit. It is important to note that the Mobile I-limit appears to be quite tough. Not even state organization and a literate bureaucracy allowed the mobile, Ethiopian capitals to infringe that limit (Fig. 5.3). Clearly there are advantages to being mobile but the options for growth appear to be locked into a steep decrease to low density as group size increases. Not even literacy appears to offer a way out of that constraint. The remaining issue to consider is whether the impact of political power projected from outside, combined with an influx of immense commercial wealth, will serve to allow communities to begin a shift to large settlement areas and high densities beyond their otherwise necessary C-limits and I-limits. The issue is how long such a situation could persist.

METHODOLOGY

I will first review the nature of the evidence, followed by an appraisal of a continental sample of large settlements. The appraisal will first look at eastern and southern Africa and then concentrate on West Africa, concluding with the critical case of the Yoruba in the late eighteenth and in the nineteenth century AD, up to the time of direct British, colonial intervention in 1897.

RELIABILITY OF EVIDENCE

As I have noted on frequent occasions in previous papers, population estimates and settlement plans tend to be partial, unreliable, and problematic. However, it is precisely these data which are commonly used to refer to the size and extent of the communities. Rather than be merely sceptical, I propose to use the evidence at a gross level of generality to find out whether it indicates issues of sufficient consequence to deserve more detailed and rigorous reappraisal.

First, the unreliability of the data needs some discussion. Plans continue to be a problem, both because of scale errors (for example a recent instance of 1 kilometer recorded as 100 meters!) and because of distorted reductions and the absence of scales. We may, however, need to reappraise our opinions of the unreliability of verbal reports of area and population. Reappraisal involves two issues: the accuracy of verbal reports and the recognition of total settlement area as the sum of the area of the core and the suburbs. Measuring the area of a settlement on the ground without accurate surveying tools is clearly difficult and we should bear in mind such limitations when being critical of our predecessors. Soper and Darling (1980) regard Clapperton's figures for the size of Old Oyo as lacking good correspondence to the actual size of the site. In 1826 Clapperton gave it a circumference of 15 miles (c. 24 kilometers) and reported the settlement as a walled oval of 4 × 6 miles (c. 6.5 × 9.5 kilometers). The maximum width and length for the entire area, including walls 2 and 6, is 3.6 × 6.4 miles (c. 5.8 × 10.3 kilometers) (Fig. 5.1), so that Clapperton's estimate, from combining observation from horseback and some verbal comment from informants, should surely be considered quite a creditable effort. Clapperton's total circumference estimate was 15 miles (c. 24 kilometers) when the actual maximum circumference is 18.75 miles (c. 30 kilometers) and the inner complex of walls 2 and 3 is 13 miles (c. 21 kilometers) in circumference. Clapperton's error presumably derives from the waisted arrangement of the walls which produces a longer outer circuit than would a smooth oval. Alternatively, is his area a referent for the occupied zone at the time of his visit, i.e. a slight overestimate of the inner enclosure? Even so, his figures do give an approximation of the enormous size of the city and clearly identify it as by far the largest Yoruba city of its time.

Evidence of the considerable extent of other West African cities derives from Connah's (1975) and Darling's (1984) meticulous surveys at Benin City (Fig. 5.1), which first identified the massive enclosures of the settlement; and the work of Houseman et al. (1986) on Abomey, describing its extensive suburbs and the sequence of their development (Fig. 5.1). Given the extent and nature of Kampala with its 'suburbs' extending 'fully a mile [c. 1.6 kilometers] to the north, east and west' around the central palace (Roscoe in Gutkind, 1963: 14), the 30–40 square kilometers of Addis Ababa (Gleichen, 1898), and the considerable area of occupation discovered by Huffman around the stone-built central part of Great Zimbabwe (1977), we should reappraise the way in which we recognize the areas of the great preindustrial cities of Africa. Greatly to his credit, Bowdich (1819) provided the information for Kumasi which allows us also to perceive that it too was an extensive low-density settlement (Fig. 5.1). What Bowdich illustrated in his plan of Kumasi was its central area corresponding to the walled portion of Abomey. He also describes 'plantations' extending out for two to three miles (c. 3–5 kilometers) around the center (Bowdich, 1819: 323) which seem to be the 'suburbs' (Wilks, 1989: 375, 378) as reported for other major settlements.

Table 5.1 Yoruba urban population reports 1851–78 (after Mabogunje 1968: Table 4, p. 91)

Ibadan	1851	100,000	Hinderer
	1856	70,000	Bowen
	1878	100,000	Johnson
Ogbomosho	1853	45,000	Tucker
	1855	25,000	Bowen
	1856	40,000	Mann
Iseyin	1853	70,000	Tucker
	1856	20,000	Bowen

The larger area estimates are important because it is more likely that some of the larger population estimates refer to a population which is episodically relocating from residence units beyond the central area. For Kumasi Bowdich noted that the populace moved in and out of the central area from the 'plantations' (1819: 322). On occasion according to local sources, large numbers of people (up to 100,000 is mentioned) came into Kumasi. The transience of the population of Kampala in the early nineteenth century is also a topic of repeated comment (Gutkind, 1963: 10, 16–18). The same applies to Addis Ababa and the Ethiopian moving capitals (Pankhurst, 1961; Horvath, 1969). Pankhurst (1962: 52–3) notes annual fluctuations between 100,000 and 40,000. This may help to restrain our criticism of the frequent divergence between reports of community size for the nineteenth-century Yoruba towns (Table 5.1). Perhaps the populations were actually fluctuating due to a complex combination of the partial persistence of residential mobility and abrupt movements caused by the exigencies of warfare. The reports may simply be erroneous but the alternative should be considered, that the observers were noting, however inadequately, the effects of instability combined with some seasonal movement and episodic visits of which they were not clearly aware.

Prior to the Kirigi wars of the mid-nineteenth century AD, seasonal movement for agriculture was apparently an habitual part of traditional Yoruba residence. People lived outside their towns for substantial parts of the year, yet retained formal residence associations in their urban community (Krapf-Askari, 1969: 30). But in times of conflict, especially in the central region, the practice was erratic due to the risks of being outside the city walls. While outfield residence was revived in some Yoruba communities under the *Pax Britannica* of the late nineteenth century (Krapf-Askari, 1969: 31), it did not reappear substantially in the larger towns (Eades, 1980: 45; Mabogunje, 1962: 10) such as Abeokuta and Ibadan. A quite recent remnant of this former pattern was noted by Goddard and by Lloyd in the 1950s (Krapf-Askari, 1969: 31), in Oyo where only 40 percent of the total allegiant populace of a residential compound was actually living in the town. From the 1820s to the 1890s an uneven transformation was occurring, from some form of residential mobility toward increasingly permanent residence in the larger communities.

As Bruce Fetter cogently stated in the title of his study of African census data, all this is 'Vital evidence from an unsavory witness.' He remarks that 'you can't believe it all but you ignore it at your peril' (Fetter, 1987: 83). The claims about population and the sometimes uncertain settlement plans are what we have. We may eventually be able to improve on both, the plans certainly from archaeological research, the population figures perhaps from further work on demography combined with new historical and archaeological enquiry. What we need now are directions for enquiry: some questions to ask which would allow us to interrogate systematically our sources and to decide what degrees of precision we actually need. At this stage I will take the population figures as they are and allocate them to the larger recorded residential area of the settlement that was in use at the time – as the observers often did. However flawed the data, the gross patterns may be informative. The Interaction-Communication matrix itself suggests general attributes for settlements depending on their density values and their viability as indicated by their duration.

ANALYSIS

EASTERN AND SOUTHERN AFRICA (FIG. 5.3)

The estimates for the Zulu kraals, the Tswana town of Lithako and the Ethiopian moving capitals in the nineteenth century, suggest that even transient communities which occupy a site for as long as five to ten years are just as subject to the 'Mobile' I-limit as more mobile communities which continually change their domicile or use seasonal settlement sites. Their residents do, however, also seem to have used episodic relocation during the course of a year (see below). When Burchell visited the Tlhaping capital of Lithako (Lithako II) in 1812 (1822: 360–1), it had been at its current site for only six years. Between 1802 and 1806 the community was in a settlement at Kruman where it was visited by a Dutch team under Lichtenstein (1930). When first seen, in 1801 (Lithako I), by the team of Somerville, Truter, and Daniell, it was not far from its 1812 location. One can gain the impression from more recent reports that Lithako was continually occupied on the one site for over 20 years. However, Burchell is emphatic that it had relocated in the interim (Burchell, 1822: 217–18; Hardie, 1981: 37).

In the late nineteenth century Count Gleichen drew a plan of the city of Addis Ababa just as the formerly transient residential system solidified into

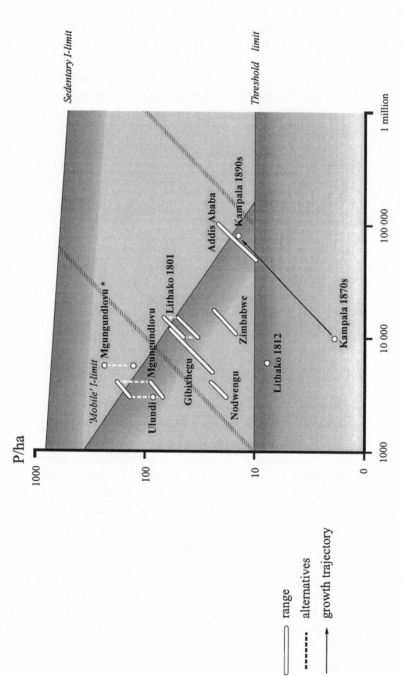

Fig. 5.3 Overall residential densities for Eastern and Southern African settlements. Note: Mgungundlovu* – represented high density estimate from maximum estimated population.

permanence. In 1881, Menelik II had been resident at Entoto at the top of the ridge above Addis. After a brief stay on the slopes below Entoto, Menelik shifted the capital down to its new location at Addis Ababa in 1886 (Johnson, 1974: 34–5). Only in 1892 was Addis finally made into a permanent capital, when its former 'mobile' pattern began to solidify into durable residential buildings. Mid-nineteenth-century Kampala was also a transient settlement. The *kibuga* (the royal residence of the ruler of Buganda) was usually located near the northern shore of Lake Victoria. Between 1860 and 1885 it was successively at Banda-Balogo, then at Rugaba hill in the 1870s in conjunction with another site, only coming onto Mengo hill in the mid 1880s (Gutkind, 1963: 10). The aggregate density of the settlement around the palace compound was very low until the arrival of European and Islamic residents in the late nineteenth century.

In addition to such relocations, some members of the Zulu and Tswana communities are also known to have moved seasonally between places of residence. Hardie points out that living in a large settlement did not inhibit the mobility of the Tswana (1981: 37). As well as relocating every few years, members of the community might have as many as three domiciles. Some lived for a large part of the year on their distant farmlands, others looked after cattle on stations well away from the main settlement. Only in the dry winter was a settlement fully occupied (Hardie, 1981: 41–2). For the Zulu there are consistent reports of episodic moves by the paramount chief to other kraals (Bryant, 1949; Binns, 1963). Mathers reports a royal progress from Bulawayo (presumably Gibixhegu) when Shaka went to stay with those of his queens who lived in other kraals (1891: 95). Any such visits would take a substantial number of warriors and followers out of the royal kraal. Following Gardiner's visit to Mgungundlovu in early 1835, Dingane moved to the nearby kraal of Imbelli-belli and was next encountered by Gardiner at the Congella kraal in May (1836: 61, 159). By July, Dingane was back at Mgungundlovu, but in the interim the huts had been demolished and the kraal rebuilt so that the hut rows extended further out from the cattle byres and the central open area (1966 edition: 199, 204). The kraal was abandoned and burned by Dingane three years later, after he murdered Retief's party and came under threat from the Boers (Ballard, 1988: 36–7).

DISCUSSION

The Tlhaping settlements at Lithako I and II are particularly interesting cases and suggest that the Tswana towns would repay a detailed study in order to gain a better understanding of the constraints on interaction in large transient communities. Lithako I (in 1801) was said to be as extensive as Cape Town by Somerville and Turter (Hardie, 1981: 31; Walton, 1956: 52). At the time, Cape Town was probably only about 2 to 2.5 square kilometers including its small extension of garden suburb to the southwest, though a maximal area of 3 square kilometers could be claimed if the utilized hill slopes and shore are included (Fransen and Cook, 1980: 37–8). Between 1802 and 1812 the Tlhaping split (Hardie, 1981: 37). Lichtenstein only reports a community of 5000 (Larsson, 1990: 49), presumably at the Kruman settlement referred to by Burchell (1822: 360–1). Burchell also estimated only 5000 at Lithako II, near the old site of Lithako I. If these figures and the large areal extent for Lithako II reported by Burchell are even a rough approximation, the Tlhaping would appear to have been trying to function at a very high residential density in 1801 and then dropped to a much lower density after the split. Lithako II is said by Burchell to have included large areas of unoccupied and undisturbed ground (1822: 361–2), consistent with a comparatively low, aggregate intensity of usage. I suspect that Somerville and Turter may have underestimated the extent of Lithako I in their comparison to Cape Town, which would make the earlier density lower, but it would have had to seem astonishingly large to the European observers to have provided a density as low as Lithako II. The implication of the 1801 report is that there was less open space in that settlement than is reported by Burchell for Lithako II in 1812.

The calculated population estimates for Great Zimbabwe in the fourteenth century AD fall well within the mobile/transient range. If, however, the community were permanently sedentary then, on a settlement area of about 7 square kilometers, the Interaction-Communication model specifies that the community could only function at less than ten persons per hectare, i.e. with no more than 7000 people. Great Zimbabwe will be a critical test case both for methods of estimating population and for our ability to identify whether or not its population made frequent use of episodic and/or seasonal relocation. We should not assume that durable structures are an index of permanent sedentism (Edwards, 1989; Fletcher, 1995: 168–70, 176–9), since they also serve mobile residence patterns quite well. The elite can have moved between different seasonal residences, and large portions of the community may also have lived near their fields in the crop season or at outstations where they looked after the cattle. Huffman has repeatedly noted the ecological and health problems which would result from a population of over 10,000 people at Great Zimbabwe (1972, 1987). The precise work by Sinclair et al. (1993) and by the research department at the Great Zimbabwe site will be of great value in tackling a major issue in the operation of human communities. If some forms of mobility allowed sustained use of the same settlement site for several centuries, and could carry community sizes of over 15,000 at maximum densities up to about 60 persons per hectare, then the implications for state formation, urban growth, and regional ecology are considerable.

Gardiner's estimate of 5500 people for Mgungundlovu in mid to late 1835 does not currently fit the model and requires more discussion. The higher density estimate derives from a small area estimate of about 20 to 22 hectares –

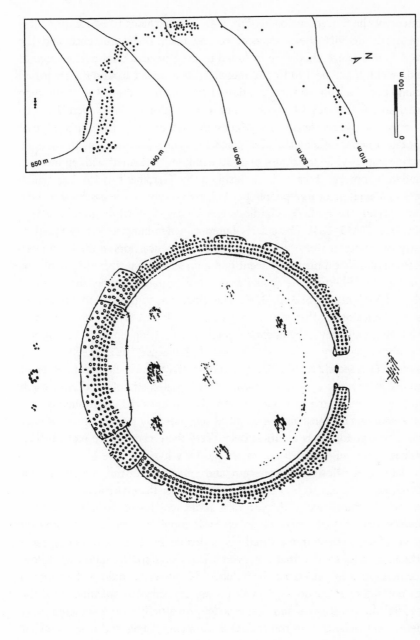

Fig. 5.4 Mgungundlovu, South Africa. Plans. *Left*: sketch of kraal after Stuart (1880s–1890s). *Right*: excavation plan after Parkington and Cronin (1979).

the extent of the fenced enclosure (Fig. 5.4). This excludes ritual locations just to the north, activity areas adjacent to the main enclosure fence and the garbage dumps which should be included in the immediate, interactive area of the settlement. If a zone 100 to 150 meters wide is added around the enclosure to include the ritual site and the location of the funerary site to the south, then the total area was about 44 hectares. For a population of 5500 even this area only brings the overall density for Mgungundlovu down to the upper edge of the mobile I-limit. Other estimates place Dingane's kraal within the mobile interaction zone. While the figure of 5500 would be consistent with an increase in Dingane's power, it cannot be justified by Gardiner's reasoning which presumes an average of five people per hut, two of whom are assumed to be a warrior's wives (1836: 206). Gardiner emphasizes that Mgungundlovu is a military kraal (1836: 123). The elderly Lunguza, when interviewed by Stuart in the early twentieth century, was emphatic that most warriors in the kraal were not married and that a man who went home on leave tried to find someone to occupy his hut, otherwise he would find it full of garbage when he returned (Webb and Wright, 1976: 308, 328). This does not suggest high occupancy levels and indicates a rather low intra-group cohesion! It also neatly illustrates an interesting exigency of residential mobility. Following on from Parkington and Cronin's survey and excavations (1979), we now need further archaeological research to identify the total activity area and the number of huts in use at any one time in the kraal. More detailed ethnohistorical research should help to clarify the residence pattern. Given the strict constraints on the operable densities of transient communities suggested by the Ethiopian moving capitals, Mgungundlovu is a critical case. Were there many more women than the celibacy 'rule' suggests? If so, where did they live?

The key implication of the eastern and southern African sample is that residential mobility has to be defined broadly rather than narrowly, because it has to include 'transience' – the use of a settlement for up to a decade by a community that in part operates on episodic mobility. This broad category seems, however, to lie within a strictly bounded range of viable densities, since the Ethiopian cases specify that not even literacy or state formation will allow such communities to get across the 'Mobile' I-limit. We should perhaps begin to regard mobility as the broad, prevalent class of residential operation over the past several thousand years and define sedentism strictly as the comparatively rare permanent sedentism of the enduring, agrarian villages and towns familiar from regions such as Europe, South West Asia, India, and China.

WEST AFRICA (FIG. 5.5)

The West African examples fall into two distinct groups, the smaller communities at Bono Manso and Begho between the fourteenth and the

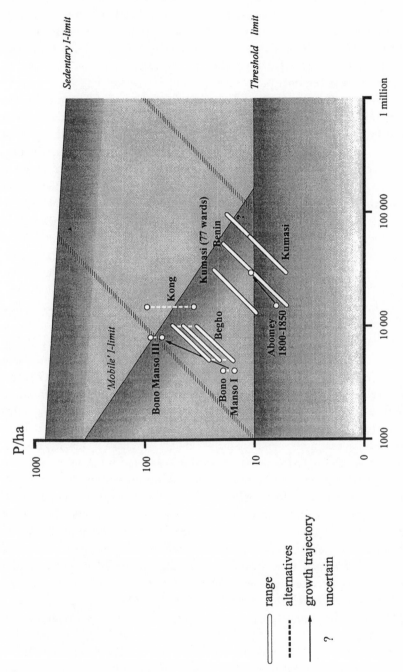

Fig. 5.5 Overall residential densities and trajectories for West African settlements.

seventeenth/eighteenth centuries AD and the large settlements of seventeenth-
century Benin and nineteenth-century Kumasi and Abomey. The populations
for the former are derived from ethnographic analogy to contemporary Brong/
Akan communities. The latter derive from travelers' reports. With Benin and
Kumasi we have the added complication that the larger estimates may refer to
some portion of a regional population and not merely/or only the extensive
urban area. The complexity is well illustrated by the data for Kumasi in the
nineteenth century (Table 5.2). Figures are available for the people *apparently*
resident in the center; estimates of a larger population living in the general
urban area; and a set of bigger figures for an episodic influx population that on
occasions fills the city – meaning the central area. A far larger regional
population is also referred to that encompasses more than the settlement as
recognized. We therefore have three descriptions of the extent of the
settlement. The central area covering about 2–3 square kilometers (Bowdich,
1819: 323) or only just over 1 square kilometer according to Wilks (1989: 375),
then an area including the 77 wards extending over roughly 12 square
kilometers, and beyond that an area including the residential plantations
mentioned by Bowdich subsuming approximately 50–55 square kilometers.
Clearly the rulers of Kumasi saw its extensive area as one place. The
Asantehene Osei Bonsu in 1817 planned new roads to be lined with houses for
resettled people, out to Bantama, and from Breman to the Mampon road (Wilks,
1989: 375). Yet Lewin records a local opinion that Kumasi was not one place
(1978: 20–1). People commuted in and out. They had 'village' and town houses.
The central population cannot therefore be securely and exclusively linked to
that area, while the maximum populations are likely to refer to an area greater
than the town since visitors from separate neighboring towns would have
attended major ceremonies and festivals. Similarly at Shaka's Gibixhegu kraal,
Flyn observed that a festival or a political crisis would bring in as many as
25,000 to 30,000 people, far more than the resident population (Bryant, 1949:
573, 579). We can, therefore, only adequately link the general populace of
Kumasi to the total area which includes the plantations. While the central
populace of about 12,000–30,000 people probably resided within the 77 wards,
that number is certainly not the total residential population of the capital, as
Bowdich and Freeman were aware. For populations of 40,000–60,000, the
aggregate density range lies near or below about ten persons per hectare for
the entire settlement including the suburbs, with a visiting peak population of
100,000 taking the figure briefly up to about 20 persons per hectare in the
course of a year.

The figures for Abomey in the period from 1800 to 1850 range from 15,000
to 30,000. When plotted against the 20–30 square kilometers of extended
settlement presented in the plans by Houseman *et al.* (1986), it also lay at and
below the ten persons per hectare threshold. In both Abomey and Kumasi

Table 5.2 Population estimates for Kumasi

	CENTER	GENERAL	MAXIMUM	REGIONAL
1816		50,000–60,000		
1817	12,000–15,000	> 30,000	100,000 (155,000)	700,000–800,000
1820	15,000–20,000			
1839	30,000	> 40,000		
1848	25,000		> 80,000	
1860	40,000?	40,000?	90,000–120,000	558,000
1874	15,000–20,000			
1901				250,000

Sources
1816   Huydecoper (*General*) (Wilks, 1989: 94)
1817   Bowdich, 1819: 322, 323, 316 (*Center, General and Maximum*)
1817   Wilks, 1989: 90 (*Regional*)
1820   Hutton (*Center*) (Wilks, 1989: 93)
1839   Freeman (*Center and General*) (Wilks, 1989: 94)
1848   Winniet (*Center and Maximum*) (Wilks, 1989: 93–4)
1860   Wilks, 1989: 88–9, 90–1, 374 (*Center, General, Maximum and Regional*)
1874   City of Kumasi Handbook 1992: 4–5 (*Center*)
1901   Wilks, 1989: 90–1 (*Regional*)

major official places and chiefly residences lay outside the distinct, central area. In Kumasi for instance the Kontihene lived in Bantama where the Royal mausoleum was located (McCleod, 1981: 41; Wilks, 1989: 379).

Benin City is profoundly problematic both in its form and the chronology of its growth. The core of the settlement is a 7.5-square-kilometer zone which Ewuare delimited by a ditch and wall in the mid-fifteenth century (Connah, 1975: 244; Egharevba, 1960: 85). This area contained the royal palace and some housing after the fifteenth century (Connah, 1975: 244; Eweka, 1992: 19–20; Roese, 1981: 166). However, some earlier palaces and chiefly residences lay outside this area, and occupation extended for several kilometers along the Benin–Ifon road and towards Sapele and Siluko (Egharevba, 1960: 14–15; Connah, 1975: 89, 243). Some even lay beyond the more extensive enclosed area of around 30 square kilometers (including the core) (Roese, 1981: 170–1). This enclosure extends westward from the core. While oral tradition states that it was built in the late thirteenth century (Egharevba, 1960: 14; Eweka, 1992: 19; Roese, 1981: 220), Connah is sceptical of this ascription (1975: 106). The date of the larger enclosure is not known. What is important to note, however, is that even in the nineteenth century there was occupation to the west and south of the central enclosure both within and beyond the larger *enceinte* (Bradbury, 1967: 12). The implication is that the whole settlement was an extended multifocal complex including at least the two innermost enclosures. This complex was also surrounded by other settlements, each with their own enclosures (Connah, 1975: 102; Roese, 1981: 171). A dispersed occupation may even have preceded the construction of the enclosures (Connah, 1975: 249). At the Reservation Road site the Ewuare boundary was built over earlier house walls (Connah, 1975: 86).

According to this perspective the 7.5-square-kilometer enclosure, which contained the royal palace in the nineteenth century, was therefore the equivalent of the walled area of Abomey. The entire settlement must have been larger. If, therefore, to provide a pragmatic basis for an area estimate, the more extensive enclosure is considered as the urban area, then the population estimates in the seventeenth and eighteenth centuries, which range from 15,000–17,000 people up to 54,000–65,000, indicate densities which bracketed the T-limit. Since the area could have been larger and the larger population estimates, as in Kumasi, are likely to refer to an influx regional population (Home, 1982: 14) and not merely to the extended urban area, the overall density was probably lower and close to the T-limit.

We are left with the intriguing possibility that if the populations of these towns were at the lower end of the reported size ranges, then the extended settlements could even have functioned as effectively permanent sedentary communities below the T-limit. The Interaction-Communication model specifies that below the T-limit a concrete information management system is not required for a sedentary community to function. What is more likely, however, is that these big communities functioned at low densities and also had episodically relocating populations, who moved both within and beyond the identified areal extent of the settlement. Quite what form this took I do not know but it is worth noting that these communities were very fragile, perhaps an indicator that residential mobility has its own limitations. Wilks identified that the regional population around Kumasi appears to have declined throughout the nineteenth century but is at a loss to explain why. Despite the period of prosperity and security from at least the 1820s to the 1860s, the regional populace fell from about 700,000–800,000 people (Wilks 1989: 88) to about 550,000 (Wilks, 1989: 90). McCleod notes that 'the city would empty on occasion as people fled to farms and villages or left because they could not afford to live there' (1981: 41). Early in the 1820s the Germans reported what was apparently a brief episode, when they observed the city in decay only three years after Bowdich saw it in prime condition (Wilks, 1989: 382). Problems of political stability, state-implemented violence and inadequate food supply seem to have plagued the city. The regional decline, despite the attraction of the capital, suggests that this was an almost unmanageable population aggregate which was having adverse behavioral effects on its region. It is not clear what these were, but resource supply and health should be further investigated. The capital may simply have been too predatory in its relentless acquisition of food. Though more obscured in the history of Benin City, there are indicators that this fragility was more than just an Ashante problem. The story associated with the Ewuare enclosure of Benin City is that he built it to keep in an urban populace that was fleeing Draconian royal mourning laws (Egharevba, 1960: 14–15). The story encapsulates a capacity for substantial portions of the community simply to depart. From the late fifteenth to the mid-sixteenth century, Benin City was torn by civil wars (Eweka, 1992: 22–3). In 1702, three-quarters of the population is supposed to have left due to a civil war (Mauny, 1961: 502).

The two settlements of Bono Manso and Begho raise a major issue about the degree to which mobility played a significant role in their residence pattern. Both clearly lie within the zone of the matrix above the T-limit and below the 'mobile' I-limit. Neither is usually considered to have had a literate administration, though some of the merchants may have been literate and an Islamic population lived in the Kramo quarter at Begho (Anquandah, 1993). Therefore, in order to function in that zone their communities must have been using some form of episodic mobility. They deserve detailed study, however, because they could be key refutations of the model. If these communities were nonliterate but were permanently sedentary, the Interaction-Communication model would be in some difficulties. Bono Manso offers an interesting clue since, as Effah-Gyamfi pointed out (1979, 1985: 209, 213–14), it is unusual in eventually contracting to a more densely occupied form (Fig. 5.6). From the perspective of the Interaction-Communication model, this shift becomes highly consequential because Bono Manso contracted to precisely the maximum areal extent at which it could have been nonliterate and permanently sedentary. It seems unlikely that it would go through such an extraordinary involution just to go from permanence at low density to the same condition at a higher density. An interesting alternative is that the demands of social control were requiring an intensity of interaction that could not be sustained in a dispersed residence pattern. If this was the case for Bono Manso, then Begho with its substantial role in long distance trade (Posnansky, 1973) and numerous nonlocal members in its community, is even more likely to have operated on episodic mobility. In this perspective we would expect a significant portion of the community to arrive and depart seasonally, through the trade network, as weather conditions affected movement. The foreigners from the Islamic north, Mande merchants, and visitors from the Volta region may have maintained small households or simply shut their houses when they went away. Only the local Brong population would have been continually in residence.

Another possibility is that the populations were much smaller than they have usually been estimated. To fit the Interaction-Communication Stress Matrix they would have to be reduced to about 2000–2500 for Bono Manso Phase I (cf. the higher estimate of 4000) and 2500–3000 for Begho. However, the only (and rather limited) support for such a claim for Begho would be the apparently substantial supply of wild fauna which entered the diet of the

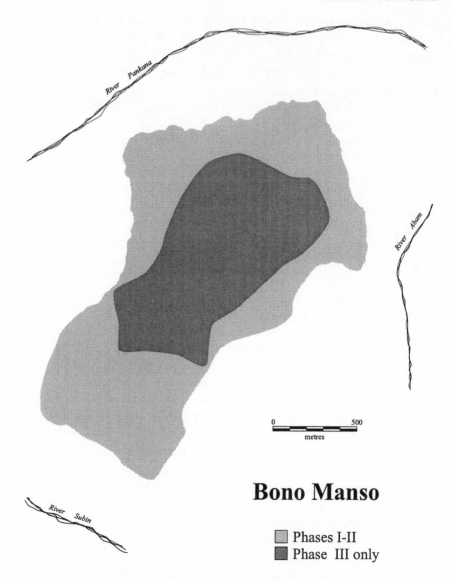

Bono Manso

▨ Phases I-II
▉ Phase III only

Fig. 5.6 Bono Manso, Ghana. Plans (after Effah-Gyamfi 1985). Note: I and
II also underlie the area of Phase III occupation.

community (Anquandah, 1993: 649). This might indicate that the populace was
not causing serious ecological stress or else was sending out long-range
hunting parties. The alternative is, of course, that the community was
episodically large, but remained small enough in other seasons to allow the
fauna to restock.

ISSUES

Whatever the precise populations of these large West African settlements, they all lie within the 'mobile' interaction zone and would have had to contain markedly larger communities if they were to be situated above the Mobile I-limit. They also do not appear to have made substantial use of material information-management systems. Kumasi's sophisticated system of transmission by word of mouth through messengers and the movements of the chiefs appears to have been an essentially nonliterate operation. The prediction would, therefore, be that some form of episodic residential relocation was going on. This is known for Kumasi and indicated by the 'brittle' residential behavior reported in the histories of Benin City from the fifteenth to the seventeenth century AD. The very low aggregate densities for Abomey and Benin City do allow, however, that in the eighteenth and nineteenth centuries they may have shifted to a more permanent mode of residence.

Overall, the West African urban communities appear to have made use of residential dispersal from the fifteenth century, e.g. Bono Manso, and perhaps even earlier given Connah's impression of the pre-Ewuare settlement pattern (1975: 243–5, 249). This is consistent with the evidence from Ife that some of the earlier Yoruba settlements (tenth–eleventh centuries onward) were extensive (Willett, 1960a) and were also functioning at low density. Ijebu Ode, for example, is reported to have had a wall in the sixteenth century (Momin, 1989: 39–40, 47), yet many of the locality names within the wall refer to open ground, fields, and groves of trees. Similarly, Old Oyo had reached its maximum extent of about 50–60 square kilometers in the seventeenth century AD, but with only patchy occupation within the enclosures immediately around the palace and small discrete clusters of occupation elsewhere within the entire enclosed space (Soper, 1978; Soper and Darling, 1980; Agbaje-Williams, 1990). This now bring us to the issue of what happened to the Yoruba towns in the nineteenth century.

YORUBA TOWNS OF THE EIGHTEENTH AND NINETEENTH CENTURY AD

By the time Clapperton visited Old Oyo in the 1820s, the wall of the northern enclosure was in ruins (Soper and Darling, 1980: 74–5) and the settlement lay within the enclosures around the palace. With an estimated population of about 20,000 on an enclosed area of approximately 20 square kilometers, the community was functioning at an aggregate density of around ten persons per hectare. If this density was also applicable in the preceding century when the settlement covered about 50–60 square kilometers, then a total population of 60,000 was possible at peak size. Though the northern enclosure only appears to have had discrete clusters of occupation, the concentrations could have been quite high within those patches and more people would have been living within the core enclosures. Residence in enclosures 1–3 had clearly declined by the time of Clapperton's visit (Willett, 1960b: 63). At a density below the T-limit, Old Oyo could have contained a permanently settled community in the eighteenth and early nineteenth centuries, even without the use of literacy. While Islamic traders and scholars were present, it remains unclear to what degree they were involved in the management of the city. Did they play a role akin to that of the Nestorian Christian Chancellors to the Mongol Khans. in the thirteenth century AD (Fletcher, 1991: 413) or did they avoid political involvement?

We know from the data on Ijebu Ode that Yoruba settlements had walled areas of more than 30 hectares prior to the nineteenth century (Momin, 1989: 45). While it seems likely that the community was operating at low density, it is not possible to give even a remote estimate. In the mid-nineteenth century Abeokuta developed from an aggregation of several settlements, presumably with extensive open space between the clusters, and is therefore likely to have had a low overall density within its boundary (Hinderer, 1872: 215). Ibadan commenced as a war camp in 1829 and rapidly collected more and more refugee groups throughout the 1830s (Mabogunje, 1968: 188), again presumably coming up from a relatively low density to fill its successive enclosures (Fig. 5.7). Two density gradients are possible for Yoruba settlements in the eighteenth and the early nineteenth centuries, one with a steep decrease in settlements of less than 1 square kilometer and a sharp change to low density and rapid increases in areal extent beyond an area of 1 square kilometer. The alternative is a gradually decreasing density gradient, across the 1 square kilometer (100 hectare) C-limit, as community size increases with the same kind of densities as have been estimated for Bono Manso and Begho. The latter seems more likely since it would have required the least alteration in residential density to create the trajectories of the 1840s and '50s. As yet I have no population and areal data for the 1830s but the trajectories for Abeokuta and Ibadan strongly indicate that they came from densities of 10–30 persons per hectare in the 1820s and 1830s (Fig. 5.8). By the 1850s Yoruba communities had reached densities of 50 to over 100 persons per hectare, well above the mobile I-limit. This surge of growth and residential packing occurred in a period of about 20 years and reached densities which were not exceeded in the next 40 years. There was some increase in maximum group size up to claimed populations of 150,000–200,000, especially for Ibadan. In the 1850s both Ilesha (Clarke, n.d., cited by Peel 1983: 35) and Ijaya (Mabogunje, 1968: 98), with densities of about 100 persons per hectare, are said to have had wide, broad, straight, or well-laid-out streets, which does not suggest extreme over-crowding. Both, however, were sacked within a decade and by the 1880s

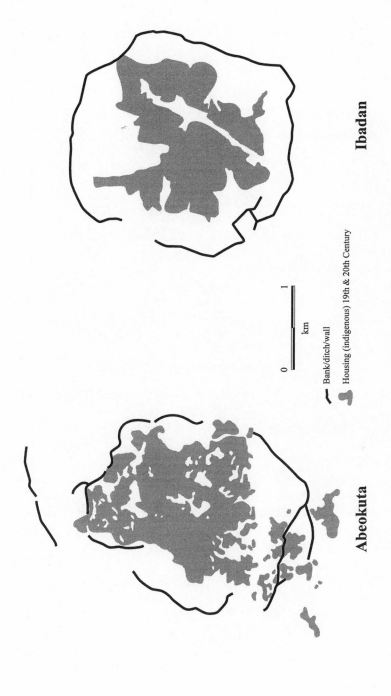

Ibadan

Abeokuta

0   1
km

— Bank/ditch/wall

⬮ Housing (indigenous) 19th & 20th Century

Fig. 5.7 Yoruba urban plans: Abeokuta (after Krapf-Askari, 1969) and Ibadan (after Schwab, 1964).

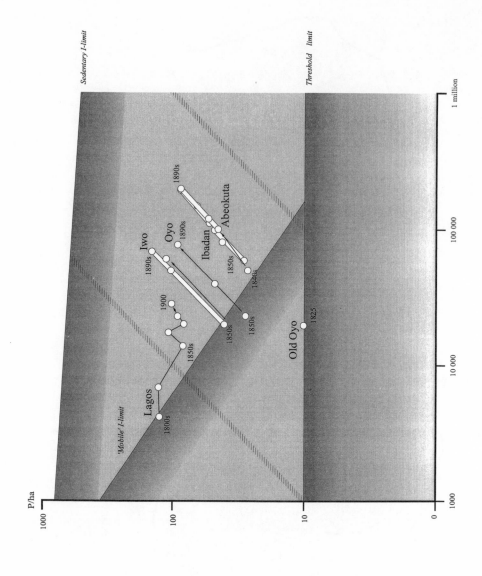

Ilesha's streets are described as, 'no more than narrow lanes where men walk in single file' (Mabogunje, 1968: 98).

By the late 1850s the Yoruba towns had moved decisively into the zone above the 'Mobile' I-limit. We cannot assume that residential mobility abruptly ceased. The I-limit boundary is not deterministic. It merely specifies that attempting to retain some form of residential mobility would itself generate extreme behavioral stress. Insecurity may have reduced the tendency to seasonal outfield residence but detailed historical evidence is needed to identify what degree of residential mobility was retained and what adverse effects it may have had. The open questions are how long communities could function at such densities with residential mobility and whether or not they were using any established system of literate administration. While literate people were increasingly present in the towns, it is unclear how significant their social role was for the entire community. We do know that Islam was beginning to be increasingly influential, especially in Ibadan and Iwo (Mabogunje, 1968: 94). In the 1870s there were 12 mosques in Oyo. Iseyin had two quarters exclusively for Muslims in 1883. Between the 1850s and the 1870s European influence was also becoming seriously intrusive. Christian missionaries moved into Abeokuta in the 1840s and a romanized script for Yoruba was created in the 1850s (Ikime, 1977: 9–11). At the same, time missionaries entered Ibadan. Simultaneously the British bombarded and took Lagos, making it a colony in the 1860s. They were supplying rapid-fire weapons to the Yoruba in the 1870s and had occupied Yorubaland by 1897 (Ajayi and Smith, 1964).

For a brief period of about 20 to 30 years the inland Yoruba towns were therefore practicing a very unusual form of residential packing. Warfare is not in itself a sufficient explanation. It is as likely to fragment and reduce communities as it is to compress and enlarge them. Instead, we must look to the way in which the Yoruba transformed their indigenous political organization and social management in the context of the war towns. Here I face questions which only a rich contextual, historical analysis can tackle. How much role did the literate religions play in the organization of these towns, or was management and control exerted through variants of traditional social mechanism using word of mouth and personal authority? To what degree did increasing commercial wealth serve to control the populace and if so how?

Fig. 5.8 (see opposite page) Trajectories for Yoruba urban settlements.
Iwo: range in 1850s was equivalent to growth recorded from minimum population estimate in 1850 to report for 1880s.
Abeokuta: range in 1850s covers entire upper half of trajectory. Estimates for 1860s and 1870s dropped back to minimum 1850s estimate.
Old Oyo: note this is the estimate and density for the central area that was still occupied in the 1820s, not for the maximum extent of the settlement.

Whatever the answers, the second half of the nineteenth century is a remarkable period in the development of urban communities. Though the towns were swiftly resumed into the literate administration of the British Empire, 20 to 30 years was nearly a lifetime of urban existence for an entire generation of Yoruba people. If, as I have argued, they previously used a more mobile residential pattern, the shift to higher density permanence, without a preexisting material system for managing information and people, must have put a devastating strain on social life. Yet the communities in these settlements functioned, some successfully waged war, and others defended themselves. They are of critical importance because they suggest that for brief periods (in archaeological terms) communities can function beyond their proposed operable limits. The Yoruba in the nineteenth century may help to indicate how and perhaps even for how long, if we can acquire sufficiently detailed histories and archaeological evidence. The overall health, mortality patterns and social conditions of the towns might help to indicate the nature of their operation. Were they mortality sinks, consuming a surplus of refugees in order to keep up their population size? Did Islam and Christianity have a noticeable impact on hygiene and public health or did elaborations of traditional practices suffice? The Yoruba displayed an immense capacity for controlling large population aggregates. They also appear to have rapidly exploited new technologies, new social mechanisms, and new integrative moral and political devices. Whether the settlements could be said to have been truly workable, and how we will define that condition, remains to be seen.

WORLDWIDE IMPLICATIONS AND ISSUES

Various forms of substantial episodic mobility, and perhaps fully seasonal mobility by much of the community, may have been more prevalent in large communities, even in those we might conventionally perceive as urban, than we have been inclined to suppose.

Great Zimbabwe and the eighteenth and nineteenth-century Yoruba towns suggest much longer durations of repeated use of one location by such communities than is generally apparent in Asia (for example among the Mongols) and North America (the Plains Indians). The very large *oppida* of Europe (such as Kelheim) in the last century before the Roman conquest of the west, may be further examples of this pattern. They were mostly of short duration (Collis, 1984). However, the Scythian settlements like Belsk (Hoddinott, 1981: 95–7) deserve review. Much earlier intriguing cases are suggested by the Cucuteni-Tripolye sites of the fourth millennium BC in Moldova and Ukraine (Ellis, 1984). This possibility allows an alternative to the proposal I made in Fletcher 1995 (pp. 198–200) that these sites, with areas up to 400 hectares, must necessarily have functioned at densities below ten persons per hectare. If they made substantial use of seasonal relocation, then they could have had higher densities and therefore higher populations. With horses conspicuously apparent, they could represent both seasonal and episodic occupation. All the four or five biggest Cucuteni-Tripolye sites were, however, in use within a 150-year period. We do not know whether they were successive or contemporaneous but they did not have long durations and had no direct descendant in the region.

The study of low-density residential urban patterns also needs to be taken seriously in the late twentieth century, since most of our major cities are on trajectories toward dispersed patterns of residence. If an essentially nonliterate community can create a low-density settlement 50 to 60 times the size of the C-limit at 1 square kilometer (100 hectares), which otherwise appears to have constrained settlements without some form of concrete information management system, then in principle the same set of conditions applies to our future. We currently use industrial, mechanized modes of communication, which on analogy to previous transitions should allow our largest compact settlements to reach a size at least 100 times greater than the C-limit of 100 square kilometers. Such a new C-limit at or beyond 10,000 square kilometers could therefore be exceeded at low density by a community still using our current modes of communication. This is the trajectory being taken by Greater New York which now exceeds 10,000 square kilometers (Fletcher, 1995: 224–5). By equivalence, if places like Benin City and Old Oyo could reach sizes in excess of 30–50 times the 1 square kilometer C-limit, then future low-density cities can get to 300,000–500,000 square kilometers! The East Coast megalopolis in the USA offers a faint image of what such a place might be like. The intriguing possibility is that such expanding, low-density descendants of permanently sedentary communities may take on more and more episodic residential mobility, as dispersal loosens the demands of behavioral consistency. The histories of African low-density urban communities surely deserve some attention as a possible mirror to the future.

CONCLUSIONS

The critical value of the study of different regions, in a cross-culturally referable analytic milieu, is that it allows us to escape the standard and otherwise apparently sensible premises which a fragmented emphasis on specific regions might otherwise maintain. African urbanism does not support the conventions of what urbanism is supposed to be, nor what trajectories it might follow. We should avoid arranging the unexpected into the expected. But to do so we seem to need a frame of reference that will encourage us to see the divergent and unexpected. We should consider the role of transience and mobility in urban life far more vigorously. There are hints of an entirely alternative pattern to the permanently sedentary system which has come to prevail over the past five millennia.

The duration of the Yoruba towns in their mid-nineteenth-century higher density form is a critical test case on the nature of interaction and communication in human communities. While 20 to 30 years is short from the perspective of a global model and an archaeological timescale, it was a lifetime for many of the people who lived in those towns. Two important points follow. First, the Interaction-Communication model specifies that the proposed limits on social viability are not deterministic. The boundaries can be crossed without all the requirements for an enduring growth but some 'cost' should be incurred for doing so. The archaeological record can, therefore, contain cases of settlements which have crossed a limit but cannot endure for long. Duration is critical. On an entirely different scale we must also look at the experience from the viewpoint of the active agents, the people who lived and died in, for and because of those towns. They, and the people who sought to rule them, had to solve the extraordinary problem of how to manage large numbers of people at quite high residential densities, apparently without an established literate apparatus of government to undertake the task. How did they do it? To what degree did they manage? What costs, whether personal, biological or economic, were incurred to keep the towns going? The Interaction-Communication model suggests that the nineteenth-century Yoruba towns may have been an impending disaster averted by some complex historical conjuncture of indigenous decisions and external forces, or alternatively were a transient phase and would have moved back to dispersal had colonial control not intervened. The means whereby the Yoruba rulers exerted control and the ways in which the populace communicated, ran their economy and engaged in social life, deserve serious attention in cross-cultural studies as a remarkable instance of people's capacity to act and their resistance to the behavioral constraints on human community life.

The remarkable achievement of indigenous African communities was to harness mobility to the formation of the state and the functions conventionally ascribed to urbanism. As a consequence, large communities could function without the need for elaborate systems of information management systems and were able to retain locational flexibility. Colonization removed the mobility option, making many of the urban developments from the twelfth to the nineteenth century in southern and western Africa look like marginal options. Great Zimbabwe, the option of the moving capitals of Ethiopia, and the Yoruba towns of the fifteenth to nineteenth century, suggest another story.

ACKNOWLEDGMENTS

First, my especial thanks to Graham Connah for organizing the conference in such a congenial environment at the Humanities Research Centre in Canberra. Much credit to Graeme Clarke as a gracious host. This study had its ancestry in the encouragement given me by Merrick Posnansky many years ago to begin an overview of the physical nature of African indigenous urban communities. For enabling me to start on this long and fascinating task, my sincere thanks. My thanks also to Murielle Sarenas for her interest in Yoruba towns and the work she did to pull the material together. My thanks to Julian Cobbing for suggesting that I pay particular attention to the Tswana towns.

This paper was completed while I was at the Smithsonian Institution, Washington DC, as a research collaborator in the Anthropology Department in the Museum of Natural History and an academic guest of the Arthur M. Sackler and Freer Galleries of Art. I am indebted to Bruce Smith for the opportunity to work in such a congenial place. My thanks in particular to Dr Milo Beach and Dr Tom Lentz for allowing me to be a guest scholar at the Sackler. For the kindness of the staff of the Sackler library and research office I am most grateful. Thanks to Andrew Wilson for the splendid work on the illustrations. My thanks also to Mayda in the Anthropology library, to the library staff of the Museum of African Art in the Smithsonian Institution, and to Aidan of the Haddon Library in Cambridge, who gave me valuable assistance with problematic sources.

BIBLIOGRAPHY

Adams, R. McC. (1981) *Heartland of cities*. Chicago, Chicago University Press.

Agbaje-Williams, B. (1990) Oyo ruins of NW Yorubaland, Nigeria. *Journal of Field Archaeology* 17(3): 367–73).

Ajayi, J.F.A. and Smith, R.S. (1964) *Yoruba warfare in the nineteenth century*. Cambridge, Cambridge University Press.

Anquandah, J. (1993) Urbanization and state formation in Ghana during the Iron Age. In Shaw, T., Sinclair, P., Andah, B. and Okpoko, A. (eds). *The archaeology of Africa. Food, metals and towns*. London, Routledge, pp. 642–51.

Ballard, C. (1988) *The House of Shaka. The Zulu monarchy illustrated*. Marine Parade, South Africa, Emoyeni Books.

Bascom, W. (1955) Urbanization among the Yoruba. *The American Journal of Sociology* LX (5): 446–54.

Binns, C.T. (1963) *The last Zulu kings*. London, Longman.

Bowdich, T.E. (1819) (1966 edition). *Mission from Cape Coast Castle to Ashantee*. London, Frank Cass.

Bradbury, R.E. (1967) The kingdom of Benin. In Forde, D. and Kaberry, P.M. (eds) *West African kingdoms in the nineteenth century*. London, Oxford University Press, pp. 1–35.

Bryant, A.T. (1949) *The Zulu People, as they were before the White Man came*. Pietermaritzburg, Shuter and Shooter.

Burchell, W.J. (1822) (1953 edition). *Travels to the interior of Southern Africa*. 2 vols. London, The Batchworth Press.

City of Kumasi Handbook (1992) *The City of Kumasi. Past, present and future*. Legon, Institute of African Studies.

Clark, W.C. (1989) Managing Planet Earth. *Scientific American* 261(3): 19–26.

Clarke, W.H. (n.d.) Travels and explorations of William H. Clarke. Kentucky, Ms in Southern Baptist Theological Seminary Library, Louisville.

Collis, J. (1984) *Oppida, earliest towns north of the Alps*. Sheffield, Department of Prehistory and Archaeology, Sheffield University.

Connah, G. (1975) *The archaeology of Benin. Excavations and other researches in and around Benin City, Nigeria*. Oxford, Clarendon Press.

Darling, P.J. (1984) *Archaeology and history in southern Nigeria*. 2 vols. Oxford, BAR International Series 215(i) & (ii).

Eades, J.S. (1980) *The Yoruba today*. Cambridge, Cambridge University Press.

Edwards, P.C. (1989) Problems of recognising earliest sedentism: the Natufian example. *Journal of Mediterranean Archaeology* 2(1): 5–48.

Effah-Gyamfi, K. (1979) Bono Manso Archaeological Research Project – 1973–76. *West African Journal of Archaeology* 9: 173–86.

Effah-Gyamfi, K. (1985) *Bono Manso: An archaeological investigation into early Akan urbanism*. African Occasional Papers No. 2. Calgary, University of Calgary Press.

Egharevba, J. (1960) *A short history of Benin*. 3rd edn. Ibadan, Ibadan University Press.

Ellis, L. (1984) *The Cucuteni-Tripolye Culture: a study in technology and the origins of complex society*. Oxford, BAR International Series 217.

Eweka, E.B. (1992) *The Benin Monarchy. Origin and development*. Benin City, Seber Printers.

Fetter, B. (1987) Decoding and interpreting African census data: vital evidence from an unsavoury witness. *Cahiers d'Etudes Africaines* 105–106, XXVII(1–2): 83–105.

Fletcher, R.J. (1981) People and space: a case study on material behaviour. In Hodder, I., Isaac, G.L. and Hammond, N. (eds) *Pattern of the past: studies in honour of David Clarke*. Cambridge, Cambridge University Press, pp. 97–128.

Fletcher, R.J. (1986) Settlement archaeology: world-wide comparisons. *World Archaeology* 18(1): 59–83.

Fletcher, R.J. (1991) Very large mobile communities: interaction stress and residential dispersal. In Gamble, C. and Boismer, B. (eds) *Ethnoarchaeological approaches to mobile campsites: hunter-gatherer and pastoralist case studies*. Ann Arbor, International Monographs in Prehistory, pp. 395–420.

Fletcher, R.J. (1992) Time perspectivism, *Annales* and the potential of archaeology. In Knapp, A.B. (ed.) *Archaeology, Annales and ethnohistory*. Cambridge, Cambridge University Press, pp. 35–49.

Fletcher, R.J. (1995) *The limits of settlement growth. A theoretical outline*. Cambridge, Cambridge University Press.

Fransen, H. and Cook, M.A. (1980) *The old buildings of the Cape*. Cape Town, Balkema.

Gardiner, A.F. (1836) (1966 edition). *Narrative of a journey to the Zoolu Country in South Africa*. Cape Town, Struick.

Gleichen, Count. (1898) *With the Mission to Menelik*. London, Edward Arnold.

Gutkind, P.C.W. (1963) *The Royal Capital of Buganda. A study of internal conflict and external ambiguity*. The Hague, Mouton and Co.

Hardie, G.J. (1981) *Tswana design of house and settlement. Continuity and change in expressive space*. PhD thesis, Boston University. Ann Arbor, University Microfilms.

Hinderer, A. (First publ. c. 1872) Seventeen years in the Yoruba Country. London, Religious Tract Society.

Hoddinott, R.F. (1981) The Thracians. London, Thames and Hudson.

Home, R. (1982) City of Blood revisited. A new look at the Benin Expedition of 1897. London, Collings.

Horvath, R.J. (1969) The wandering capitals of Ethiopia. Journal of African History 10(2): 205–19.

Houseman, M., Legonou, B., Massy, C. and Crepin, X. (1986) Note sur la structure évolutive d'une ville historique. Cahiers d'Etudes Africaines 104, XXVI(4): 527–46.

Huffman, T.N. (1972) The rise and fall of Zimbabwe. Journal of African History 13(3): 353–66.

Huffman, T.N. (1977) Zimbabwe: Southern Africa's first town. Rhodesian Prehistory 7: 9–14.

Huffman, T.N. (1987) Symbols in stone. Unravelling the mystery of Great Zimbabwe. Johannesburg, Witwatersrand University Press.

Ikime, O. (1977) The fall of Nigeria: the British conquest. London, Heinemann.

Jacques, C. (1990) Angkor. Paris, Bordas.

Johnson, M.E. (1974) The evolution of the morphology of Addis Ababa, Ethiopia. PhD thesis, University of California. Ann Arbor, University Microfilms.

Krapf-Askari, E. (1969) Yoruba towns and cities. An enquiry into the nature of urban social phenomena. Oxford, Clarendon Press.

Larsson, A. (1990) Modern houses for modern life. The transformation of housing in Botswana. Department of Building Function Analysis Report R.1. Lund, Sweden, University of Lund, School of Architecture.

Lewin, T.J. (1978) Asante before the British. The Prempean years 1875–1900. Lawrence, The Regents' Press of Kansas.

Lichtenstein, M.H.K. (1930) Travels in South Africa, Vol. 2. Cape Town, The Van Reibeck Society.

Mabogunje, A.L. (1962) Yoruba towns. Based on a lecture entitled 'Problems of a preindustrial urbanization in West Africa' given before the Philosophical Society on 12 April 1961. Ibadan, Ibadan University Press.

Mabogunje, A.L. (1968) Urbanization in Nigeria. London, University of London Press.

McLeod, M.D. (1981) The Asante. London, British Museum Publishers.

Mathers, E.P. (1891) Zambesia, England's El Dorado in Africa. London, King, Sell and Railton.

Mauny, R. (1961) Tableau géographique de l'Ouest Africain au Moyen Age. D'après les sources écrites, la tradition et l'archéologie. Dakar, Mémoires de l'Institut Français d'Afrique Noire 61.

Momin, K.N. (1989) Urban Ijebu Ode. An archaeological, topographical, toponymical perspective. West African Journal of Archaeology 19: 37–50.

Pankhurst, R.K.P. (1961) Menelik and the foundation of Addis Abba. Ethiopian Observer II(1): 103–17.

Pankhurst, R.K.P. (1962) The foundation and early history of Addis Ababa. Ethiopian Observer VI(1): 3–61.

Parkington, J. and Cronin, M. (1979) The size and layout of Mgungundlovu 1829–1838. Goodwin Series (Cape Town) 3: 133–48.

Peel, J.D.Y. (1983) Ijeshas and Nigerians. The incorporation of a Yoruba kingdom 1890s–1970s. Cambridge, Cambridge University Press.

Posnansky, M. (1973) Aspects of West African trade. World Archaeology 5: 149–62.

Roese, P.M. (1981) Erdwälle und Gräben im ehemaligen Königreich von Benin. Anthropos 76: 166–209.

Roscoe J. (1922) *The soul of Central Africa.* London, Cassell.

Schwab, W.B. (1964) Berichte und kleine Mitteilungen. *Erdkunde. Archiv für Wissenschaftliche Geographie* xviii(1/4).

Sinclair, P.J.J., Pikirayi, I., Pwiti, G. and Soper, R. (1993) Urban trajectories on the Zimbabwean Plateau. In Shaw, T., Sinclair, P., Andah, B. and Okpoko, A. (eds) *The archaeology of Africa: food, metals and towns.* London, Routledge, pp. 705–31.

Soper, R.C. (1978) Carved posts at Old Oyo. *The Nigerian Field* 43: 12–21.

Soper, R. C. and Darling, P. (1980) The walls of Old Oyo. *West African Journal of Archaeology* 10, 61–81.

Walton, J. (1956) *African villages.* Pretoria, van Shaik.

Webb, C. de B. and Wright, J. (1976) *The Stuart Archives* 1. Pietermaritzburg, Shuter and Shooter.

Wilks, I. (1989) *Asante in the nineteenth century. The structure and evolution of a political order.* Cambridge, Cambridge University Press.

Willett, F. (1960a) Ife and its archaeology. *Journal of African History* 1(2): 231–48.

Willett, F. (1960b) Investigation at Old Oyo 1956–7: an interim report. *Journal of the Historical Society of Nigeria* 2: 59–77.

CHAPTER 6

CLIMATE AND HISTORY IN WEST AFRICA

George E. Brooks

Ecological changes determined by rainfall patterns have had such profound consequences in West Africa that alternating wet and dry phases may be used to demarcate historical periods. Seven ecological-historical periods between approximately 18,000 BC and c. AD 1860 can be identified.

Between 18,000 and 9000 BC the Sahara was hyperarid and the southern margins of the desert extended hundreds of kilometers further south than its present limits. Around 12,000 years ago, rainfall began to increase, transforming West and North Africa.

The period from c. 9000 to c. 300 BC was characterized by two long wet periods with an intervening arid period (c. 6000–c. 5500 BC). Gatherer-hunter-fisher groups exploited abundant resources, and cattle, sheep, and goats were introduced from North Africa during the wet phase from c. 5500 to c. 2500 BC. As the 'Green Sahara' desiccated after c. 2500 BC, many of its inhabitants moved away, diffusing their economic, social, and cultural heritage among the peoples of North Africa, the Nile Valley, and West Africa. During the latter part of the era, groups living in the southern Sahara domesticated millet, sorghum, and other crops. Trans-Saharan links were promoted by the Phoenician trade diaspora across the Mediterranean from c. 1200 BC.

During the transitional arid period extending from c. 300 BC to c. AD 300, people along the bend of the Niger River participated in an expanding matrix of commercial networks traversing ecological zones. As rainfall in the Sahara increased during the early centuries AD, camel caravans established trade links with North Africa.

Greater rainfall between approximately AD 300 and 1100 facilitated the expansion of trans-Saharan trade and enabled herders to bring zebu cattle and Arabian horses across the desert. Flourishing commerce contributed to the development of Ghana, Takrur, Kanem, and other states in the Sahel and savanna. Long-distance trade and the development of elite cultures and urban centers with highly skilled artisans extended into the forest zone.

A period of diminished rainfall that extended from c. 1100 to c. 1500 spurred Mande-speaking and Hausa-speaking traders and smiths to extend commercial networks progressively further south. As tsetse fly habitats receded south, horse warriors pillaged along trade routes and founded conquest states.

A brief period of increased precipitation (c. 1500–c. 1630) improved pasturelands and crop yields. More favorable conditions in the Sahara enabled a Moroccan expedition to conquer the northern part of Songhai, but it was unable to conquer territories further south because of sleeping sickness and other diseases.

A two-and-a-half century dry period with numerous droughts and famines began around 1630, tragically coinciding with a growing European demand for African slaves in the Americas. As areas of tsetse infestation receded south, Fula cavalry dominated the battlefields. Had European imperialists not intervened, Muslim Fula states might have been able to establish hegemony over most of West Africa.

The current West African drought, which began in 1968, has impoverished the inhabitants of West Africa and imperilled the environments of vast territories by exacerbating the consequences of unregulated deforestation and widespread degradation of soils to feed rapidly augmenting populations (Fig. 6.1). The fragility of West Africa's ecology is such that a few years of drought — or of plentiful rainfall — can significantly alter environmental conditions and threaten or ameliorate the livelihood of its peoples. The pattern of human life in West Africa has for millennia been strongly influenced by prevailing climate periods.

West Africa extends 3200 kilometers east of Cape Verde across the savanna zone to Lake Chad, and 1400 kilometers north from the Gulf of Guinea to the bend of the Niger River — from mangroves to desert, traversing forest,

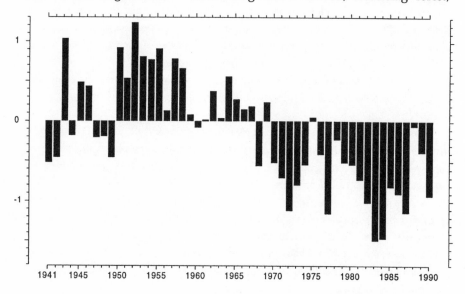

Fig. 6.1 Time series (1941–90) of yearly average of normalized April–October rainfall departures for 20 sub-Saharan stations between 11 and 18 degrees north of the Equator and west of 10 degrees east longitude. (After Ropelewski, Lamb and Portis, 1993: 2196.)

savanna-woodland, savanna, and Sahel ecological zones (Fig. 6.2; Lake Chad begins approximately 400 kilometers east of this map). Most of the inhabitants of this vast and geographically diverse territory speak languages belonging to the Niger-Congo language family, with Afroasiatic speakers living to their north across the Sahel and Sahara. Nilo-Saharan speakers occupy the north-east and east, with a remnant population of Songhai along the bend of the Niger River (Greenberg, 1970).

West Africans' life patterns derive from the cycle of wet and dry seasons. The beginning and end of the rainy season are unpredictable year by year, as is the amount of precipitation. Annual rainfall patterns are linked to decades-long and centuries-long cycles as yet imperfectly charted by climatologists. The amount of rainfall in West Africa each year is determined by the northern limit of the advancing Inter-Tropical Convergence Zone (ITCZ) during the rainy season (Church *et al.*, 1971: 29–36, Fig. 5; Ojo, 1977: 87–8; Hayward and Oguntoyinbo, 1987: 114–17). Ecological changes influenced by rainfall patterns over centuries and millennia have had such profound consequences that wet and dry periods may be used to demarcate eras of historical developments: periodizations of West African history independent of European-derived chronologies.

Figure 6.2 depicts a provisional reconstruction of rainfall patterns and ecological zones during the past two millennia, excluding the years *c.* 1860–*c.* 1930 and 1960 to the present. The isohyets on the map are derived from Jackson (1961: Map 5), with isohyets for the period 1930–1960 serving as references for projected rainfall patterns in past times: isohyets for wet periods assume 20 percent more rainfall; those for dry periods assume 20 percent less. These are arbitrary estimates subject to modification by new research data, but so far have proved generally congruent with information obtained from written and oral sources and with findings in recent scholarship (Brooks, 1993: 10 and Appendix A; Nicholson, 1979; Kadomura, 1992, 1994; McIntosh, 1993; Webb, 1995). The period from *c.* 1860 to the present challenges periodization because of variable and transient rainfall patterns, greatly increased population-to-land ratios, overgrazing of pasturelands, destruction of rainforests, and other factors (Brooks, 1995: 165–70).

West Africans' livelihoods have long been characterized by skillful adaptation to environments and microenvironments. Moors and Berbers herd camels, goats, sheep, and donkeys in the southern Sahara and northern Sahel zone, and exchange livestock and salt from Saharan mines for cereals grown by flood-recession farmers dwelling along the bends of the Senegal and Niger rivers and the southern side of Lake Chad. Fula herding zebu cattle practice transhumance across the Sahel and northern savanna zones, maintaining symbiotic relationships with Mande, Hausa, and other cultivators.

Farmers in the savanna and savanna-woodland zones cultivate sorghum,

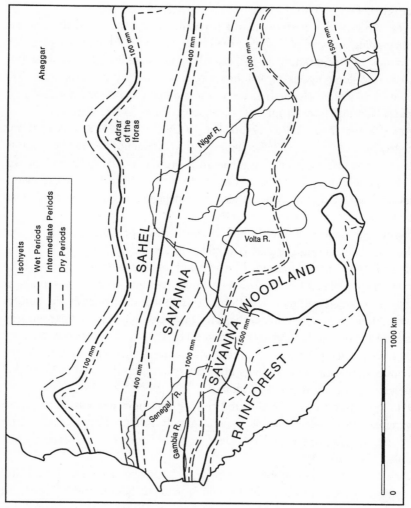

Fig. 6.2 Rainfall patterns and ecological zones (after Brooks, 1993: 10).

millet, dry rice, cotton, and numerous other crops. Those dwelling along the *ria* ('sunken') coast extending south from the Sine-Saloum estuary to merge with the forest zone, are some of the most proficient padi rice growers in the world, but east of the Bandama River is yam country. Peoples living along the Atlantic littoral from Mauritania to Nigeria include numerous fishing societies which supplement their livelihoods with salt-making and coastwise and riverine commerce.

Soils in West Africa are of marginal fertility and are generally strongly impregnated with iron and alumina oxides. Farmers practice shifting or recurrent agriculture in these ferruginous soils, sensibly cultivating land for only a few years at a time before allowing plots to revert to natural fallow for seven to eight years or longer to regain fertility. Land depleted of nutrients by excessive cultivation or burn-offs by herders and subsequent exposure to the elements, leaching by rains and baking by the sun, develops an almost impenetrable lateritic crust that sustains only sparse vegetation (Church, 1980: 76–90; Martin, 1991: 53–6).

The ecological-historical eras described following are presented with the caveat that much remains to be learned of rainfall patterns and their consequences for West Africans, especially for the early periods (the same applies to other parts of the African continent, e.g. Miller, 1982; Schoenbrun, 1994; Huffman, 1996).

c. 18,000–c. 9000 BC: THE HYPERARID SAHARA

While glaciers spread south across Eurasia and North America, the climate of the northern part of the African continent was so arid that dunes were created as far as 500 kilometers south of the present limit of mobile Saharan dunes. Major rivers ceased their flow in mid-course and Lake Chad, the largest of the West African lakes, dried up completely. It appears that West Africa north of 11 degrees North latitude was virtually uninhabited during this period (McIntosh and McIntosh, 1981: 604).

Rainfall began to increase around 12,000 years ago, transforming the ecologies of West and North Africa.

c. 9000–c. 300 BC: PALAEOLITHIC AND NEOLITHIC

This era was characterized by two long wet periods with an intervening arid period (McIntosh and McIntosh, 1981: 604, Fig. 2).

By 8000 BC, the Sahara had been transformed into a mosaic of shallow lakes and marshes linked by permanent streams. During the wet phase extending to approximately 6000 BC, gatherer-hunter-fisher groups moved west from the region of the upper Nile valley to the mid-Sahara, exploiting the abundant resources of the grasslands, swamps, and shallow lakes. The people of this 'aqualithic culture' probably spoke proto-Nilo-Saharan languages. During the five-century arid period that began around 6000 BC, some groups abandoned the Sahara while others took refuge in oases and other hospitable microenvironments, from which locales their descendants dispersed with the coming of the Atlantic Wet Phase that lasted from approximately 5500 to 2500 BC (Sutton 1974; McIntosh and McIntosh 1983: 229–32; Ehret, 1993).

The renewal of the 'Green Sahara' during the Atlantic Wet Phase enabled proto-Nilo-Saharan groups to expand west to the Atlantic Ocean. Proto-Mande speakers migrated north from West Africa, and proto-Afroasiatic speakers (ancestors of the 'Berbers') moved south into the Sahara bringing cattle, sheep, and goats that over time were acquired by other groups. Numerous rock paintings and engravings found in areas of the Sahara uninhabitable in recent times depict life during the Atlantic Wet Phase (Lhote, 1958; Sutton, 1974; McIntosh and McIntosh, 1983: 229–36). Recent advances in linguistic and genetic studies are contributing more information regarding numerous unresolved issues concerning groups living in the Sahara during this era.

With the ending of the Atlantic Wet Phase, the desiccating Sahara was gradually abandoned, its former inhabitants diffusing their shared economic, social, and cultural heritage among the peoples of North Africa, the Nile valley, and West Africa. Groups migrating south introduced cattle, goats, and sheep (and, somewhat later, grain cultivation) to sub-Saharan Africa, to be dispersed south through the continent into favorable environments during the millennia following (Kopytoff, 1987: 9–10).

Groups living in the southern Sahara along the receding shorelines of shallow lakes intensified their collection of wild grains, some of which they began to cultivate. These groups included proto-Mande speakers around Tichit who cultivated millet sometime after 2000 BC, and other groups to the east (proto-Nilo-Saharan speakers?) who domesticated sorghum. These and other foods came to be grown widely across the Sahel and savanna zones extending to the Nile River valley (Munson, 1980: 462–3; Shaw, 1981: 102–5, Fig. 10; McIntosh and McIntosh, 1983: 238–9).

The extent of the dispersal of Mande speakers in past times is indicated by the locations of present-day groups, the easternmost of which are small remnants remote from the large populations to the west (Fig. 6.3). The pattern of diffusion of surviving Mande groups suggests that the ancestors of Southwestern and Southeastern speakers early adopted cultivation of millet and sorghum and migrated south in search of areas with higher rainfall, while the ancestors of Northern speakers remained for a time in the Sahel and margins of

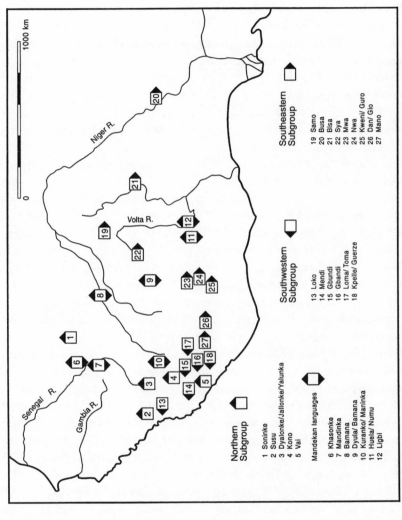

Fig. 6.3 Mande subgroups and languages (after Brooks, 1993: 30 and Greenberg, 1963: Maps A and B).

the Sahara as gatherer-hunters and herders. In all probability, there were significant population increases among Mande-speaking groups from this period onward, the domestication of rice before 300 BC providing an additional staple to sustain growing populations (McCall, 1971a; McIntosh and McIntosh, 1983: 238; Brooks, 1989: 28).

How far south Mande farmers ventured during the long period of desiccation cannot be determined since it is likely that numerous Mande speakers were absorbed by other groups over the centuries, but probably most remained within the savanna zone as it shifted south. Migration into the savanna-woodland zone would have required adaptation to unfamiliar environmental conditions for cultivation and animal husbandry. The social and cultural attributes of Mande groups are likewise speculative, but the diffusion of horizontal masks, smithing, and power associations may date from this era, as discussed following.

The Phoenician trade diaspora across the Mediterranean that began in approximately 1200 BC introduced a number of cultigens and technological developments to Berber groups in North Africa. Berbers who acquired horse-drawn chariots ranged the Sahara from the seventh to the fourth centuries BC, after which the Sahara became too desiccated to traverse. Dramatically portrayed rock paintings and engravings (probably made by observers, not the charioteers) show Berbers engaged in hunting and warfare along two principal trans-Saharan routes (Oliver and Fage, 1988: Map 4 on p. 40). Also depicted are carts pulled by steers whose functions are unclear: they may have been used for the transportation of salt and copper (Lhote, 1982; Munson and Munson, 1969; Munson, 1980: 462–5).

Trans-Saharan links facilitated the spread of ironworking to West Africa by 500 BC, probably by itinerant Berber smiths who in association with Mande apprentices founded the endogamous blacksmith groups that spread widely in West Africa (McIntosh and McIntosh, 1981: 610). Almost certainly smiths served as the prototype for *nyamakalaw* (smiths, leatherworkers, and bards), occupational specialists set apart from the rest of their society by their craft skills, knowledge of occult powers, and endogamous marriage patterns. The social differentiation of leatherworkers and bards probably dates to a considerably later period than that of smiths, as discussed following.

During the two millennia following, Mande smiths dispersed widely, trading their manufactures and exploiting gold deposits. Smiths and their potter wives, whose expertise likewise fused the fundamental elements of fire, earth, and water, exercised leadership roles among many host groups through control of 'power associations' (Brooks, 1993: Chapter 4). Mande smiths carved sculptures, and the diffusion of horizontal masks in West Africa raises tantalizing questions regarding past movements of Mande smiths and their influence (McNaughton, 1991: map on p. 42; McNaughton, 1992: 82–3).

Among groups that remained in the Sahara, people living in the Aïr massif engaged in copper mining during the first millennium BC, but with whom the ore was traded has yet to be determined (McIntosh 1994: 173). Also to be established are the origins and early development of the Nok culture in northern Nigeria. Charcoal associated with iron and tin working has been used to date Nok artefacts to as early as *c.* 500 BC, but numerous terracotta sculptures attest to an earlier evolution of expertise and range of styles in pottery making. At present one can only speculate about Nok exchanges with other groups (Shaw, 1978: 70–82; Garlake, 1990: 130).

c. 300 BC–*c.* AD 300: A TRANSITIONAL ARID PERIOD

During this period the Sahara may have been more desiccated than at any time during the past 2000 years (McIntosh and McIntosh, 1981: Fig. 2 on p. 604). Some groups subsisted in oases, but intra-Saharan communications would have decreased and perhaps ceased in some areas. Nonetheless, developments in the Sahel and savanna zones of West Africa in this period facilitated extensive trans-Saharan exchanges when rainfall increased.

Beginning around 300 BC, settlements proliferated along the bend of the Niger River and its tributaries, inhabited by fisherfolk, cultivators, smiths, potters, and traders (McIntosh and McIntosh, 1981: 15–21; 1988: 148–51). As Figure 6.2 shows, riverine traders living in these communities could readily exchange the products of herders, cultivators, and artisans from different ecological zones. The expanding matrix of trade networks linking ecological zones was a prerequisite for the development of trans-Saharan commerce made feasible by the westward spread of camel-herding across the Sahel zone from the Nile River valley (Bulliett, 1975: 132–4).

As rainfall in the Sahara increased during the first century AD, camel caravans traveled between oases and reached North Africa. Trans-Saharan commerce is attested by gold coins issued by the Roman mint at Alexandria from AD 294 and at Carthage from AD 296 (Garrard, 1982: 447). Berber groups controlled trade, guiding caravans along routes where water sources and pasturage were available.

c. 300–*c.* 1100: INCREASED RAINFALL AND IMPROVING ECOLOGICAL CONDITIONS

With improved precipitation, cultivators and herders prospered and trade between ecological zones expanded. Landlord-stranger reciprocities facilitated long-distance coastal, riverine, and overland commerce in such commodities as salt and dried fish and molluscs from coastal areas; malaguetta pepper and kola collected in the forest zone; kola, gold, iron and iron manufactures from the savanna-woodland zone; and, from the eleventh century, cotton textiles produced in the savanna zone (Brooks, 1993: Chapters 4 & 5).

Progressively better conditions in the Sahara contributed to the progressive expansion of trans-Saharan trade (Mauny, 1961: 429–36, compare Figs 74, 75, 76 & 77). Gold, slaves, ivory, kola, and other commodities were traded across the Sahara in exchange for cloth, copper rods, swords, and other North African products. More reliable water sources and pastures permitted the herding across the Sahara of zebu cattle, which Fula pastoralists dispersed across West Africa in tsetse-free pasturelands in the Sahel and savanna zones. Following the Muslim conquest of North Africa at the close of the seventh century, Arabian horses were also brought across the Sahara to breed with the herds of 'ponies' dating from Phoenician times (McCall, 1979). Possession of larger horses conferred great prestige on rulers and elites, but it was some centuries before cavalry was deployed in warfare (Brooks, 1985: 28–34).

Flourishing interregional and trans-Saharan commerce promoted the development of states in the Sahel and savanna zones. Rulers and elites controlled, taxed, and otherwise profited from exchanges (Garlake, 1990: 24; Connah, 1987: 16). Speakers of the Soninke dialect of the Northern Mande subgroup exercised an important role in state formation between the Niger and Senegal rivers. Rulers were apparently peripatetic, moving seasonally to oversee trade, collect taxes, and undertake military campaigns. Artisans accompanying them resided in separate compounds, creating the spatial configurations of 'portable cities' (McCall and Sieber, 1969; McIntosh, 1993: 187, 218).

The Soninke of Ghana took advantage of improved conditions in the Sahara to seize the oasis of Awdaghust toward the close of the tenth century; it was not to be regained by Berbers for a half-century until they were united by the Muslim Almoravid movement (Levtzion, 1973: 29–35). In this and other Berber-Soninke conflicts, Berber groups were prevented from raiding further south by tsetse and mosquito infestations associated with the northward advance of ecological zones during wet periods (McDougall, 1985: 15). The eleventh century was notable for the spread of Islam among trading communities across the Sahel and savanna zones, and Gao, Timbuctu, and Jenne became renowned centers of trade and Islamic learning (McCall, 1971b).

It was in the region between the bends of the Senegal and Niger rivers, crisscrossed by east-west and north-south trade routes, that Mandekan dialects developed as trade languages, characterized by syntactic regularity and simplified rules facilitating communication among Mande and people belonging to other language groups (Bird, 1970). The wide diffusion of Mandekan languages (Fig. 6.3) was greatly expedited by the conquests of horse warriors during the c. 1100–c. 1500 dry period (Brooks, 1993: Chapter 6).

To the east of the bend of the Niger, trans-Saharan trade routes linked the Nile valley. Kanuri elites and traders profited from commerce with Egypt, with Hausa to the west, and with other groups living in the savanna-woodland and forest zones to the south. Cities were more numerous, especially in the area of present-day Nigeria (Connah 1987: maps on p. 19, Chapters 5 and 6; Coquery-Vidrovitch, 1993: 107–40). Surviving works in terracotta, ivory, bronze, and other materials attest to the expertise of artisans and to the diffusion of skills and styles along expanding commercial networks.

The remarkable bronzes excavated at Igbo Ukwu dated to the tenth century were found with imported glass and stone beads obtained perhaps through Egypt (McIntosh, 1994: 176). Yet to be delineated are relationships of a widely dispersed complex that included the incomparable art in terracotta and bronze produced at Ife between the twelfth and fifteenth centuries, the enormous output of bronzes by Benin's craft guilds from the fifteenth century, and other works in metal whose dates and provenance remain provisional (Shaw, 1978: Chapters 7–9; 1984: 12–13, 20; Garlake, 1990: 111–16, 126–36).

c. 1100–c. 1500 DRY PERIOD: HORSE WARRIORS AND CONQUEST STATES

From c. 1100, four centuries of diminished rainfall caused a southward shift of ecological zones, in some areas perhaps as much as several hundred kilometers (Fig. 6.2). The first part of the period saw a striking proliferation of commercial networks between ecological zones. During the latter centuries, horse warriors followed the paths of trade to pillage and found states among conquered groups.

Mande-speaking smiths moved progressively further south to exploit woodlands for charcoal-making and to gain new markets for their manufactured goods. The ecologies of the areas they migrated from, Senegambia and the lands along the northern fringes of the Futa Jallon, changed from savanna-woodland to savanna during this period. Cotton plants and horizontal looms introduced from the Nile valley transformed the economy of the savanna zone, and increasing quantities of cotton textiles were sold by Mande traders to the peoples of the savanna-woodland and forest zones (Johnson, 1977).

Spurred by the expanding markets of communities inhabited by affluent elites, Mande, Hausa, and other long-distance traders penetrated progressively deeper into the savanna-woodland and forest zones to exploit gold deposits and acquire kola, malaguetta pepper, and other commodities. Mande traders began to arrive in the Volta River region by the fourteenth century, if not earlier, and they and Hausa subsequently competed for gold and kola and other products of the area (Wilks, 1961; Posnansky, 1973: 155–8).

Wherever Mande smiths and traders settled they founded chapters of 'power associations' exercising the same functions as those in their home areas. Komo, Simo, Poro, and the affiliated Sande and Bundu female associations provided leadership and spiritual protections for Mande communities, mediated disputes, punished transgressors, protected and expedited commerce, and otherwise furthered the interests of Mande strangers. The awesome reputations of these associations persuaded members of host societies to allow the induction of their children, with the consequence that in many areas Mande acquired surpassing influence among landlord groups (Brooks, 1993: 73–7).

During the c. 1100–c. 1500 dry period, exports of gold across the Sahara dramatically increased, reflecting the expansion of West African commercial networks and increased demand in North Africa. Mediterranean trade networks were transformed by the Crusades (1095–1291) and by the depredations of the Hilalian Arab conquests which began in 1045 and continued for two centuries. During the Crusades, Italian seafarers supplanted Muslims along the trade routes of the Mediterranean Sea and European merchants gained access to North African ports. European commerce increased the demand for West African products, primarily gold, and West Africa became the leading supplier of gold to the international economy between the eleventh and the seventeenth centuries (Hopkins, 1973: 82).

While gold exports to North Africa greatly increased, the number of slaves transported across the desert diminished, an indication of the increasing difficulty of conveying captives across the desiccating Sahara (Austen, 1979: 66; 1990: 322). The oasis of Awdaghust serves as a 'rain gauge' for the ecological history of the Sahara. During the tenth century, water was sufficiently abundant at Awdaghust for the cultivation of a variety of crops, including millet, henna, and wheat, the latter a luxury available to the most affluent inhabitants (Al-Bakri translated in Hopkins and Levtzion, 1981: 62–3, 68). The oasis was abandoned by the end of the fourteenth century, after its desperate inhabitants dug their wells deeper and deeper in the futile attempt to obtain water. Awdaghust was not resettled until two centuries later during the c. 1500–c. 1630 wet period (McDougall, 1985: 10; Posnansky, 1993).

During the latter part of the c. 1100–c. 1500 dry period, cavalry forces commanded the battlefields of the Sahel and savanna zones. By the thirteenth and fourteenth centuries, pastoralists in the Sahel zone owned numerous horses and had acquired the necessary skills for training warhorses and deploying them in battle (Law, 1980: 7–9; Harris, 1982: 81–5; Webb, 1993: 223–5). As the northern limits of tsetse fly infestation (approximately the 1000-millimeter isohyet) receded during the dry period, horse warriors pillaged progressively further south along trade routes and founded conquest states. Possession of horses was synonymous with military power and rulership, with control of the means of both destruction and production (Goody, 1971: Chapter 3).

West of the Niger bend, Mandekan-speaking horse warriors founded conquest states tributary to the Mali Empire (thirteenth–fifteenth centuries). Bulking and artisanal centers among host societies in the savanna and savanna-woodland zones were especially attractive prizes for Mandekalu conquerors, who used them as headquarters to administer conquered territories and levy taxes on traders.

Wherever they settled, Mandekalu imposed Mandekan languages and tripartite social structures comprising: (1) elites and free people; (2) endogamous occupational groups (nyamakalaw): smiths, leatherworkers, and bards; and (3) large numbers of slaves, either captured during conquests or obtained through commerce. Nyamakalaw groups provided essential services to the Mandekalu overlords. Smiths and leatherworkers manufactured the weapons and tack needed by horsemen. Bards exercised an important role as publicists who rationalized the social and cultural practices Mandekalu imposed on subjugated peoples, and, through the praise poetry they created for their patrons, disseminated Mandekan languages (Brooks, 1993: 99–106).

Elites' patronage promoted the skills of leatherworkers, smiths, weavers, dyers, and other artisans whose products were traded greater and greater distances, including to North Africa. Security of trade routes increased the wealth of traders and artisans that was then subject to tax by rulers. As the appreciative Muslim traveler ibn Battuta reported on Mali in 1352, 'The traveler here has no more reason than the man who stays home to fear brigands, thieves, or ravishers' (Davidson, 1966: 82).

Comparable developments occurred east of the Niger bend. Oyo's cavalry gained control of the savanna north-west of Ife, intercepting Ife's long-distance trade and causing its decline (Shaw, 1984: 20). Mounted Hausa warriors dominated the Sahel and savanna zones, enabling elites and traders to enrich themselves from trans-Saharan commerce and a growing commerce with the Volta region and other areas to the south. During the fourteenth century, Kanuri horsemen conquered Borno south-west of Lake Chad, where rainfall was greater (Shinnie, 1965: 69–72, map p. 69; Garlake, 1990: 123–4).

Progressive desiccation contributed to the disintegration of the Mali Empire. During the first half of the fifteenth century, Berbers pressed south, raiding Malian territory and capturing Timbuctu. Songhai horsemen conquered west from the bend of the Niger, and Malian territory along the White Volta River was conquered from the south-east by Mossi, who were able to maintain horse herds with the retreat of the tsetse-fly line (Roy, 1995). During the latter part of the fifteenth century, Berber control of Timbuctu was supplanted by that of the Songhai, who combined the use of cavalry with control of the Niger by river craft (Levtzion, 1973: 80–4).

By the fifteenth century, iron-smelting, though not iron-working, had virtually ceased north of the Gambia River, and the Futa Jallon massif had become a major area of iron production. Large quantities of iron bars were carried north to former areas of production along caravan routes and coastwise and riverine networks. As the forests of the Futa Jallon were cleared by Mande smiths and cultivators, groups of Fula pastoralists with ndama cattle moved south, to be followed by large-scale migrations during the c. 1630–c. 1860 dry period (Brooks, 1993: 52–3, Map 6).

Portuguese seafarers began trading with the inhabitants of the Atlantic littoral during the last half-century of the c. 1100–c. 1500 dry period. The Portuguese quickly developed a thriving commerce with the Jolof Empire, exchanging horses for slaves, and with Kruan-speaking groups along the coast of modern-day Liberia, bartering for malaguetta pepper in exchange for iron bars, metalware, cloth, and other commodities previously obtained via Mande caravan routes. Expanding trade with European vessels along the coast and navigable rivers initiated a long process of reorienting West African commercial networks toward the Atlantic (Chauveau, 1986; Brooks, 1993: Chapter 7).

c. 1500–c. 1630: AN ECOLOGICAL REVERSAL

Around 1500, rainfall significantly increased for approximately a century and a third. Although a relatively brief span of time in ecological terms, this wet period had important consequences for West Africa, including the expansion of trans-Saharan trade.

As increased rainfall brought about the northward advance of the tsetse-fly line, perhaps by 200 kilometers or more during this period (Fig. 6.2), the advance of horse warriors was arrested. The most rapid ecological changes probably occurred in the Sahel and savanna zones, where several years of increased precipitation would have significantly improved grazing areas to the advantage of pastoralists. For cultivators, increased rainfall yielded more dependable and abundant harvests (including those from American cultigens as they were introduced), and higher productivity contributed to population increases.

Coastal and riverine groups expanded their trade with Europeans, who were obliged to observe longstanding African landlord-stranger reciprocities regarding commerce and social and cultural patterns. Where Europeans were permitted to live in African communities to engage in trade, they were denied access to caravan networks linking interior markets, as in years to come were most of their Eur-African descendants.

As the Sahara became easier to traverse the number of slaves exported from West Africa to North Africa increased to an estimated 3000+ annually between 1501 and 1600, compared with an estimated 2500+ between 1401 and 1500 (Austen, 1990: 322). During the sixteenth century, significantly larger quantities of gold were also transported across the Sahara (Pereira, 1990: 189). Increased rainfall in the Sahara enabled Songhai's cavalry to prevail over Berber groups far into the desert, capturing Teghaza and Agades, just as Ghana's forces had captured Awdaghust five centuries earlier during the previous wet period (Mauny, 1961: map facing p. 514; Kaba, 1981: map on p. 459); conversely, improved conditions along trans-Saharan routes made Songhai vulnerable to attack from Morocco.

This attack came in 1590–1591 when a Moroccan force equipped with firearms (cannon and arquebuses) crossed the Sahara, defeated Songhai forces, and occupied the bend of the Niger River. The Moroccans were unable to conquer territories further south because of Songhai resistance and losses of horses and men to sleeping sickness, malaria, and other diseases endemic along the river valley and the advancing savanna-woodland zone (Kaba, 1981: 469; Cissoko, 1968; Map 1). Moroccan pillaging may have contributed to an increased shipment of slaves across the Sahara, but Austen's revised estimates for the years 1601–1700 are the same as those for 1501–1600: 3000+ annually (1990: 322).

The c. 1500–c. 1630 wet period also had significant consequences for the peoples of Senegambia. The northward movement of tsetse fly during the sixteenth century decimated the cavalry forces of the Mandinka-ruled states and the Jolof Empire. Mandinka and Wolof elites continued to purchase new mounts to replace those lost to sleeping sickness, which pertinacity redounded to the profit of Portuguese traders and Cabo Verdean horse breeders (Brooks, 1993: 200).

c. 1630–c. 1860 DRY PERIOD: DROUGHTS, FAMINES, AND ACCELERATED SLAVE TRADING AND RAIDING

A two-century dry period with numerous droughts and famines began around 1630, its economic and social consequences exacerbated by increases in human and domestic animal populations during the preceding wet period (Brooks, 1985: Part V). Fortuitously and tragically for the peoples of West Africa, the onset of drought conditions coincided with a rapidly growing European demand for African slaves in the Americas, a circumstance that fostered warfare, slave raiding, and the corruption of judicial processes whereby innocent people as well as criminals and deviants were sold into trans-Atlantic slavery.

The period saw drought and famine conditions in Senegambia and the area of the Niger bend during the 1640s, several years of drought around the Niger bend towards 1670, and drought in Senegambia in the 1670s. During the 1680s people sold themselves into slavery to avoid death by famine, and Europeans were told that conditions in the 1640s had been worse. Senegambia suffered droughts in each decade from the 1710s to the 1750s, in the 1770s and 1780s, and frequent famines between 1790 and 1840. Lake Chad experienced rapid falls in lake levels around 1680–1690, 1740–1760, and 1800–1840, attesting to desiccation in the area of northern Nigeria (Nicholson, 1979: 44–7; Curtin, Supplementary Evidence, 1975: 3–5; Becker, 1985).

The number of people sold into trans-Atlantic slavery increased steadily through the seventeenth and eighteenth centuries, from approximately 7500 a year between 1601 and 1625 to more than 60,000 annually during the 1760s and 1770s, and continued at comparable numbers until the beginning of the 1840s (Curtin, 1969: 119, 216, 266, Fig. 26; Lovejoy, 1982: 496–7). Meantime, despite continuing desiccation, Austen estimates that the trans-Saharan slave trade significantly increased: from 3000 + annually from 1601 to 1700, to 5500 + from 1701 to 1800 (1990: 322).

Comparison between the projected extension of ecological zones during the c. 1100–c. 1500 and c. 1630–c. 1860 dry periods and the scattered populations of Southeastern and Southwestern Mande-speaking groups depicted on Figure 6.3 suggests that the survival of these groups (and numerous West Atlantic, Gur, Kwa, and other groups) owes much to their location south of the tsetse-fly line, where Mandekalu horse warriors were unable to penetrate. The same would also seem true for the southernmost Northern Mande groups, Susu/ Jallonke/Yalunka and Vai/Kono, likewise protected from Mandekan-speaking cavalry (Brooks, 1989: 36–7).

During the c. 1630–c. 1860 dry period, cultivators along the Senegal River valley who during the c. 1500–c. 1630 wet period had switched to higher-yielding maize reverted to growing sorghum and millet. Herders forced south from desiccating Saharan and Sahelian pasturelands burned extensive woodland areas along the Senegal River to eliminate tsetse infestation and to increase the area of pasturage for their livestock (Webb, 1995: 7–8). In the Futa Jallon highlands, improvident slash-and-burn cultivation and twice-annual burning-off of pasturelands caused progressive deterioration of soils into infertile lateritic hardpan (Richard-Molard, 1956: 49; Church, 1980: 66–7, 291–3).

As areas of tsetse infestation receded south, Fula herders followed and in many areas became increasingly interspersed among groups of cultivators. Cavalry warfare spread across West Africa and, in contrast to the c. 1100–c. 1500 dry period, Fula, not Mandekalu, dominated the battlefields of western Africa and in northern Nigeria conquered the Hausa states.

Inspired by Torodbe marabouts, Fula horse warriors conquered vast areas across the Sahel, savanna, and savanna-woodland zones. In the wake of their victories Torodbe founded almamates, i.e. states committed to Islamic principles. These included Bundu in the 1690s; and Futa Jallon in the 1720s, which became a lodestar for Muslims across West Africa. There was also Futa Toro in 1776; Usuman dan Fodio's conquests of Hausa states in northern Nigeria 1804–1811 and, until halted by tsetse infestations, Fula and Hausa horsemen subsequently pillaging southward at the expense of Yoruba, Nupe, Igala, and other groups (Hodgkin, 1960: Map 3). In addition there were Umar Tal's conquests along the upper Niger and upper Senegal river valleys beginning in 1852 (Robinson, 1985: Map 1.1). Had colonial powers not intervened during the last quarter of the nineteenth century, Muslim Fula might have established hegemony over most of West Africa.

From the latter part of the eighteenth century the industrial growth of Europe and the United States stimulated demand for West Africa's palm oil, timber, groundnuts, camwood, ginger, and other sylvan and agricultural products. These commodities were produced near the coast or along navigable rivers, to the advantage of littoral groups over the peoples of the interior (Brooks, 1970: 186–7, 198–206; Hopkins, 1973: Chapter 4). One of the unforeseen consequences of timber-felling and subsequent land-clearing for cultivation was the spread of tsetse to areas formerly free of infestation (Dorward and Payne, 1975).

The most important West African exports during the nineteenth century were groundnuts and palm oil, the former grown in the Sahel and savanna zones, the latter a forest product. Ongoing desiccation permitted the cultivation of groundnuts further and further south: from Senegambia in the 1830s to Guinea-Bissau, Guinea-Conakry, and Sierra Leone during the 1840s (Dorward and Payne, 1975: 249; Goerg, 1986; Bowman, 1987). As commerce in groundnuts expanded, French, Franco-African, and African traders from Senegal increasingly dominated western African markets against their British, Anglo-African, and Krio rivals. Meantime, British vessels monopolized trade in palm oil along the Bight of Benin (Dike, 1956; Jones, 1963). The commercial hegemonies achieved by French and British traders with the support of naval forces prepared the way for France's and Britain's subsequent territorial annexations (Brooks, 1975: 43–52).

ACKNOWLEDGMENTS

I am indebted to John A. Harrington Jr and Peter J. Lamb for their outstanding presentations in the 'Africans' vulnerability to environmental change' seminar at Indiana University, chaired by Emilio F. Moran, Director of the Anthropological Center for Training and Research on Global Environmental Change (ACT), during spring semester 1994, and for their helpfulness in providing copies of offprints, papers, and slides. John Hollingsworth prepared Figure 6.2 and Figure 6.3. Robert Ehlers and Daniel F. McCall made informed and constructive comments on earlier drafts of this chapter. Elaine C. Rivron contributed numerous editorial improvements.

I dedicate this chapter to the memory of J. Gus Liebenow (1925–1993) who, as a pathbreaking scholar in the study of African polities, founding member of the African Studies Association and its president 1977–78, founder and director (1961–72) of Indiana University's African Studies Program and a tireless advocate for its faculty and students, and worldwide traveler undertaking research and addressing African concerns, contributed immeasurably to the development of scholarship concerning the African continent.

BIBLIOGRAPHY

Austen, R.A. (1979) The trans-Saharan slave trade: a tentative census. In Gemery, H.A. and Hogendorn, J.S. (eds) *The uncommon market: essays in the economic history of the Atlantic slave trade*. New York, Academic Press, pp. 23–76.

Austen, R.A. (1990) Marginalization, stagnation, and growth: the trans-Saharan caravan trade in the era of European expansion, 1500–1900. In Tracy, J.D. (ed.) *The rise of merchant empires: long-distance trade in the early modern world, 1350–1750*. Cambridge, Cambridge University Press, pp. 311–50.

Becker, C. (1985) Notes sur les conditions écologiques en Sénégambie aux 17e et 18e siècles. *African Economic History* 14: 167–216.

Bird, C.S. (1970) The development of Mandekan (Manding): a study. In Dalby, D. (ed.) *Language and history in Africa*. New York, Africana Publishing Corporation, 146–59.

Bowman, J.L. (1987) 'Legitimate commerce' and peanut production in Portuguese Guinea, 1840s–1880s. *Journal of African History* 28(1): 87–106.

Brooks, G.E. (1970) *Yankee traders, old coasters, and African middlemen*. Boston, Boston University Press.

Brooks, G.E. (1975) Peanuts and colonialism: consequences of the commercialization of peanuts in West Africa, 1830–1870. *Journal of African History* 16(1): 29–54.

Brooks, G.E. (1985) *Western Africa to c. 1860 AD: a provisional historical schema based on climate periods*. Bloomington, Indiana University African Studies Program.

Brooks, G.E. (1986) A provisional historical schema for Western Africa based on seven climate periods (c. 9000 BC to the 19th Century). *Cahiers d'Etudes Africaines* XXVI (1–2): 43–62.

Brooks, G.E. (1989) Ecological perspectives on Mande population movements, commercial networks, and settlement patterns from the Atlantic Wet Phase (c. 5500–2500 BC) to the present. *History in Africa* 16: 23–40.

Brooks, G.E. (1993) *Landlords and strangers: ecology, society, and trade in Western Africa, 1000–1630*. Boulder, Westview Press.

Brooks, G.E. (1995) Climate, ecology, and trade in Western Africa during the past two millennia. *Proceedings for African/American/Japanese Scholars Conference for Cooperation in the Educational, Cultural, and Environmental Spheres in Africa*. Tokyo, Institute for the Study of Languages and Cultures of Asia and Africa (ILCAA), Tokyo University of Foreign Studies, pp. 153–78.

Bulliett, R.W. (1975) *The camel and the wheel*. Cambridge, Mass, Harvard University Press.

Chauveau, J-P. (1986) Une histoire maritime Africaine est-elle possible? *Cahiers d'Etudes Africaines* 101–102: 173–235.

Church, R.J.H. (1980) *West Africa: a study of the environment and of man's use of it.* 8th edn, London, Longman.

Church, R.J.H., Clarke, J.I., Clarke, P.J.H. and Henderson, H.J.R. (1971) *Africa and the islands.* London, Longman.

Cissoko, S.M. (1968) Famines et épidémies à Tombouctou et dans la Boucle du Niger du xvie au xviiie siècle. *Bulletin de l'Institut Francais d'Afrique Noire/Institut Fondamentale d'Afrique Noire* 30(3): 806–21.

Connah, G. (1987) *African civilizations: precolonial cities and states in tropical Africa: an archaeological perspective.* Cambridge, Cambridge University Press.

Coquery-Vidrovitch, C. (1993) *Histoire des villes d'Afrique noire: des origines à la colonisation.* Paris, Albin Michel.

Curtin, P.D. (1969) *The Atlantic slave trade: a census.* Madison, Wis., University of Wisconsin Press.

Curtin, P.D. (1975) *Economic change in precolonial Africa: Senegambia in the era of the slave trade.* Madison, Wis., University of Wisconsin Press.

Davidson, B. (1966) *African kingdoms.* New York, Time, Inc.

Dike, K.O. (1956) *Trade and politics in the Niger Delta, 1830–1885.* Oxford, Clarendon Press.

Dorward, D.C. and Payne, A.I. (1975) Deforestation, the decline of the horse, and the spread of tsetse fly and trypanosomiasis (*nagana*) in nineteenth century Sierra Leone. *Journal of African History* 16(2): 239–56.

Ehret, C. (1993) Nilo-Saharans and the Saharo-Sudanese Neolithic. In Shaw, T., Sinclair, P., Andah, B. and Okpoko, A. (eds) *The archaeology of Africa: food, metals and towns.* London, Routledge, pp. 104–25.

Garlake, P. (1990) *The kingdoms of Africa.* 2nd edn, New York, Peter Bedrick Books.

Garrard, T. (1982) Myth and metrology: the early trans-Saharan gold trade. *Journal of African History* 23(4): 443–61.

Goerg, O. (1986) L'Exportation d'arachides des 'Rivières du Sud' puis de Guinée (1842–1913): de produit dominant à produit secondaire. In Liesegang, G., Pasch, H. and Jones, A. (eds) *Figuring African trade.* Berlin, D. Reimer, pp. 297–320.

Goody, J. (1971) *Technology, tradition, and the state in Africa.* For the International African Institute, London, Oxford University Press.

Greenberg, J.H. (1963) *The languages of Africa.* Bloomington, Indiana University Research Center in Anthropology, Folklore, and Linguistics.

Greenberg, J.H. (1970) *The languages of Africa.* 3rd. edn, Bloomington, Indiana University Research Center for the Language Sciences.

Harris, R. (1982) Review of Law, R. *The horse in West African history* (1980). *Africa* 52(1): 81–5.

Hayward, D.F. and Oguntoyinbo, J.S. (1987) *The climatology of West Africa.* London, Hutchinson.

Hodgkin, T. (1960) *Nigerian perspectives: an historical anthology.* London, Oxford University Press.

Hopkins, A.G. (1973) *An economic history of West Africa.* London, Longman.

Hopkins, J.E.P. and Levtzion, N. (eds) (1981) *Corpus of early Arabic sources for West African history.* Cambridge, Cambridge University Press.

Huffman, T.N. (1996) Archaeological evidence for climatic change during the last 2000 years in Southern Africa. *Quaternary International* 33: 55–60.

Jackson, S.P. (1961) *Climatological atlas of Africa.* Lagos, CCTA/CSA.

Johnson, M. (1977) Cloth strips and history. *West African Journal of Archaeology* 7: 169–78.

Jones, G.I. (1963) *The trading states of the Oil Rivers.* London, Oxford University Press.

Kaba, L. (1981) Archers, musketeers, and mosquitoes: the Moroccan invasion of the Sudan and the Songhay resistance (1591–1612). *Journal of African History* 22(4): 457–75.

Kadomura, H. (1992) Climatic change in the West African Sahel–Sudan Zone since the Little Ice Age. In Mikami, T. (ed.) *Proceedings of the International Symposium on the Little Ice Age Climate*. Tokyo, Department of Geography, Tokyo Metropolitan University, pp. 40–5.

Kadomura, H. (1994) Climatic changes, droughts, desertification and land degredation in the Sudano–Sahelian Region: a historico-geographical perspective. In Kadomura, H. (ed.) *Savannization processes in tropical Africa II*. Tokyo, Department of Geography, Tokyo Metropolitan University, pp. 203–28.

Kopytoff, I. (1987) *The African frontier: the reproduction of traditional African societies*. Bloomington, Indiana University Press.

Law, R. (1980) *The horse in West African history*. Oxford, Oxford University Press.

Levtzion, N. (1973) *Ancient Ghana and Mali*. London, Methuen.

Lhote, H. (1958) *A la découverte des fresques du Tassili*. Grenoble, Arthaud.

Lhote, H. (1982) *Les chars rupestres sahariens: des Syrtes au Niger, par les pays Garamantes et des Atlantes*. Toulouse, Editions de Hesperides.

Lovejoy, P.E. (1982) The volume of the Atlantic slave trade: a synthesis. *Journal of African History* 23(4): 473–501.

McCall, D.F. (1971a) The cultural map and time-profile of the Mande-speaking peoples. In Hodge, C.T. (ed.) *Papers on the Manding*. Bloomington, Indiana University Research Center for the Language Sciences, pp. 27–98.

McCall, D.F. (1971b) Islamization of the Western and Central Sudan in the eleventh century. In McCall, D.F. and Bennett, N.R. (eds) *Aspects of West African Islam*. Boston, Boston University African Studies Center, pp. 1–30.

McCall, D.F. (1979) The horse in West African history. *L'Uomo* III(1): 41–69.

McCall, D.F. and Sieber, R. (1969) Unpublished seminar discussion at Indiana University.

McDougall, E.A. (1985) The view from Awdaghust: war, trade, and social change in the Southwestern Sahara, from the eighth to the fifteenth century. *Journal of African History* 26(1): 1–31.

McIntosh, R.J. (1993) The Pulse Model: genesis and accommodation of specialization in the Middle Niger. *Journal of African History* 34(2): 181–220.

McIntosh, R.J. and McIntosh, S.K. (1988) From siècles obscurs to revolutionary centuries on the Middle Niger. *World Archaeology* 20(1): 141–65.

McIntosh, S.K. (1994) Changing perceptions of West Africa's past: archaeological research since 1988. *Journal of Archaeological Research* 2(2): 165–98.

McIntosh, S.K., and McIntosh, R.J. (1981) West African prehistory (from c. 10,000 BC to AD 1000). *American Scientist* 69: 602–13.

McIntosh, S.K. and McIntosh, R.J. (1983) Current directions in West African prehistory. *Annual Review of Anthropology* 12: 215–58.

McIntosh, S.K., McIntosh, R.J. and Bocoum, H. (1992) The Middle Senegal Valley Project: preliminary results from the 1990–91 field season. *Nyame Akuma* 38: 47–61.

McNaughton, P.R. (1991) Is there history in horizontal masks? A preliminary response to the dilemma of form. *African Arts* XXIV(2): 40–53, 88–90.

McNaughton, P.R. (1992) From Mande Komo to Jukun Akuma: approaching the difficult question of history. *African Arts* XXV(2): 76–85; 99–100.

Martin, C. (1991) *The rainforests of West Africa: ecology – threats – conservation*. Basle, Birkhauser Verlag.

Martin, P.M. and O'Meara, P. (eds) (1977) *Africa*. Bloomington, Indiana University Press.

Mauny, R. (1961) *Tableau géographique de l'Ouest Africain au moyen age*. Dakar, Institut Francais d'Afrique Noire.

Miller, J.C. (1982) The significance of drought, disease, and famine in the agriculturally marginal zones of West-Central Africa. *Journal of African History* 23(1): 17–61.

Munson, P.J. (1980) Archaeology and the prehistoric origins of the Ghana Empire. *Journal of African History* 21(4): 457–66.

Munson, P.J. and Munson, C.A. (1969) Nouveaux chars à boeufs rupestres du Dhar Tichitt (Mauritanie). *Notes Africaines* 122: 62–3.

Nicholson, S.E. (1979) The methodology of historical climate reconstruction and its application to Africa. *Journal of African History* 20(1): 31–49.

Ojo, O. (1977) *The climates of West Africa*. London, Heinemann.

Oliver, R.O. and Fage, J.D. (1988) *A short history of Africa*. 6th edn, London, Penguin Books.

Pereira, J.C. (1990) *Le troc de l'or à Mina pendant les règnes du roi Jean III et du roi Sébastien*. Paris, Foundation Calouste Gulbenkian, Centre Cultural Portugais.

Posnansky, M. (1973) Aspects of early West African trade. *World Archaeology* 5(2): 149–62.

Posnansky, M. (1993) Tokyo, Personal communication.

Richard-Molard, J. (1956) *Afrique Occidentale Française*. Paris, Editions Berger-Levrault.

Robinson, D. (1985) *The holy war of Umar Tal: the Western Sudan in the mid-nineteenth century*. Oxford, Clarendon Press.

Ropelewski, C.F., Lamb, P.J. and Portis, D.H. (1993) The global climate for June to August 1990: drought returns to Sub-Saharan West Africa and Warm Southern Oscillation Episode conditions develop in the central Pacific. *Journal of Climate* 6(11): 2188–212.

Roy, C.D. (1995) Resistance and receptivity to change in African art: the case of the Mossi and the Bwa. Unpublished paper presented at Indiana University.

Schoenbrun, D.L. (1994) The contours of vegetation change and human agency in Eastern Africa's Great Lakes Region: c. 2000 BC to c. AD 1000. *History in Africa* 21: 269–302.

Shaw, T. (1978) *Nigeria: its archaeology and early history*. London, Thames and Hudson.

Shaw, T. (1981) The Late Stone Age in West Africa. In Allan, J.A. (ed.) *The Sahara: ecological change and early economic history*. Outwell, Cambridgeshire, Middle East and North African Studies Press, pp. 93–130.

Shaw, T. (1984) *Filling gaps in Afric maps: fifty years of archaeology in Africa*. Bloomington, Indiana University African Studies Program.

Shinnie, M. (1965) *Ancient African kingdoms*. London, E. Arnold.

Sutton, J.E.G. (1974) The aquatic civilization of Middle Africa. *Journal of African History* 15(4): 527–46.

Webb, J.L.A. (1993) The horse and the slave trade between the Western Sahara and Senegambia. *Journal of African History* 34(2): 221–46.

Webb, J.L.A. (1995) *Desert frontier: ecological and economic changes along the Western Sahel, 1600–1850*. Madison, University of Wisconsin Press.

Wilks, I. (1961) The northern factor in Ashanti history: Begho and the Mande. *Journal of African History* 2(2): 25–34.

CHAPTER 7

IRON IN AFRICA: METAL FROM NOWHERE

James Woodhouse

There has been a large range of literature published on the origins of iron in Africa, based on a very limited range of localities, with the sites of Meroë in the Sudan, Taruga in Nigeria, Kemondo Bay in Tanzania, Akjoujt in Mauritania, and Agadez in Niger providing the key information. Traditional views have been based on the idea that iron metallurgy could not have developed independently in Africa, because of the lack in most of the continent of a copper-working tradition before the more difficult process of iron production. The site of Meroë was seen as a possible conduit for diffusion of iron from Egypt. However, this site appears to be later and very different from Taruga in the west. It was therefore suggested that Carthage in North Africa was the best alternative as a diffusion conduit, but no temporally relevant iron-working sites have been excavated in this area. More recently, claims for an indigenous development have been put forward based on an advanced and complex metallurgical process suggested by experimental work in Tanzania. However, this work has been criticized for lack of control in the experimentation and unsupported leaps in interpretation. Several sites in Burundi, Rwanda, and Niger have produced interesting, early dates for iron, which may make indigenous metallurgy more likely. Further fieldwork is needed to clarify the situation, but is often restricted due to ongoing civil conflicts. A complete, and critical review of the current ethnographic and archaeological data is required, examining the multidisciplinary evidence, rather than looking at a limited range of information and sites, if a coherent picture is to be created.

The beginnings of metallurgy have always been seen as one of the key landmark changes in human development. In Africa the intensification of many other activities, such as deforestation and agriculture have, for example, been linked to the introduction of 'better' tools made of iron. We must, however, consider the evidence for early iron metallurgy in terms of production scale, social placement, and timescale before making such statements.

The introduction of iron would not have created a sudden change in African societies. Stone tools would probably have still dominated working practices for at least a millennium, even for shaping iron objects (Fagg, 1952; Pole, 1975; Holl, 1993), with iron products limited to ceremonial, artistic, or high value goods. This has created a need to see this as a transitional period sometimes called the Stone-to-Iron Age. The question is why iron did not become more widely used in this early period when the technology and ore were available. The answer may depend on the origin of iron-smelting and working technology; if there was a pristine indigenous development of metallurgy, a slower introduction might reflect initial low yields with slowly growing knowledge and skill.

The origins of metallurgy in Africa have been the subject of many publications; from the early ethnographic study of Cline (1937) to more recent synthetic works, the most notable of which are those of Tylecote (1975a) and Kense (1983). These interpretive attempts have been severely limited by a paucity of archaeological data; across the continent there are relatively few metalworking sites that have produced dates before 600 AD. Within this group there are a number of sites that have dates which are questionable, because of contamination, 'old wood', or problems with radiocarbon laboratories. This lack of real data has led to a few key sites being used to create the basis of continent-wide theories regarding the origins of metallurgy. The relevant sites are widely spaced across Africa covering over 3000 kilometers east to west, with the key areas being around Meroë in the Sudan, Kemondo Bay in Tanzania, Agadez in Niger, Taruga in Nigeria, and Akjoujt in Mauritania.

The proliferation of theories concerning metallurgical origins, based on such limited data, provided the impetus for the title of this chapter. The aim of the chapter is not just to review current published material and theoretical models, but to examine the basis of interpretations and try to follow the paths of logic used to develop current ideas on African origins for metallurgy. Additionally, I will examine the fundamental requirements for the development of metallurgy, particularly ironworking, in an African context, looking at the range and relevance of the available evidence from an array of disciplines. The purpose of this is not to create a 'new' theory or to develop set notions for how metallurgy developed, but to examine the various interpretations of the data and to suggest possibilities for future research.

A TYPICAL AFRICAN FURNACE

The range of furnaces found in archaeological contexts has been suggested to be very varied (Kense, 1983; Pole, 1985; Sutton, 1985); however, most of the excavations have uncovered little more than a 'bowl' or 'hearth.' This is probably due to excavators choosing furnaces that are partly visible on the surface, and which are therefore already eroded. The use of geophysical techniques, particularly magnetometer surveys, may provide excavators with the opportunity to discover more intact furnaces, not visible from surface features. As it is, the upper structure and ancillary working parts of a furnace are almost never recovered. This is particularly true of the bellows arrangements; although both bag and bowl types have been documented ethnographically (Cline, 1937; Brown, 1995), archaeologically only bowl bellows have been found, and then only in a few cases, such as those seen at Meroë (Tylecote, 1970).

The range of ethnographic data which has been recorded concerning metallurgy in Africa is large. As Kense (1983) observed, Cline's very good review of ethnographic ironworking examples in 1937 already had over two hundred references. However, this material, as Sutton (1985) pointed out, must be used with caution as much of the early literature is unclear and can be misleading. The mass of new data which now exists also means that no complete synthesis of ethnographic studies has been undertaken, the best attempts being the 1983 work of Kense and the recent annotated bibliography by Lawal (1995). The one clear observation from this body of work is that there is no such thing as a 'typical' African iron-smelting furnace. Even within particular regions there can be a large range of variability in construction and operating methods, due to both technical and cultural factors. The variety of furnace design and operation has restricted any attempts to create meaningful typologies across Africa. The lack of a standard type and range of variation seems to be one of the few things agreed by most of the scholars working on African metallurgy (Childs and Schmidt, 1985; Kense and Okoro, 1993).

Because of the lack of reliable archaeological data, the African ethnographic examples and even European examples have been relied on heavily in the interpretation of archaeological sites. The reconstructions of the physical structures have mostly been based on European types of bloomery furnaces (Coghlan, 1956; Cleere, 1972; Martins, 1978), with the working practice being recreated from modern African ethnographic examples (Tylecote, 1970; 1975b). The notable exception to this is the work of Schmidt with Avery and Childs (Schmidt and Avery, 1978, 1983, 1996; Schmidt and Childs, 1995; Avery and Schmidt, 1996a 1996b; Childs and Schmidt, 1985) on the Kemondo Bay sites in Tanzania. These were reconstructed using completely African data derived from ethnographic reconstruction experiments. These will be considered later.

A EUROPEAN EXAMPLE

The use of European reconstructions is understandable; with such a poor African archaeological database Europe was the area that was best understood. The early work of Tylecote (1975a, 1975b) on the evidence from Fagg's excavations at Taruga in Nigeria (Fagg, 1969) is a good example of the European bias that resulted. Tylecote likened the furnaces at Taruga to those seen in Jutland from the fourth century AD. However, he attached a warning to his observation that his comparisons should not be taken literally, similarities were observed but no cultural connection was inferred! Tylecote used the European evidence for classification and reconstruction, rather than relying on African ethnographic examples for the upper structure. Tylecote's reconstruction is much more conservative than that of Schmidt and Avery (1983), who were trying to suggest much greater similarities between Taruga and Kemondo Bay. With such limited remains found on many sites, the reconstruction of the furnace structure has great scope for variation as was demonstrated by Schmidt and Avery. Both reconstructions have merit but neither has the evidence to make them meaningful (Fig. 7.1).

The basic three-type system of bowl, dome, and shaft furnaces, developed for the classification of European iron-smelting sites, as seen in Coghlan (1956) and Cleere (1972), has been used in an African context with little or no modification. This system has been used to good effect to create typologies within Europe, helping to show progression in the knowledge of iron. However, modifications have been needed to accommodate even the scope of European development (Martins, 1978).

The relevance of such a system of classification to a continent as large and diverse as Africa has been questioned; Sutton (1985) particularly noted the unsuitability of this form of classification. In trying to fit such a wide range of size and shape variations into a narrow typological system, the social and technological importance of these differences may well be overlooked. The lack of upper structure at most sites means that reconstructions must be used when looking at typologies, this has already been shown to be subjective. Yet visual characteristics have been very important in the development of hypotheses concerning the origins of African iron, particularly with those advocating the diffusion of the technology to Sub-Saharan Africa.

DIFFUSIONIST THEORIES

The development of theories of diffusion started with the Nubian site of Meroë. Early observations suggested that this was an important area for metallurgy. Garstang in 1911 noted large quantities of black slag material, with a high metallic content. He suggested that the 'very imperfect refining of ore' reflected a 'primitive' smelting technology and therefore pointed to an early date for the site (Garstang, Sayce and Griffiths, 1911: 21). At this time copper and ironworking were known from sites in Egypt, so the assumption that iron diffused from Egypt through Meroë and into Sub-Saharan Africa was made. Without the benefit of scientific dating methods, and given the little that was known of the archaeology of tropical Africa, this train of thought seemed quite reasonable.

With the introduction of radiocarbon dating and the excavation of additional

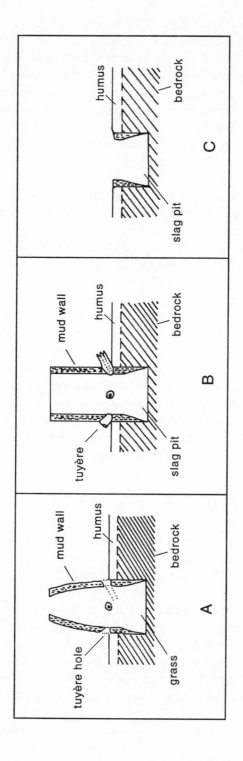

Fig. 7.1 Possible furnace reconstructions for Taruga, Nigeria. A: After Schmidt and Avery (1983: 431). B: After Tylecote (1975a: 5). C: Extent of furnace remains excavated at Taruga (after Tylecote, 1975b: 49–50).

sites this position changed. Meroë has dates from the base of slag mounds of 2464 ± 73 bp (770–510 BC) but no furnace remains have yet been found at these levels. The first smelting furnace remains are dated to 1680 ± 80 bp (AD 240–440) (Shinnie, 1985). The furnaces found at Meroë were brick-built, a method used until at least the seventh century AD at this site (Shinnie, 1974), with an inner lining, and a pit for tapping the slag away from the bloom. The walls tapered in toward the top and the hearth narrowed at the base. The furnaces used an induced draft with several bowl bellows feeding each furnace. Some of the remains have very good preservation of the upper structure. These furnaces were like those seen in Roman-influenced Egypt, suggesting that the original ideas for their origins were correct. The dates and typology of furnaces at Meroë, however, contrasted with those that Tylecote (1975b) published from the site of Taruga in Nigeria, with a furnace date of 2250 ± 100 bp (410–170 BC) and a general site date of 2390 ± 140 bp (770–380 BC). These dates related to very different nonslag-tapping furnaces, which showed little or no similarity to those at Meroë. The furnaces were built from piled mud rather than brick, with no inner lining. The hearth tapered out at the base, but the preservation of the upper structure was so poor at this site that no comparison should be made. The furnaces did use several tuyères but no bellows bowls have been found. This led Tylecote (1975a: 5) to question the idea that Meroë was the conduit for the diffusion of iron into Sub-Saharan Africa. Instead, he suggested that the Egyptian-influenced iron-smelting at Meroë was prevented from spreading further due to geographical factors.

Still Egypt and Meroë were hardly isolated from Sub-Saharan Africa and trading did occur (Welsby, 1996), suggesting that transfer of ideas was possible. The areas to the south and west certainly had ore and did practice iron-smelting, in Nigeria (Tylecote, 1975b; Connah, 1981), the Gulf of Guinea (Nigeria, Cameroon, Gabon) (Maret and Thiry, 1996), and the interlacustrine area, by the fifth century BC, and possibly earlier in Rwanda and Burundi (Van Grunderbeek, Roche and Doutrelepont, 1983), which leads one to question what 'geographical factors', if any, prevented the expansion of iron from Meroë.

Tylecote, however, did not believe that iron metallurgy could develop independently in two regions, especially since Sub-Saharan Africa seemed to have no previous pyrometallurgical tradition in copper. The lack of copper or bronze made Tylecote (1975a) believe that diffusion from outside Africa was the answer: the furnaces at Taruga suggested a common source with European furnaces, which most likely entered Africa from the Mediterranean coast. He went as far as to state 'one cannot accept the possibility of independent development in this case [Nigeria] as there was no pyrometallurgical tradition to build on' and that diffusion from Carthage was the 'only acceptable hypothesis' (Tylecote, 1975a: 4). This is an idea that has endured despite an absence of supporting evidence.

It is believed that the Phoenicians at Carthage had knowledge of iron by the early first millennium BC, when they arrived in this area, assuming that their technology was equivalent to the Phoenician civilization in general (Tylecote, 1975a: 5). The problem is that no ironworking or smelting sites from this pre-Roman period have been found. However, funerary stelae at Carthage do mention both iron and copper smelters, and there are also depictions of metalworking tools (Tylecote, 1975b: 55). We do not know what level of technology the Phoenicians at Carthage possessed, so are unable to make typological comparisons with Sub-Saharan Africa. There have been two routes suggested for the diffusion of iron across the Sahara. The first is south to the Aïr mountain region in Niger, and the other is along the western coast to the Akjoujt area in Mauritania, where Munson (1976) suggested the Lybico-Berbers had invaded between 700 and 400 BC. Both these routes involve Berber groups transferring the ironworking knowledge across the desert region. The sites of Akjoujt in Mauritania and Agadez in Niger are at the end of these routes and are the only ones in Sub-Saharan Africa with early copper-working. This is more likely to suggest that if the Berbers were smelting anything, it was copper. However, these ideas are based mainly on 'geographical feasibility' and 'classical references' rather than on archaeological evidence (Miller and Van Der Merwe, 1994).

Oliver and Fagan (1975), Mauny (1978), and Law (1980) have used rock art depictions of chariots to support the idea that Lybico-Berbers were the facilitators for the diffusion of iron. The suggestion was made that the rock art depicted Berber chariots 'traveling' (Oliver and Fagan, 1975: 59–69) across the desert and that they would have required metal parts in order to survive in such harsh conditions. There are two problems with this argument. First, the rock art depictions change greatly across the desert. Toward the south the depictions become 'less artistically and more schematically drawn' (Mauny, 1978: 279), and are barely recognizable as chariots (Grébénart, 1988). It has therefore been suggested that the people creating the drawings may not have seen the chariots and only had a 'symbolic' knowledge of them (Camps, 1982). Second, the depictions of chariots do not actually show the use of metal, it was merely an assumption that all-wooden chariots would not survive. This idea has been tested and it has been shown that they are usable, but only for short periods or on level surfaces (Grébénart, 1988: 92). Even if the use of metal in the chariots is accepted, this still does not necessarily mean that the Berbers had a working knowledge of iron, it may just have been that they traded with people that did. As at Punic Carthage, no Berber iron-working sites have been found.

INDIGENOUS THEORIES

The variety and range of furnaces found in Africa has often led to ideas of indigenous experimentation. It has been suggested that as the technology was diffused across the continent, it was slowly modified (Kense and Okoro, 1993; Maret and Thiry, 1996). The question is why people should experiment with a technology they have only just acquired. One answer to this may be that there was a local invention of the technology, with experimentation at each new stage, to improve the quality of the smelt. However, Okafor (1993) has suggested that the early Nigerian furnaces were more efficient than later ones. Another possibility is that the variations and changes are simply a response to very different environmental conditions and raw materials found over the continent. Rowlands (1971), Sutton (1985) and Miller and Van Der Merwe (1994) have suggested that some of the changes in furnace shape and size seen across the continent may be a response to different ore grades. A lower grade ore would require a larger furnace to produce the same quantity of workable iron as a higher grade ore would produce in a small furnace.

Some changes may be seen as strictly cultural with no practical function intended. Modifications to the appearance of a furnace could be one way of integrating an outside technology into a culture. However, the changes are more than just cultural adaptations, some of the variations found are distinct technological modifications requiring very different operating practices. The development of these is more difficult to explain as modifications to suit changes in the environment or cultural integration.

The chronology of the archaeological furnaces has proved difficult and does not fit very well with the diffusionist theories. The earliest iron furnace from Meroë is known from 1680 ± 80 bp (AD 240–440), which is later than generally accepted dates from the sites of Taruga at 2250 ± 100 bp (410–170 BC) (Tylecote, 1975b), and Samun Dukiya at 2250 ± 100 bp (410–170 BC) (Fagg, 1972) in Nigeria, Do Dimi in Niger at 2628 ± 120 bp (930–750 BC) (Grébénart, 1985), and Otumbi in Gabon at 2640 ± 70 bp (910–780 BC) (Peyrot and Oslisly, 1987; Clist, 1995). However, the furnace remains at these early sites are generally poor, being little more than hearth bases with no upper structure, tuyères, or bellows. The furnaces do not appear to use any form of slag-tapping pit which would make them more like those at Taruga than Meroë. Since Carthage is believed to have had smelting technology only by the early first millennium BC (Tylecote, 1975b: 55), this makes diffusion to Niger difficult in such a short time span. However, the resolution problems with radiocarbon dating make it impossible to argue such precise cases with any confidence. As can be seen in Table 7.1, the one-sigma calibrated range is often several hundred years (McIntosh and McIntosh, 1988: 91), and is sometime in excess of five hundred years (calibrated to 1 sigma using OxCal v2.18, giving

Table 7.1 Earliest radiocarbon dates for iron in Africa (furnaces, slag and artifacts)

	Date	Standard Error ±	Calibrated Range (1 sigma)	Site	Country
bc	1665	205	2300–1700	Muganza	Rwanda
bc	1230	155	1680–1260	Rwiyanje	Burundi
bc	1210	135	1620–1260	Mubuga	Burundi
bc	905	285	1450–750	Rwiyanje	Burundi
bc	870	100	1130–840	Oliga	Cameroon
bc	865	165	1220–820	Kabacusi	Rwanda
bc	760	130	1090–770	Oliga	Cameroon
bc	680	160	990–520	Ghwa Kiva	Cameroon
bc	678	120	930–750	Do Dimi	Niger
bc	591	104	810–520	Taruga	Nigeria
bc	550	60	790–530	Doulo Igzawa 1	Cameroon
bc	538	84	790–520	Taruga	Nigeria
bc	514	73	770–510	Meroe	Sudan
bc	450	50	910–780	Otumbi	Gabon
bc	450	90	550–390	Ekne Wan Ataran	Niger
bc	440	140	770–380	Taruga	Nigeria
bc	430	110	600–380	Oliga	Cameroon
bc	380	60	520–260	Ghwa Kiva	Cameroon
bc	375	135	800–200	Okolo	Cameroon
bc	360	100	550–200	Obobogo	Cameroon
bc	355	90	520–340	Nsukka	Nigeria
bc	350	100	520–200	Moanda	Gabon
bc	341	123	550–150	Taruga	Nigeria
bc	330	270	800–50	Oyem	Gabon
bc	319	116	510–160	Taruga	Nigeria
bc	310	110	420–110	Meroe	Sudan
bc	300	100	410–170	Samun Dukiya	Nigeria
bc	300	100	410–170	Taruga	Nigeria
bc	280	80	390–200	Nkometou	Cameroon
bc	280	120	410–110	Taruga	Nigeria
bc	280	120	410–110	Meroe	Sudan
bc	260	90	390–190	In Talaylen	Niger
bc	250	60	370–190	Okolo	Cameroon
bc	230	80	370–170	Nsukka	Nigeria
bc	230	110	380–110	Oliga	Cameroon
bc	210	180	400 BC–AD 30	Jenne-Jeno	Mali
bc	210	95	260–110	Samun Dukiya	Nigeria
bc	200	60	250–110	Oliga	Cameroon
bc	200	80	260–110	Oliga	Cameroon
bc	200	210	450 BC–AD 150	Kemondo Bay	Tanzania
bc	190	65	250–100	Ndindan	Cameroon
bc	176	110	260–40	Tiekene Bassoura	Senegal
bc	170	70	240–50	Obobogo	Cameroon
bc	170	150	370–0	Obobogo	Cameroon
bc	160	60	210–40	Marc du Flex	Congo
bc	160	60	210–40	Oliga	Cameroon

Table 7.1 continued

	Date	Standard Error $\pm$	Calibrated Range (1 sigma)	Site	Country
bc	150	70	310–30	Doulo Igzawa 1	Cameroon
bc	140	90	210 BC–AD 10	Teguef N Agar	Niger
bc	130	70	200–0	Oliga	Cameroon
bc	130	90	210 BC–AD 20	Nsukka	Nigeria
bc	115	320	500 BC–AD 350	Zoui	Chad
bc	110	60	170–0	Ndindan	Cameroon
bc	105	70	170 BC–AD 10	Obobogo	Cameroon
bc	92	126	210 BC–AD 90	Taruga	Nigeria
bc	70	75	120 BC–AD 70	Rafin Ndoko	Nigeria
bc	60	90	120 BC–AD 80	In Talaylen	Niger
bc	60	140	200 BC–AD 140	Daboya	Ghana
bc	40	65	90 BC–AD 70	Obobogo	Cameroon
bc	30	60	90 BC–AD 80	Tiekene Bassoura	Senegal
bc	30	180	200 BC–AD 250	Amkoundjo	Chad
bc	25	125	170 BC–AD 180	Rop Rock Shelter	Nigeria
bc	10	60	40 BC–AD 120	Toungour	Chad
bc	10	80	90 BC–AD 120	Oliga	Cameroon

68.2 per cent confidence that the true date falls between this range; if the 2 sigma calibration is used, there is a 95.4 per cent confidence, but the range becomes too great to be meaningful). This problem is compounded by the flattening of the calibration curve between 800 and 500 BC, which has created a discontinuity in African iron dates (McKeating and Phillipson, 1996).

DATING AND ASSOCIATION

In recent years a number of new sites have been published with early dates, from Cameroon, Gabon, Democratic Republic of Congo, Rwanda, and Burundi (Van Grunderbeek, Roche and Doutrelepont, 1983; Maret and Thiry, 1996). Some of these have had to be dismissed because of problems with contamination and laboratory problems, or inconsistency with data from the same area (Maret and Thiry, 1996). As previously noted, generally accepted dates from Otumbi in Gabon of 2640 ± 70 bp (910–780 BC) (Peyrot and Oslisly, 1987; Clist, 1995) and Do Dimi in Niger of 2628 ± 120 bp (930–750 BC) (Grébénart, 1985) make the argument for diffusion from Carthage difficult. However, the dates from Rwanda and Burundi are even more of a problem. The sites of Muganza, with a date of 3615 ± 205 bp (2300–1700 BC) and of Kabacusi with 2815 ± 165 bp (1220–820 BC), in Rwanda, and of Rwiyanje with 3180 ± 155 bp (1680–1260 BC) and 2855 ± 285 bp (1450–750 BC) and

Mubuga with 3160 ± 135 bp (1620–1260 BC), in Burundi, would change the picture in favor of an indigenous development. Only the hearth pits have been found at these sites, which again makes any comparison with technology from other areas very difficult. However, the hearths do not appear to have any form of slag-tapping pits associated with them, unlike those at Meroë. The work of Van Grunderbeek, Roche and Doutrelepont (1983) fixes smelting in this region to the early part of the first millennium BC, which in itself must question the likelihood of a diffused technology (Table 7.1). Unfortunately the current political situation in this region prohibits further investigations at this time.

In addition to furnace dates there have been new dates for slag and artifacts, not in association with furnaces, from the Congo and Cameroon. There is one date from the first millennium BC in the Congo, at the site of Marc du Flex, of 2110 ± 60 bp (210–40 BC) (Lanfranchi, 1991). However, the Cameroon has produced twenty-three dates from the first millennium BC, the earliest of which are at Obobogo with 2310 ± 100 bp (550–200 BC), Oliga with 2820 ± 100 bp (1130–840 BC), 2710 ± 130 bp (1090–770 BC), and 2380 ± 110 bp (600–380 BC), Okolo with 2325 ± 135 bp (800–200 BC) (Holl, 1991), Doulo Igzawa 1 with 2500 ± 60 bp (790–530 BC), Ghwa Kiva with 2630 ± 160 bp (990–520 BC) and 2330 ± 60 bp (520–260 BC) (MacEachern, 1996). These dates would also change the picture in favor of an indigenous development. However, they do not provide us with any information about the iron-smelting technology.

There have also been several early first millennium AD sites in Ghana (Penfold, 1970; Posnansky, 1975; Shaw, 1969), but even earlier dates (Davies, 1973) are believed to be intrusive by the excavator. However, this appears to be because the dates are too early rather than because of poor context.

The early radiocarbon dates for sites both in arid and humid Africa have been challenged on the grounds of contamination (Maret and Thiry, 1996). The samples from arid zones have been particularly questioned because of the possible use of 'old wood' from ancient forest fires. However, in humid zones 'old wood' is likely to decay before it could be reused (Maret and Thiry, 1996). Posnansky and McIntosh (1976) also questioned Do Dimi dates because they came from mixed charcoal, not single samples. Dates that contradict diffusionist theories are often not accepted; we must question if this is based on reasonable evidence, or simply results from an unwillingness to accept new data that contradict long-held ideas.

PREHEATING AND ASSOCIATED ARGUMENTS

Several more technical arguments have been advanced for the indigenous development of iron. The use of a 'bloomery direct steel process' has been claimed to be unique to Sub-Saharan Africa and to represent a pristine technological development (Schmidt and Childs, 1995). This process involves a one-step method of producing steel within a bloom, without the need to add or remove carbon by secondary processes, as with European blast furnaces in which the cast iron, which cannot be hot or cold worked (Sassoon, 1963), requires decarburizing to make steel. Recent research has, however, shown that the process of bloomery direct steel production is also found in Europe from 500 BC (Killick, 1996) and is thus not a uniquely African development.

Schmidt and Avery (1978, 1983, 1996) and Schmidt and Childs (Schmidt and Childs, 1995; Childs and Schmidt, 1985) have produced a complex argument for an 'advanced' smelting technology in Africa predating that found in Europe. Their work has been centered on excavations in the Kemondo Bay sites and ethnographic reconstructions with the Haya people, both in Tanzania. This contentious argument is based on the production of a 'carbon steel' and cast iron by a direct steel process. By using long deeply-inserted tuyère pipes, creating a 'preheating' effect, the furnace is said to have been able to reach much higher temperatures than usually found in bloomery production. In addition to this Schmidt and Childs (1995) have suggested the use of carbonized grass reed beds, creating a 'carbon boil' to improve carbon content, and the existence of an unusual iron chemistry because of smelting with fuel with a high phosphorous content.

Some of the terminology used by Schmidt and Avery can be misleading. 'Carbon steel' suggests a product that is different and superior to normal steel found in other processes, but steel by definition has a set range of carbon content, typically less than 2 per cent (Eggert, 1987). The term 'carbon boil' has been used to suggest a violent reaction between oxygen and carbon which assists the reduction process. This term is more commonly used with blast-furnace technology, the carbon boil is there employed to decarburize cast iron. Use of the term in the African context suggests a connection with blast-furnace technology which does not exist, the two methods are very different.

The use of long tuyères or air pipes in Haya furnaces to preheat the incoming air and improve the burn has been suggested (Schmidt and Avery, 1983). This has been likened to the preheating used since the eighteenth century in European blast furnaces. However, the latter involved the use of large quantities of tubing and a cylinder which directed the waste gases to heat the air (Eggert, 1987), a process which is in no way similar to what Schmidt and Avery are proposing.

The temperature of the air within the tuyères was measured using thermocouples, and these registered an increase of up to 600°C. This increase would lessen the energy reduction in the furnace used to heat incoming air, thus giving the furnace more energy to reach higher temperatures with less fuel. However, the method of measuring the temperature has been criticized by

Rehder (1986; 1996). Solid objects like the thermocouples will pick up heat by radiation from the tuyère wall, whereas the air primarily takes heat by convection. Rehder calculated that the increase by convection would only be about 22°C, which would have a negligible effect. Avery and Schmidt (1996a, 1996b) now suggest that, as the bellows were valveless and not sealed to the tuyères, an oscillating effect would be created, increasing the time the air was in the tuyère. Such an effect, however, would draw air from the furnace, lowering the energy within, then mix this with the incoming air, heating it but not adding energy to the system. In this situation the air in the tuyère may be hotter but cannot increase the temperature within the furnace, as it is only replacing what it has already taken out.

The unusual chemistry in Haya furnaces is said to lower the melting and reduction temperatures of iron and thus to assist the smelt. The blooms from these furnaces are said to contain some cast iron, creating a denser bloom than those from a solid state reduction process (Schmidt and Childs, 1995). If this is the case then preheating is not required, as the suggested lowering from a melting point of 1540°C for iron to 1147°C would bring cast-iron production within the range of normal bloomery furnaces, which can reach more than 1300°C. If the preheating is used with this suggested chemistry, then an entirely cast-iron bloom should be produced. The production of small quantities of cast iron has been seen at other African bloomery furnaces which have normal chemistry and no preheating. The production of cast iron is usually seen as a problem or mistake, as this cannot be hammer-worked without decarburization to steel.

Schmidt and Avery have found long tuyère pipes, grass impressions, and high phosphorous content at the Kemondo Bay sites which date to 2150 ± 210 bp (450 BC–AD 150). Their reconstruction of these is similar to the Haya furnaces, suggesting a continuity of over 2000 years. It seems unrealistic to suggest that no changes would have taken place in this timescale even with no changes in the environmental conditions. They have also suggested that the Kemondo Bay furnaces were similar to those at the site of Taruga, which had some grass impressions. Tylecote (1975a: 6) suggested that grass or straw may have been used in the furnaces at Taruga to aid the separation of slag from the bloom. However, as Schmidt and Avery themselves demonstrated (1983), furnace bases can be reconstructed in many ways. The claims made that this was a more efficient and advanced technology producing a better bloom have not been proven. No measurement of charcoal burnt was made, so claims that this technology was more efficient are unfounded. The technology and chemistry may have been different, but the resultant bloom does not seem to have been sufficiently different to warrant their claims (Rehder 1986, 1996). The Kemondo Bay sites are 400–500 years later than those at Taruga and Do Dimi, so the smelting in Tanzania may, of course, have been the result of experimentation based on earlier technology. In sum, there is no basis for the claims of a unique and indigenous technology at Kemondo Bay based solely on extant information.

COPPER

One of the main arguments for the diffusion of iron from outside Africa is the lack of any early 'Copper Age' in Sub-Saharan Africa. Nevertheless, the areas of Akjoujt in Mauritania and Agadez in Niger both have early copper-working. Akjoujt in the west of Mauritania has a range of dates for copper-smelting in the early to mid first millennium BC. The dates for Akjoujt of 2350 ± 110 bp (800–250 BC), 2360 ± 110 bp (600–360 BC), 2400 ± 110 bp (600–390 BC), 2430 ± 110 bp (600–400 BC) and 2522 ± 123 bp (810–510BC) (Willett, 1971) and 2460 ± 100 bp (770–480 BC) and 2500 ± 100 bp (800–520 BC) (Flight, 1973) are well grouped but fall after the first dates for ironworking in Niger and Nigeria, which would suggest that this is a separate technology not linked to African ironworking. However, two dates at Akjoujt have been produced that are just earlier than the first commonly accepted dates for iron, these are 2700 ± 100 bp (990–790 BC) (Flight, 1973) and 2776 ± 126 bp (1100–810 BC) (Willett, 1971). Both these dates are seen, by the excavators, as being too old in relation to the other material from the sites, but could possibly be older than ironworking.

Copper artifacts have been found in association with lithic material at another site in Mauritania. The site of Khatt Lemaiteg has projectile points, a bracelet, and a stone bead attached to a wire loop which are in the same style as objects found at Akjoujt. These artifacts are associated with 'Habitation 2' on this dune site, which dates to 3310 ± 200 bp (1890–1390 BC) (Vernet, 1992). This site was believed to have been inhabited by stone-tool-using 'nomadic' pastoralists and the excavator believes that the copper artifacts are intrusive, perhaps introduced by a later group from Akjoujt. This argument is based on the premise that Khatt Lemaiteg's ceramics do not match those associated with copper-working at Akjoujt. However, as there are no other artifacts from the Akjoujt facies, it seems unlikely, but not impossible, that a group would leave its copper goods but none of its ceramics. If these older dates are correct, then copper-working in Mauritania may be much older than previously believed, possibly predating iron metallurgy (Table 7.2). It is interesting to note that the copper ores in this region have a high iron content, which would have been difficult to remove before smelting (Oliver and Fagan, 1975). The iron would act as a flux improving the copper smelt, but in the process some prills of iron (droplets of slag or globules of metal) may have been formed. It is possible this could have led to the development of iron-smelting.

Table 7.2 Earliest radiocarbon dates for copper in Africa (furnaces, slag and artifacts)

	Date	Standard Error ±	Calibrated Range (1 sigma)	Site	Country
bc	1360	130	1890–1390	Khatt Lemaiteg	Mauritania
bc	826	126	1100–810	Akjoujt	Mauritania
bc	750	100	990–790	Akjoujt	Mauritania
bc	750	70	920–800	Agadez	Niger
bc	678	120	930–750	Agadez	Niger
bc	572	123	803–406	Akjoujt	Mauritania
bc	550	100	800–520	Akjoujt	Mauritania
bc	540	90	790–520	Azelik	Niger
bc	530	90	780–510	Azelik	Niger
bc	510	100	770–480	Akjoujt	Mauritania
bc	480	110	600–400	Akjoujt	Mauritania
bc	450	110	600–390	Akjoujt	Mauritania
bc	410	110	600–360	Akjoujt	Mauritania
bc	400	110	800–250	Akjoujt	Mauritania

Data for copper-working at Agadez in Niger has been more contentious, with Grébénart (1983, 1987, 1988) proposing two early copper phases in this area. Copper I had dates from furnaces for the late second to early first millennium BC, but on reexamination these furnaces were seen to be charred tree stumps from an ancient forest fire in copper-rich soil (Killick *et al.*, 1988). However, furnace number 8 at the site of Afunfun 175, with a date of 3660 ± 100 bp (2200–1900 BC), does appear to be a humanly made feature and is possibly a furnace base. Nevertheless, this date is still questionable, as there is a possibility that old wood from the original forest fires was used in later smelting processes.

The Copper II sites have better associations, with 17 dates which are mostly grouped between 800 and 200 BC. Ironworking also would seem to have existed during this same period, with four dates in the first millennium BC from the same region (Grébénart, 1987) and a date of 2628 ± 120 bp (930–750 BC) at Do Dimi (Grébénart, 1988). The copper-working dates from Copper II may be possibly a few hundred years earlier than iron in this area, but the resolution offered by radiocarbon dating does not strongly suggest a pre-iron pyrometallurgical tradition. Two dates for native copper-working have come from this area, suggesting cold or hot hammering was practiced between 2500 BC and 1500 BC (Grébénart, 1988).

LINGUISTICS AND THE BANTU EXPANSION

There has been a limited use of linguistics in connection with metallurgy; the only area that has had serious consideration is the origins of metal in the Bantu groups. The suggestion has been that the spread of iron across central and southern Africa was linked to the Bantu expansion during the early first millennium BC (Huffman, 1970). This was supported by the idea that large-scale forest clearance would require metal tools. This idea appears to have no archaeological evidence to support it and the assumption that large-scale clearance would require metal tools is untested. Stone tools would probably be more efficient than some early iron implements. Indeed, early linguistic claims for Proto-Bantu possessing words for metal have been rejected in recent years (Vansina, 1995; Maret, 1996). The Bantu homelands have been agreed to be in the grassfields of Cameroon. The expansion has been placed from around 1500 BC from the core homelands, prior to the introduction of metal. One of the core sites for the Proto-Bantu is Obobogo in the Cameroon, and this site has also produced several early dates ranging from 2900 ± 100 bp (1260–980 BC) to 3625 ± 165 bp (2300–1750 BC) (Maret, 1982, 1985). However, these have been dismissed because of contamination problems (Maret, 1996). The Fundong smelting site in the Cameroon grasslands provides a good date from the second century AD (Rowlands and Warnier, 1993). Bantu-speakers appear to be an unlikely facilitator of metallurgical expansion; the early dates in Rwanda and Burundi would seem to predate their arrival in these areas.

TECHNOLOGY, INDUSTRY AND SCALE OF PRODUCTION

There are several key technological requirements for smelting iron in a bloomery furnace, which is not melting the metal from the ore but reducing it by chemical reaction. In this, temperature is a key factor: the reduction reaction starts to occur at 1150–1200°C but iron does not start to melt until 1540°C. Interestingly, the 1200°C temperature is obtainable within open pit fires (Van Noten, 1985). But temperature is not the only requirement, equally important are correct atmospheric conditions. The gas balance within the furnace is critical, a reducing environment with low carbon dioxide (CO_2) content and excess of carbon monoxide (CO) must be maintained. The basic process of reduction can be explained in its most simple form as iron oxide (ore) reacting with carbon monoxide to produce metallic iron and carbon dioxide or:

$$FeO + CO = Fe + CO_2$$

This is a simplistic representation as different ores will have more complex compositions and carbon will react with the ferric iron; it would be better expressed by

$$Fe_2O_3 + 3CO = 2Fe + 3CO_2$$

However, the basic requirement to reduce the oxygen content by reaction with carbon monoxide is at odds with temperature production. A reaction interface with oxidation and reduction zones needs to be created. Oxygen is needed to burn the fuel (charcoal) to create the temperature, but too much oxygen introduced from the bellows will stop the reduction or reverse it and reoxidize the iron ore (Fig. 7.2).

The different parts of a furnace are designed to meet these two requirements and to maintain them. Any meaningful typology of furnaces needs to consider if variations and changes affect this smelting operation. Changes in production quantities may require a change in physical structure but not in operating practices. This can be seen in the work of Van Noten (1985) with the Madi of northeastern Democratic Republic of Congo. The Madi used an open pit furnace to produce iron in an ethnographic reconstruction. When questioned how they would increase the yield of the furnace, they said that walls of clay would be built up around the edge of the furnace to the required level. This would effectively change a open pit furnace into a low shaft furnace, with no change in operating procedures.

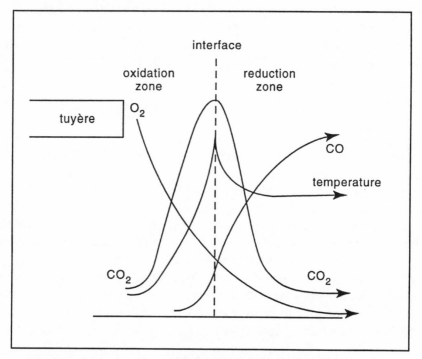

Fig. 7.2 Schematic diagram of reduction and oxidizing zones during the operation of an iron-smelting furnace. (Modified from Childs and Schmidt, 1985: 125.)

The function of furnace walls thus needs to be examined; the Madi experiment suggests that the primary purpose of the upper structure is as a container to hold ore and charcoal in place. Secondary functions of walls in some furnaces include the maintenance of temperature and assistance with the creation of a reduction zone. However, as the Madi have produced usable iron products in open pits, upper furnace walls are not a requirement of smelting. Furnace shape has been seen as an important factor in the development of typologies especially in Europe. However, this may not be an indication of technological development, but a cultural manifestation with furnace shape being part of the overall decoration used to integrate a new process into a specific group. The placement and size of tuyères in relation to the fire-bed or pit would be of more relevance in a technological development sequence. These would change the control of the reduction zone and therefore the size and quality of the bloom. It is thus essential to differentiate furnace elements which are technological and furnace elements which are stylistic.

The materials used in construction and operation are likely to be adaptations to new environments rather than representative of developmental stages. These are likely to have little relevance to a typology aimed at finding changes in iron-smelting and the development of a technological spread across the continent. I agree with Kense and Okoro (1993) that the 'discovery' of new furnace types has little meaning in an African context. However, a usable typology may be possible if a detailed technological study of African furnaces was undertaken with material and shape variations only considered when they affect the operating procedures of the furnace.

The variations in bellows types may also provide little technological information. Of course only bowl bellows have survived archaeologically due to differential preservation. The change between bag and bowl bellows may be due to the relative importance or availability of materials, as essentially they perform the same function. Sutton (1976) noted that different size tuyères, presumably with different size bellows, can be used at the same time on a single smelt. The operation of the later natural draft furnaces may depend on the environmental conditions at the time: if there was not a suitable wind to create a draft, bellows may have been used to assist the operation.

The changes in the size of furnaces seen across the continent, and often on the same site, have also been used to suggest chronologies, particularly for individual sites. The smaller furnaces are often believed to represent the earliest occurrence of smelting in an area. Within a site this might be a reasonable assumption, but caution must be used and other means of corroboration are needed. There are other reasons for the change in size of furnaces. Different grades of ores found across the continent could necessitate changes in the size of the furnace used to obtain the same size bloom (Sutton, 1985). Goucher (1981) calculated that four furnaces would use a 1-kilometer radius of forest in 40 days of smelting. This may suggest that smaller furnaces are a later reaction to reduced resources. Davies (1966) suggested that the lack of fuel in Sub-Saharan West Africa required blooms to be transported across the desert from the north. The scale of production on a site may not be represented by the size of the furnace or the quantities of slag. Meroë has often been seen as one of the industrial centers of Africa, based on the quantities of slag found at that site. The ore quality and efficiency of the smelting at this site have not been fully examined, however, so the quantity of iron produced at Meroë is unclear. Meroë is likely have been one of the most important and relatively productive sites in early African ironworking, but we must somehow quantify production at smelting sites in order to create a truly rigorous comparison. Bachmann (1982: 5) has suggested an equation for calculating production levels from slag quantities, but slag can also have differential preservation, if the iron content is high then the slag will oxidize or rust (Mapunda, 1995), so caution is required.

The amount of iron produced at any early ironworking site is likely to have been modest, even at a site such as Meroë. The amount of iron produced on a site must be considered with regards to the timescale of operation. The site of Meroë is known to have been producing iron from the middle first millennium BC to at least the middle first millennium AD. If the total production is divided by the operational timescale then the cultural significance of iron in this area changes. The level of production was probably low, but shows a surprising level of continuity, suggesting that iron was a high-status product rather than a material produced on an industrial scale. This suggestion might be supported by the tomb of King Harsiotef, dated from c. 404–369 BC, which contained miniature iron weapons in place of the copper ones previously used (Shinnie, 1985: 30). This argument assumes static production levels across the occupation of the site, it does not take into account production development or change of status for iron in the culture. The argument is not meant to be taken literally, but merely used to suggest that statements about production at other sites be reconsidered.

POSSIBLE IMPETUS FOR INDIGENOUS DEVELOPMENT

Having considered the basic requirements of temperature and reducing environment, one must pose the question: could these conditions have been created to facilitate the development of metal-smelting in the absence of any previous pyrometallurgical tradition? The temperature conditions required of 1150–1200°C are very close to those observed from open natural draft fires. Current work at the Institute of Archaeology, University College London (Austin, personal communication) has regularly recorded temperatures of 900°C in open natural fires when properly constructed. The use of a pit when clamp-firing pottery is likely to attain this temperature for extended periods. These observations have been made from fires created in England. Observations of African potters firing ceramics in clamps with a shallow pit have shown temperatures in excess of 900°C (Tobert, 1982; Woods, 1982). The conditions in Africa during the dry season are more likely to be conducive to the maintenance of temperatures, particularly in areas which have strong seasonal winds. The temperatures within pottery and normal fires are known to fluctuate, as they do within furnaces.

The difficulty with an indigenous development without previous pyrometallurgical knowledge begins when the temperature is linked to the need for a reducing environment to produce metal. However, there are possibilities that the control of the environment within a fire was already understood in relation to the use of some iron ores. Crushed haematite had been used as a slip on pottery from 4000 BC onwards in several parts of Africa. This material was used to create both red and black surfaces on the ceramics. In order to create a black finish, the conditions needed to be regulated to give a reducing environment. Experiments in England with a similar process have shown that the correct conditions can be created in a simple fire if it is properly controlled (Middleton, 1986). Temperatures of 940°C were recorded while the reducing environment was in existence (Dawson and Kent, 1986). The control displayed by African potters was often remarkable, with part of a pot regularly firing black in a reducing environment and the rest regularly firing red in an oxidizing environment (Krause, 1985).

If the conditions were correct, it may only have required one instance for the idea of iron-smelting to germinate and inspire experimentation. It is possible that small quantities of metallic iron prills could have been formed in the firing of pottery with haematite slips. The use of bellows would have assisted the production of iron but may not necessarily have been required. Any upper structure for a furnace would not have been necessary, and could have been a later development, as it is possible to smelt in a open bowl furnace (Van Noten, 1985; Clare, 1986). Forest fires in copper-rich areas such as Agadez could also have provided the impetus for experimentation. After all, the remains found by Grébénart (1983, 1985) appeared to the excavator to be smelting furnaces on first inspection, as the copper-rich soil had produced some metallic copper. Sassoon (1964) suggested that magnetite in the form of black river sand may have attracted early experimenters because of its metallic luster.

CONCLUSION

The archaeological and ethnographic material needs to be reviewed, taking care to isolate the technological furnace elements from separate stylistic differences.

In the past only limited ethnographic examples have been used to support the archaeological data and to put forward theories for the origins of metallurgy. A comprehensive reassessment of the ethnographic data would be a mammoth task, but if we are to move closer to a clear understanding of African origins, it requires doing. In conjunction with this, we need more complete surveys for all areas of the continent, with a clear picture of where different ores are found and their respective grades. Todd and Charles (1978) have demonstrated the benefits of chemical and element analysis which can assist in provenancing both artifacts and ores. We may be able to target future research more accurately and to expand our interpretations of current furnace data.

We need to move away from the intricate arguments over individual sites and start to build larger multidisciplinary models for questions concerning origins. It is unlikely in the extreme that a single site will be found that has a pristine technology; no single site will solve all our problems.

There are two basic arguments for the origins of metallurgy in Sub-Saharan Africa. The ideas for diffusion may become more acceptable if additional research was to add new data on Meroë or the Maghreb. Some of the dates for copper or copper-working in Mauritania are interesting, and may point to an early 'Copper Age' that has been previously missing from Africa. Much more work is required in the copper belts of Africa in Mauritania, Niger, and Zambia. From the other side of the continent there is still the possibility for iron to have diffused from Egypt to Meroë, then west into Chad and Niger, following the east-west Sahelian trade route. Thus, more research in southern Chad, for example, would be welcome.

The other argument for origins is that of a pristine technological development of smelting in Sub-Saharan Africa. The usual area for ideas of indigenous development centers around Nigeria and Niger, and with the sites of Taruga and Do Dimi this has seemed to be a likely candidate. This has been strengthened by the new dates associated with slag from the Cameroon, at Obobogo, Oliga, Okolo, Doulo Igzawa 1, and Ghwa Kiva. However, early dates have come from Rwanda and Burundi at Rwiyanje, Mubuga, and Muganza, which create another possible center for development if these dates are believed (Fig. 7.3). Before a clear picture can be developed much more research needs to be undertaken both on the existing data and in the field with excavation.

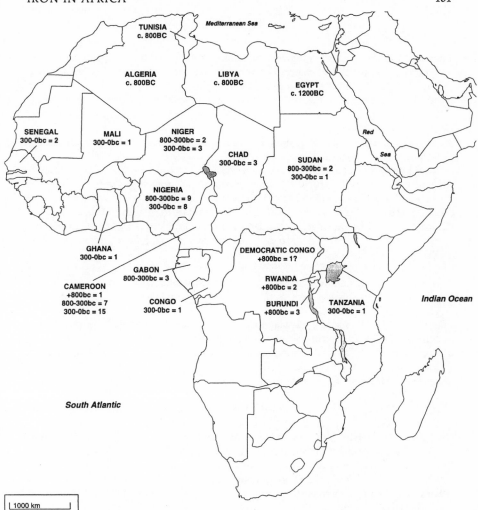

Fig. 7.3 Distribution of uncalibrated radiocarbon dates for ironworking sites from the first millennium BC across Africa. Showing number of sites within ranges: + 800 BC; 800–300 BC; 300–0 BC. *'Circa'* dates are derived from textual sources. Radiocarbon dates for which contamination has been alleged are marked with a question mark.

BIBLIOGRAPHY

Austin, P. (1996) Personal communication from Phillip Austin on experimental open fires for his PhD. (Wood charcoal from hearth deposits: taphonomy and interpretive models.) Institute of Archaeology, University College London.

Avery, D.H. and Schmidt, P.R. (1996a) Preheating: practice or illusion. In Schmidt, P.R. (ed.) *The culture and technology of African iron production.* Gainesville, University Press of Florida, pp. 267–76.

Avery, D.H. and Schmidt, P.R. (1996b) Use of preheated air in ancient and recent African iron smelting furnaces: a reply to Rehder. In Schmidt, P.R. (ed.) *The culture and technology of African iron production.* Gainesville, University Press of Florida, pp. 240–6.

Bachmann, H.G. (1982) *The identification of slags from archaeological sites.* Institute of Archaeology Occasional Publication 6. London, Institute of Archaeology.

Brown, J. (1995) *Traditional metalworking in Kenya.* Oxford, Oxbow Monograph 44.

Camps, G. (1982) Le cheval et le char dans la préhistoire Nord-Africaine et Saharienne. In Camps, G. and Gast, M. (eds) *Les chars préhistoriques du Sahara.* Aix-en-Provence, Université de Provence, pp. 9–22.

Childs, S.T. and Schmidt, P.R. (1985) Experimental iron smelting: the genesis of a hypothesis with implications for African prehistory and history. In Haaland, R. and Shinnie, P. (eds) *African iron working: ancient and traditional.* Bergen, Norwegian University Press, pp. 121–41.

Clare, T. (1986) A charcoal burn and attempt at smelting iron with an open bowl furnace. *Bulletin of the Experimental Firing Group* 5: 12–14.

Cleere, H.F. (1972) The classification of early iron-smelting furnaces. *Antiquaries Journal* 52: 8–23.

Cline, W. (1937) *Mining and metallurgy in Negro Africa.* Menasha, Wisconsin, George Banta Publishing.

Clist, B. (1995) *Gabon: 100 000 ans d'histoire.* Sépia, Centre Culturel Français Saint-Exupéry (Gabon).

Coghlan, H.H. (1956) *Notes on prehistoric and early iron in the Old World.* Oxford, Occasional Papers on Technology 8, Pitt Rivers Museum, University of Oxford.

Connah, G. (1981) *Three thousand years in Africa: man and his environment in the Lake Chad Region of Nigeria.* Cambridge, Cambridge University Press.

Davies, O. (1966) Comments on the Iron Age in Sub-Saharan Africa. *Current Anthropology* 7: 470–1.

Davies, O. (1973) *Excavations at Ntereso, Gonja, Northern Ghana.* Pietermaritzburg, Natal Museum.

Dawson, D. and Kent, O. (1986) Experiments in reduction firing: the Bickley Project. *Bulletin of the Experimental Firing Group* 5: 34–41.

Eggert, M.K.H. (1987) On the alleged complexity of early and recent iron smelting in Africa: further comments on the preheating hypothesis. *Journal of Field Archaeology* 12: 377–82.

Fagg, A. (1972) A preliminary report on an occupation site in the Nok Valley, Nigeria: Samun Dukiya, AF/70/1. *West African Journal of Archaeology* 2: 75–9.

Fagg, B.E.B. (1969) Recent work in West Africa. *World Archaeology* 1: 41–50.

Fagg, W. (1952) Ironworking with a stone hammer among the Tula of Northern Nigeria. *Man* 76: 51–3.

Flight, C. (1973) A survey of recent results in the radiocarbon chronology of Northern and Western Africa. *Journal of African History* 14: 531–54.

Garstang, J., Sayce, A.H. and Griffiths, F.W. (1911) *Meroë, the city of the Ethiopians.* Oxford, Oxford University Press.

Goucher, C.L. (1981) Iron is iron 'til it is rust: trade and ecology in the decline of West African iron-smelting. *Journal of African History* 22(1): 179–89.

Grébénart, D. (1983) Les métallurgies du cuive et du fer autour d'Agadez (Niger) des origines au début de la période médiévale: vues générales. In Echard, N. (ed.) *Métallurgies Africaines: nouvelles contributions*. Paris, Société des Africanistes, pp. 109–25.

Grébénart, D. (1985) *Le Néolithique Final et les débuts de la métallurgie*. Niamey, Études Nigériennes No. 49, Institut de Recherches en Sciences Humaines.

Grébénart, D. (1987) Characteristics of the Final Neolithic and Metal Ages in the region of Agadez (Niger). In Close, A. (ed.) *The prehistory of arid North Africa*. Dallas, Southern Methodist University Press, pp. 287–316.

Grébénart, D. (1988) *Les premiérs métallurgistes en Afrique Occidentale*. Abidjan, Nouvelles Éditors Africaines.

Holl, A. (1991) Cameroon. In Lanfranchi, R. and Clist, B. (eds) *Aux origines de l'Afrique Centrale*. Sépia, Centre Culturel Français de Libreville, pp. 193–6.

Holl, A. (1993) Transition from Late Stone Age to Iron Age in the Sudano–Sahelian Zone: a case study from the Perichadian plain. In Shaw, T., Sinclair, P., Andah, B. and Okpoko, A. (eds) *The archaeology of Africa: food, metals and towns*. London, Routledge, pp. 330–43.

Huffman, T.N. (1970) The Early Iron Age and the spread of the Bantu. *South African Archaeological Bulletin* 25: 3–21.

Kense, F.J. (1983) *Traditional African iron working*. Calgary, African Occasional Papers No. 1, University of Calgary.

Kense, F.J. and Okoro, J.A. (1993) Changing perspectives on traditional iron production in West Africa. In Shaw, T., Sinclair, P., Andah, B. and Okpoko, A. (eds) *The archaeology of Africa: food, metals and towns*. London, Routledge, pp. 449–58.

Killick, D. (1996) On claims for 'advanced' ironworking technology in precolonial Africa. In Schmidt, P.R. (ed.) *The culture and technology of African iron production*. Gainesville, University Press of Florida, pp. 247–66.

Killick, D., Van Der Merwe, N., Gordon, R. and Grébénart, D. (1988) Reassessment of the evidence for early metallurgy in Niger, West Africa. *Journal of Archaeological Science* 15: 367–94.

Krause, R.A. (1985) *The clay sleeps: an ethnoarchaeological study of three African potters*. Alabama, University of Alabama Press.

Lanfranchi, R. (1991) Congo. In Lanfanchi, R. and Clist, B. (eds) *Aux origines de l'Afrique Centrale*. Sépia, Centre Culturel Français de Libreville, pp. 209–12.

Law, R. (1980) Wheeled transport in pre-colonial West Africa. *Africa* 50(3): 249–62.

Lawal, I.O. (1995) *Metalworking in Africa south of the Sahara: an annotated bibliography*. Westport, Greenwood Press.

MacEachern, S. (1996) Iron Age beginnings north of the Mandara Mountains, Cameroon and Nigeria. In Pwiti, G. and Soper, R. (eds) *Aspects of African archaeology. Papers from the 10th Congress of the PanAfrican Association for Prehistory and Related Studies*. Harare, University of Zimbabwe Publications, pp. 489–95.

McIntosh, S.K. and McIntosh, R.J. (1988) From stone to metal: new perspectives on the later prehistory of West Africa. *Journal of World Prehistory* 2(1): 89–133.

McKeating, A. and Phillipson, D. (1996) *Metal in Africa*. Cambridge, Cambridge Africana No. 1. University of Cambridge.

Mapunda, B.B. (1995) Iron Age archaeology in the south eastern Lake Tanganyika region, southwestern Tanzania. *Nyame Akuma* 43: 46–57.

Maret, P. de (1982) New survey of archaeological research and dates for West-Central and North-Central Africa. *Journal of African History* 23: 1–15.

Maret, P. de (1985) Recent archaeological research and dates from Central Africa. *Journal of African History* 26: 129–48.

Maret, P. de (1996) Pits, pots and the far-west streams. In Sutton, J.E.G. (ed.) *The growth of farming communities in Africa from the Equator southwards. Azania Special Volume* 29–30: 318–323.

Maret, P. de and Thiry, G. (1996) How old is the Iron Age in Central Africa? In Schmidt, P.R. (ed.) *The culture and technology of African iron production.* Gainesville, University Press of Florida, pp. 29–39.

Martins, I. (1978) Some reflections on the classification of prehistoric and medieval iron-smelting furnaces. *Norwegian Archaeological Review* 11(1): 27–47.

Mauny, R. (1978) Trans-Saharan contacts and the Iron Age in West Africa. In Fage, J.D. (ed.) *Cambridge History of Africa, Vol 2: From c. 500 BC to AD 1050.* Cambridge, Cambridge University Press, pp. 272–341.

Middleton, A. (1986) Surface finishes on 'haematite-coated' pottery from southern England. *Bulletin of the Experimental Firing Group* 4: 49–54.

Miller, D.E. and Van Der Merwe, N.J. (1994) Early metal working in Sub-Saharan Africa: a review of recent research. *Journal of African History* 35: 1–36.

Munson, P.J. (1976) Archaeological data on the origins of cultivation in the southwestern Sahara and their implications for West Africa. In Harlan, J.R., de Wet, J.M.J. and Stemler, A.B.L. (eds) *Origins of African plant domestication.* The Hague, Mouton, pp. 187–209.

Okafor, E.E. (1993) New evidence on early iron-smelting from southwestern Nigeria. In Shaw, T., Sinclair, P., Andah, B. and Okpoko, A. (eds) *The archaeology of Africa: food, metals and towns.* London, Routledge, pp. 432–48.

Oliver, R. and Fagan, B. (1975) *Africa in the Iron Age.* Cambridge, Cambridge University Press.

Penfold, D.A. (1970) Excavations of an iron-smelting site at Cape Coast. *Transactions of the Historical Society of Ghana* 12: 1–15.

Peyrot, B. and Oslisly, R. (1987) Paléoenvironnement et archéologie au Gabon: 1985–1986. *Nsi* 1: 13–15.

Pole, L.M. (1975) Iron-working apparatus and techniques: Upper Region of Ghana. *West African Journal of Archaeology* 5: 11–39.

Pole, L.M. (1985) Furnace design and the smelting operation: a survey of written reports of iron smelting in West Africa. In Haaland, R. and Shinnie, P. (eds) *African iron working: ancient and traditional.* Bergen, Norwegian University Press, pp. 142–63.

Posnansky, M. (1975) Ghana. *Nyame Akuma* 7: 15–23.

Posnansky, M. and McIntosh, R.J. (1976) New radiocarbon dates for northern and western Africa. *Journal of African History* 17(2): 161–95.

Rehder, J.E. (1986) Use of preheated air in primitive furnaces: comment on the views of Avery and Schmidt. *Journal of Field Archaeology* 13: 351–3.

Rehder, J.E. (1996) Use of preheated air in primitive furnaces: comment on the views of Avery and Schmidt. In Schmidt, P.R. (ed.) *The culture and technology of African iron production.* Gainesville, University Press of Florida, pp. 234–9.

Rowlands, M.J. (1971) The archaeological interpretations of prehistoric metal working. *World Archaeology* 3: 210–24.

Rowlands, M. and Warnier, J.P. (1993) The magical production of iron in the Cameroon Grassfields. In Shaw, T., Sinclair, P., Andah, B. and Okpoko, A. (eds) *The archaeology of Africa: food, metals and towns.* London, Routledge, pp. 512–49.

Sassoon, H. (1963) Early sources of iron in Africa. *South African Archaeological Bulletin* 18: 176–80.

Sassoon, H. (1964) Iron-smelting in the hill village of Sukur, north-eastern Nigeria. *Man* 64: 174–80.

Schmidt, P.R. and Avery, D.H. (1978) Complex iron smelting and prehistoric culture in Tanzania. *Science* 201: 1085–9.

Schmidt, P.R. and Avery, D.H. (1983) More evidence for an advanced prehistoric iron technology in Africa. *Journal of Field Archaeology* 10: 421–34.

Schmidt, P.R. and Avery, D.H. (1996) Complex iron smelting and prehistoric culture in Tanzania. In Schmidt, P.R. (ed.) *The culture and technology of African iron production*. Gainesville, University Press of Florida, pp. 172–85.

Schmidt, P.R. and Childs, S.T. (1995) Ancient African iron production: new evidence demonstrates that Sub-Saharan African iron technology, already known to be distinctive, had to cope with a difficult iron chemistry. *American Scientist* 83: 524–33.

Shaw, C.T. (1969) An iron-smelting furnace excavated in Ghana. *Bulletin of the Historical Metallurgy Group* 3(20): 48–54.

Shinnie, P.L. (1974) Meroë. *Nyame Akuma* 4: 26–7.

Shinnie, P.L. (1985) Iron working at Meroë. In Haaland, R. and Shinnie, P. (eds) *African iron working: ancient and traditional*. Bergen, Norwegian University Press, 28–35.

Sutton, J.E.G. (1976) Iron working around Zaria. *Zaria Archaeological Papers* 8.

Sutton, J.E.G. (1985) Temporal and spatial variability in African iron furnaces. In Haaland, R. and Shinnie, P. (eds) *African iron working: ancient and traditional*. Bergen, Norwegian University Press, pp. 164–96.

Tobert, N. (1982) Pyrometric readings: an example from Western Sudan. *Bulletin of the Experimental Firing Group* 1: 5–7.

Todd, J.A. and Charles, J.A. (1978) Ethiopian bloomery iron and the significance of inclusion analysis in iron studies. *Journal of the Historical Metallurgy Society* 12(2): 63–87.

Tylecote, R.F. (1970) Iron working at Meroë, Sudan. *Bulletin of the Historical Metallurgical Group* 4: 67–73.

Tylecote, R.F. (1975a) The origin of iron smelting in Africa. *West African Journal of Archaeology* 5: 1–9.

Tylecote, R.F. (1975b) Iron smelting at Taruga, Nigeria. *Journal of the Historical Metallurgy Society* 9: 49–56.

Van Grunderbeek, M-C., Roche, E. and Doutrelepont, H. (1983) *Le Premier Age du Fer au Rwanda et au Burundi: archéologie et environnement*. Brussels, IFAQ.

Van Noten, F. (1985) Ancient and modern iron smelting in Central Africa: Zaire, Rwanda and Burundi. In Haaland, R. and Shinnie, P. (eds) *African iron working: ancient and traditional*. Bergen, Norwegian University Press, 102–20.

Vansina, J. (1995) New linguistic evidence and the Bantu Expansion. *Journal of African History* 36: 173–95.

Vernet, R. (1992) *Les sites Néolithiques de Khatt Lemaiteg, Amatlich en Mauritanie occidentale*. Paris, CMA.

Welsby, D.A. (1996) *The Kingdom of Kush: the Napatan and Meroitic Empires*. London, British Museum Press.

Willett, F. (1971) A survey of recent results in the radiocarbon chronology of western and northern Africa. *Journal of African History* 12(3): 339–70.

Woods, A. (1982) Smoke gets in your eyes: patterns, variables and temperature measurements in open firings. *Bulletin of the Experimental Firing Group* 1: 11–25.

CHAPTER 8

PRECOLONIAL TRADING SYSTEMS OF THE EAST AFRICAN INTERIOR

Henry W. Mutoro

The precolonial trading systems of the East African interior have a great antiquity and can best be understood by employing a multidisciplinary approach including archaeology, oral traditions, linguistic evidence and documentary sources. Two types of trade, namely subsistence-oriented and nonsubsistence-oriented or long-distance trade, can be identified. In general, the nonsubsistence-oriented trade was a response to demands for unevenly distributed resources at both local and international levels. This is demonstrated by some of the coastal and hinterland settlements for which there is evidence for periods of prosperity. Archaeological evidence from the pre-tenth-century AD settlements on the coast, and documentary evidence of the same period, show how this prosperity emanated from trade transactions between the coast and the interior in response to industrial and labor-force demands in the lands beyond the Indian Ocean, particularly the Orient and Mediterranean Europe.

The steadily expanding market for commodities from the interior, particularly ivory and slaves, provided by the international maritime trade especially after the fifteenth century, brought new opportunities for the expansion of long-distance trade. These created and strengthened contacts between the East African interior and the coast, in order to satisfy the needs of the expanding markets in Europe and the Orient. For instance, the Akamba, the Nyamwezi, and the Yao caravans, to name just a few, collaborated with the Mijikenda, the Swahili, and Arab caravan traders to deplete the interior of its resources for the markets overseas. Trade with the interior not only increased in volume but also witnessed the supplementing of traditional commodities with new ones. From the coast, for example, interior communities got luxury items such as cloth, beads, porcelain, glass, and later guns, which had not been seen in the interior before. In addition to these were cowrie shells, now as a form of currency, certain foodstuffs, and salt. These were exchanged for interior products of the hunt and for slaves. It seems that interior communities never took the first initiative in the international trade that characterized this region in the period under review. The initiative was always taken by coastal communities in response to industrial growth and labor-force demands overseas. Analyzing the balance sheet of this trade, it may be concluded that precolonial African societies in the interior were not what we would

now call astute business people with long-term investment programs. There is little
evidence to show that they benefited very much from these transactions, in spite of the
active role that they played.

Trade and exchange of goods and services are as old as human society itself.
They are the universal human practices by which certain basic commodities and
services, which may be lacking or which are inequitably distributed in one
region, are accessed from societies that have them in another region. In the
past, during times of famine, extended droughts, flooding, and epidemics, trade
and exchange became the only remedy. In addition, during times of plenty,
trade and exchange in the surplus helped to bring together different human
communities for greater sociocultural and economic growth. This occurred at
local, regional, and international levels.

The precolonial trading systems of the East African interior can be broadly
classified into two categories: local trade and long-distance or international
trade. However, these categories were intertwined in such a way that they
cannot be discussed in isolation from each other. Both local and long-distance
trade centered initially on transactions by barter in agricultural and domestic
or wild animal products, but they were not restricted to local products. In
most cases neighboring villages benefited from transactions which extended
over hundreds of miles and involved food commodities that were not
produced by the local communities themselves. Be that as it may, long-
distance trade, which is the major concern of this chapter, appears to have
been aimed at accumulation. It was by and large market-oriented (Gray and
Birmingham, 1970: 3) and traversed larger territories, combining dealings in a
wider range of items such as agricultural products, iron, pottery, slaves,
mineral products such as salt, and wild animal and plant products obtained by
hunting and gathering. It was also characterized by the introduction of exotic
trade items such as sea shells, porcelain, glass beads, cotton cloths, and
firearms, which had never previously been seen in the interior. The long-
distance trade introduced for the first time specialized traders who traversed
large areas of the interior searching for items that were in high demand on the
coast by traders coming in from overseas. The coast in this way became a
zone of interaction between two cultural streams, one coming from the
interior and one from across the Indian Ocean (Sheriff, 1987: 13). The
initiative in this trade was always taken by coastal traders in their effort to
satisfy the expanding demands by overseas markets for products from the
interior of East Africa.

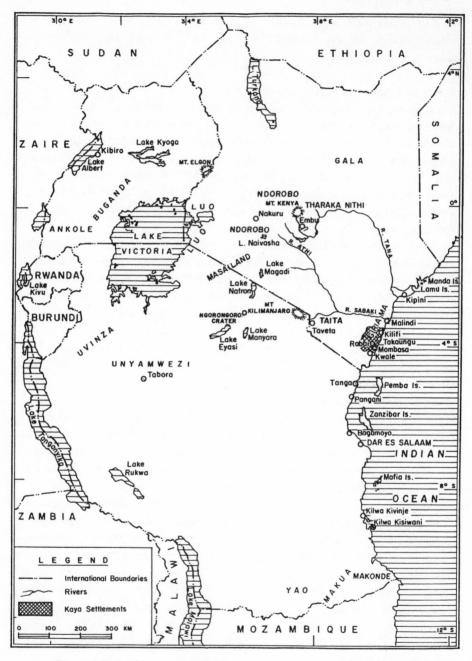

Fig. 8.1 East Africa: coast and interior.

SOURCES OF INFORMATION

In precolonial Africa, one can best understand trade and exchange by using a multidisciplinary approach based on archaeology, ethnolinguistics, oral traditions, and written sources. In the archaeological record, precolonial trade can be documented from the presence of those foreign or exotic items which preserve well after being discarded. Such include pottery, stone implements, beads, glass objects, shells, iron, and coins. When found, these can be physically and stylistically analyzed and sourced to their areas of origin. In most cases trade and exchange objects are found in smaller quantities than locally manufactured objects. Trade commodities such as salt do not preserve well in the archaeological record, but they can be documented on the basis of circumstantial evidence, such as the presence or absence of salt pans. The resultant data can then be verified by use of oral traditions, ethnoarchaeology, ethnolinguistics and written sources. Oral traditions generally consist of historical information which has been passed by word of mouth from one generation to the next. They are particularly reliable sources for periods not exceeding 500 years (Vansina, 1965: 20). In its narrowest sense, ethnoarchaeology is the study of the behavior patterns of present-day communities in order to understand extinct communities, provided there is continuity between the present and the past in the communities being studied. Used properly, ethnoarchaeological studies can shed valuable light on African precolonial communities. Ethnolinguistics involves the study of a society's basic language vocabulary in relation to its borrowed vocabulary or loan words. In many instances, loan words in a given language are an indication of the community's level of socioeconomic and cultural interactions with its neighbors. Documentary or written sources consist of texts, written preferably by eyewitnesses, concerning the events that occurred during precolonial times. In many cases, the authors only got the information from others who had themselves witnessed the events occur. As will be demonstrated, documentary sources are an important source of information, particularly when dealing with later historical periods. In addition to these sources, one needs to isolate and also study precolonial settlements' catchments, in order to understand which commodities were readily available and how economic their exploitation was. This process entails a systematic excavation and analysis of the remains recovered, before conclusions can be made about the economic potential of any given area. Site catchment studies are based on the assumption that, other things being equal, 'the further the area is from the site, the less it is likely to be exploited and the less rewarding is its exploitation, because the energy consumed in the movement to and from the site will tend to cancel that derived from the source' (Vita-Finzi and Higgs, 1970: 5). It was those items whose exploitation became uneconomic to some communities that formed a large bulk of the trade goods handled by others.

ENVIRONMENTAL BACKGROUND

The interior of East Africa is characterized by a varied topography that supports extensive biodiversity. The fauna and flora of this region has today been adversely affected by human activities, such as farming, pastoralism, poaching, charcoal burning, and cutting of mangroves for export. As a result what we see today is not a true picture of the rich environment that existed in precolonial times. Evidence from the sources discussed above attest to the existence of thick and moist rain forests, as well as rich savanna vegetation that teemed with different forms of fauna and flora. The fauna comprised a wide variety of animals, such as elephants, rhinoceros, lions, leopards, buffaloes, and many species of antelope. The flora consisted of different tree species such as mangroves, Mvule, the Mbambakofi, Msandarusi (gum copal), Mgure (teak), cinnamon, frankincense, and myrrh. There were also minerals such as gold and salt which were found in abundance. It was from this rich environmental background that the commodities handled by the interior trade of East Africa were ultimately derived. These trade goods, plus slaves, were exchanged for manufactured luxury items such as beads, cloth, porcelain and glass objects, brought from overseas through the ports of the East African coast.

PRE-TENTH-CENTURY AD TRADE CONTACTS WITH THE INTERIOR

Contacts between the coast and the interior of East Africa span a long time period. The earliest known evidence comes from a pastoral neolithic site near Ngorongoro Crater in north-western Tanzania. The items recovered there included cowrie shells, which had been cut for attachment, and two sizes of nacre-disc beads made from other marine mollusc shells. These exotic trade items were found in association with locally made ceramic vessels that were contemporary with the human interment dated to 300 BC (Leakey, 1931: 281). From another burial site at Ngorongoro Crater, M.D. Leakey (1943: 189) also found five marine-shell (*Mitra* sp.) objects which had perforations for suspension. In Kenya, coastal objects have so far been reported from the Nakuru Neolithic Burial site (Leakey, 1931: 281), Hyrax Hill neolithic site (Onyango-Abuje, 1977), and from a pastoral neolithic site in the Lake Turkana area (C. Nelson, University of Nairobi, personal communication). The findings from the Nakuru Neolithic Burial site included agate beads and short cylinder faience beads, while from Hyrax Hill a hoard of coins was recovered but has not yet been properly examined. More evidence of contacts between the coast and the interior, dating from the third to the ninth century AD, has also been found. This is local pottery which in the region of its distribution belongs to two traditions. The earlier of these traditions is named Kwale ware after the type site Kwale, near the coast south west of Mombasa, from where it was first reported (Soper, 1967). Kwale ware at the type site has been dated to the third century AD. This ware and its different variants have also been reported from a number of sites in the interior of East Africa (Soper, 1979; Siiriäinen, 1971). The second pottery tradition is known as Tana Ware (Horton, 1984, 1996; Horton and Mutoro, 1987; Mutoro, 1987; Abungu, 1989), or Triangular Incised Ware (Chami, 1994). Its geographic distribution extends from Mogadishu in Somalia down to the site of Chibuene in Mozambique (Sinclair, 1982). Dated between the fourth and the ninth century AD, this pottery tradition stretches over 300 kilometers into the interior from the coast of East Africa. It has a distinct range of forms with incised decoration, often with pendent triangles below the rim. More systematic research, in wider parts of the interior of East Africa in the future, will no doubt reveal additional evidence for coast–interior contacts to that which is known at the present time. Be that as it may, the different forms of evidence obtained so far are a clear manifestation of trade contacts between the coast and the interior. These presumed contacts were intensified as the demand increased for ivory and slaves to be brought from the interior to the coast, for onward transmission to overseas markets. The intensification of these contacts brought prosperity to coastal communities. This prosperity can be seen in an increase in the number of settlements, an expansion in settlement sizes to cater for an increasing population, and an improvement in house types from mud and thatch to stone structures. There was also a significant increase in the use of exotic objects.

The first period of prosperity within Eastern Africa which can be supported by the archaeological evidence lies in the mid-ninth century AD. During this time, sites such as Manda and Shanga (Chittick, 1984; Horton, 1984, 1996), show considerable evidence of craft activities, iron-smelting, beadworking, shell-collecting and cleaning, and pottery manufacture. Local pottery in these sites accounts for over 95 percent of the total assemblage. Animal bones, particularly of domestic stock (cattle, sheep, and/or goats) abound. There is also a variety of imports, especially pottery from the Persian Gulf area, India, and China. In the assemblage there are moreover several commodities from the African interior. These include rock crystals of exceptional clarity from which crystal beads were made, haematite for smelting iron, and pottery. It is relevant to ask what the source of this prosperity was.

Available documentary evidence suggests that at about AD 960 there occurred a radical industrial change in the Orient and in Mediterranean Europe. It appears that within a span of a single decade, workshops were set up for processing elephant ivory products and the royal courts of both Islamic and Christian Europe became flooded with numerous ivory carvings. This is supported by the evidence from the Byzantine Empire, which alone includes over 200 surviving pieces of elephant ivory dating to this period (Cutler, 1985: 31). In Latin Christendom, evidence for growth in the ivory trade is provided by the court of the Holy Roman Emperor, from which have survived the Reichinau Ivories, of which the earliest date to shortly after the coronation of Otto I, in AD 962 (Beckwith, 1964: 127). In Islamic Spain, remarkable but short-lived ivory-carving developed during this period also. Dated pieces include two from Madinet al-Zahra, which have dates between about AD 962 and 966 (Pinder-Wilson and Brooke, 1973a). Ivory-carving in Sicily, under the Fatimid control, also developed during this period with workshops spreading throughout southern Italian cities (Pinder-Wilson and Brooke, 1973b). Statistical data shows that the tusks from which this ivory was derived were large and had a minimum diameter of 110 millimeters. The question is: where did all this ivory come from?

It is probable that the ivory came from the savanna lands of the East African interior following two possible routes. The first was the sea route through the Indian Ocean from the East African coast. The second was the Red Sea trading route to the interlacustrine region of Eastern Africa via Aksum. With the Fatimid control of Cairo and the Mediterranean from about AD 969, the Red Sea route became safer than it had been and important as a conduit through which slaves and ivory from the interior could be ferried abroad. Most of the ivory that reached the Mediterranean world through this route was large, with a minimum diameter of 110 millimeters. The Indian elephant, whose ivory could have been a possible candidate, has smaller diameter tusks than the elephant of the East African savanna. It is from this latter source, therefore, that this type of ivory must ultimately have been derived. The Indian Ocean route remained similarly important, with ivory from the interior of East Africa being ferried to Siraf, Samarra, and Baghdad. In addition to ivory, rhinoceros horns and tortoise-shell (actually obtained from sea turtles) were also exported. According to Hay (1972: 104), 'a single dhow of eighty tons ... could take on sufficient elephant tusks to furnish every room in a Maharaja's palace with ivory chairs and tables, enough rhino horns to keep a dozen sultans in aphrodisiacs for a year ... as well as tortoise shells for making cabinet inlays.'

Gold was the next most important item of trade from the interior of East Africa. Although the best evidence for the supply of gold to the Indian Ocean trade during this time comes from excavated sites in the interior of Southern Africa, it is apparent that the East African coastal settlement at Kilwa was an important center in this trade. The gold trade was already established in Sofala by about AD 950. After his visit to the coast in AD 916, al-Masudi mentioned Sofala as the center for gold from the interior (Freeman-Grenville, 1962: 150). About AD 950 Buzarg ibn Shahriyar mentioned Sofala as a place where gold is 'worked in galleries by men, like ants' (Freeman-Grenville, 1981: 38). These activities appear to have been entirely controlled by the local interior communities and their Swahili and Arab middlemen on the coast. This is supported by traditions recorded by De Barros in the sixteenth century AD. According to De Barros (Freeman-Grenville, 1962: 91), foreigners from the Orient known as Emozaids were attracted to the coast of East Africa because of its fame for trade in gold. The inhabitants of Sofala also became aware of the high demand for gold, and were keen to exchange their gold and ivory for cloth and other luxury items with the coastal middlemen, who in turn traded with the Emozaids. A symbiotic relationship developed between these communities but with each operating within its respective settlements. There is no evidence to show that Emozaids moved into the unpopulated areas inland of Kilwa, to set up settlements and control the gold trade with the coast.

Slaves from the interior of East Africa, taken to the Orient via the coast of East Africa, were also an important item of trade prior to the tenth century AD. There was an excessive demand for slave labor to reclaim the marshlands of southern Iraq between the seventh and ninth centuries, and many slaves from East Africa were taken there to meet this demand. As a result of the severe exploitation and oppression that they suffered at the hands of their masters, these slaves revolted in AD 868, overthrew the Abbasid dynasty and took control of southern Iraq for 14 years before they were ultimately suppressed in 883. It is estimated that more than half a million slaves were slaughtered before calm was restored in the region (Hitti, 1956: 467–8). This Zanj Revolt, as it became known, had a substantial impact on the export of slaves from the interior of Eastern Africa through the coast. By breaking up the Abbasid dynasty, the slave revolt not only ensured the failure of one of the few cases of agricultural exploitation based on slave labor in Muslim history (Sheriff, 1987: 13), but also increased the awareness of the slave traders as to the type of slaves to be brought to the area in the future. The end product of this was a drastic decline in the demand for slaves until after the fifteenth century, when all the necessary precautions and machinery had been put in place.

FIFTEENTH- TO NINETEENTH-CENTURY TRADE CONTACTS

The period from the fifteenth to the nineteenth century casts more light on the trade of the East African interior, because of the numerous sources of information available. In addition to documentary sources, there are oral traditions, linguistic evidence, and archaeology, all of which combine to shed light on the interior trade. Here it is relevant to examine the contributions made by the Mijikenda and the Akamba of Kenya, the Nyamwezi, the Yao, and the Makua of Tanzania, as well as the Baganda and Banyoro of Uganda. It seems that, like their predecessors, these and other interior communities again participated in long-distance trade, in the interest of the Swahili and Arab traders on the coast.

The Mijikenda (also known as the Nyika) of the Kenya coastal hinterland were mixed farmers. They tilled the land, kept livestock, and practiced hunting and gathering. They always aimed at self-sufficiency but were frequently forced into trade with their Swahili and interior neighbors by adverse environmental conditions. In this way they maintained trade contacts with the Swahili towns, both on the coast and in the island of Zanzibar, by supplying them with ivory, gum copal, millets, sesame, tobacco, honey and bees wax, grain, and timber for building houses and dhows. In fact, all the sesame and grain products in Zanzibar are said to have come from the Mijikenda (Burton, 1872: 49). In return they received salt, beads, porcelain, cotton cloth, and foodstuffs during times of famine. This symbiotic relationship was so strong that Krapf (1850: 175) was to observe:

> All the pagan tribes situated at a small distance from the coast have constant intercourse with the Swahili and although they are perfectly independent of the Imam's government established in every Swahili village yet they have due regard to that government for the sake of their own interest ... the inland tribes cannot exist without their supplies from the coast and the tribes of the coast cannot subsist without the produce of the interior, so whatever temporary hostilities may ensue, they ensure always to become reconciled again for their mutual secular interests.

By the nineteenth century the volume of the Mijikenda trade with the Swahili and the interior had increased tremendously, with the Mijikenda playing the middleman role. New markets such as Takaungu on the south coast emerged as major trading centers, with the Mijikenda controlling all the grain exports from the interior. So much was this trade in the hands of the Mijikenda that Krapf (1850: 173) was again to observe that: '... inland trade was formerly in their hands almost exclusively.' In order to make more profit, the Mijikenda developed new subsidiary ports, like Kaya Pungu, Mtsanganyingo, and Konjora at the head of Kilifi Bay, that gave them direct access to overseas traders instead of going through the Swahili middlemen. Once that had been achieved, they started sending caravans of 200–300 men into the interior to bring out ivory, rhinoceros horns, leopard skins, gum copal, sesame, maize, and sorghum, in order to bolster the newly acquired contacts. A recent study of their site catchments (Mutoro, 1995) shows that the center of gravity for the Mijikenda trading activities during this time lay in the Kaya Rabai, Ribe, and Giriama (Fungo) triangle for the northern Makaya, and Kaya Kwale for the Digo and Duruma of the southern Makaya. The Digo and the Duruma, for instance, sent ivory caravans as far as Unyamwezi in central Tanzania and also traded with the Swahili at market centers near Tanga and other Tanzanian coastal towns (Lamphear, 1970: 96). By 1800, the port of Mombasa alone was handling 45 tons of ivory in a year. The Mijikenda continued to be middlemen to the interior-coast trade only as long as the interior communities remained oblivious to the benefits derived from trade in slaves and ivory. In fact, at first, ivory appears to have had no local value to many of the interior communities, who would give it away for free to whoever wanted it. However, once they learned that these items were not only valuable but could fetch even greater profits if traded directly with the Swahili or the Arabs without going through the Mijikenda middlemen, they made it difficult for the Mijikenda to penetrate into the interior. For example, the Oromo hunter/gatherers, who had been sending their ivory caravans to the Mijikenda market-villages, started revolting against the Mijikenda, initially by restricting the number of the Mijikenda traders they let into their territory. Later, they rejected the Mijikenda attempts to make peace and started to raid their caravans when they were found crossing Oromo territory. Similarly, they prevented Akamba ivory caravans from passing through the northern part of their territory across the Tana River plains.

Like the Oromo, the Akamba did not initially know that ivory-trading was profitable. However, once they learned that it was, they also organized their own hunting expeditions in search of elephants. By 1849 they had killed so many elephants in their neighborhood that Krapf (1860: 140) was to remark: '... many Wakamba are engaged in hunting elephants ... [and] these animals have been much destroyed in Ukambani.' The Akamba also learned that they could make more profit if they delivered the ivory direct to the coast, rather than through the Mijikenda middlemen. The Mijikenda resisted this by confining the Akamba caravans to the outlying markets of Kwa Jomvu and Shogi, while the Akamba, on their part, tried to ensure that no Mijikenda caravans passed through their territory to the interior. As principal suppliers of ivory and slaves to the coast, the Akamba traveled deep into north-eastern Tanzania and central and western Kenya to get these commodities. In north-eastern Tanzania they established themselves in the Kilimanjaro–Pare–Usambara region with a view to practicing commercial hunting. After his visit to the area, J. T. Last (1883: 16) had the following observation to make:

> Their chief object in leaving Ukambani was hunting ... [They] settle down ... and cultivate the ground for food until they have remained long enough to get a good stock of ivory and teeth by hunting, then they return home. It seems that they are continually going and coming.

In central and eastern Kenya, the Akamba hunters and traders developed special relationships with the Kikuyu, Tharaka, Mbeere, and Meru people. The Akamba traded with the Kikuyu, depending on who had had a more successful harvest. Grains, ivory, and livestock would then be exchanged by barter. The Akamba also traded with the Tharaka, Mbeere, Embu and Meru in arrowheads and arrow-poisons, in exchange for ivory. In fact, the Akamba provided coastal trade items to the Embu and Mbeere, who in turn traveled beyond Mt Kenya as far as the Winam Gulf (of Lake Victoria), the slopes of Mt Elgon, and Karamoja (north-east Uganda), to obtain ivory and tobacco which they sold to the Akamba caravans on return (Lamphear, 1970: 97). It is worth noting that as principal participants in the precolonial trade in the interior of Kenya, the Akamba, like the Mijikenda, never made any attempts at establishing political control over the communities with which they traded. If there were any accumulation and redistribution centers, these were not centrally controlled but were supervised by a small clique of wealthy individuals who had made it to the top. What these individuals wanted from their trading partners was security, a prospect of additional trading items, and luxurious living that was devoid of any meaningful long-term investments.

In Tanzania three ethnic groups, the Nyamwezi, the Yao, and the Makua, were active participants in the precolonial interior trade of Eastern Africa (Alpers, 1975; Roberts, 1970). The principal items of trade were again ivory and slaves. Like the Akamba of Kenya, the Nyamwezi of Tanzania did not initially know that ivory was of any commercial value at all. They used it only as a symbol of chieftainship, when their chiefs wore ivory bracelets or when their chiefs died and were buried between elephant tusks (Roberts, 1970: 47). The Nyamwezi hunting expeditions for ivory only started after they had learned from the Swahili and Arab caravans from the coast that ivory was in very high demand on the coast for export to India, Europe, and America. There is no doubt also that their country was by then known in Zanzibar as having plenty of ivory. In 1811 Captain Smee (Burton, 1872: Vol. 2, 510) wrote of: 'the Meeahmaizees, whose country is said to be three months journey from the East Coast of Africa; elephants abound in it ...' Unlike the Akamba, the Nyamwezi political system was controlled by a number of chiefs with limited economic resources. Many of these chiefs also participated in the ivory trade and obtained a certain share of their people's labor and produce. Part of the proceeds got from ivory-trading and mineral wealth was given to the chief. The development of trade links with the coast not only brought in new items such as guns but also new forms of wealth that were to sustain and transform the Nyamwezi socioeconomic and political systems. Old dynastic leaders soon gave way to new leaders who themselves were successful traders. With guns and a ready market on the coast, these new leaders organized hunting expeditions based on experience and achievement rather than birth. Their trade caravans were large and consisted of hundreds (and sometimes thousands) of people. By 1884 the Nyamwezi had become well established in their headquarters at Tabora. During the time of chief Mirambo they took command of virtually all the trade in central Tanzania and the interlacustrine kingdoms between Lake Victoria and the eastern part of the Democratic Republic of Congo. They also took control of the central route which passed through Tabora. The main exports along this route from the interior included ivory, slaves, and copper and gold from Katanga (south-east Democratic Republic of Congo). All caravans, be they Nyamwezi, Swahili, or Arab, had to pay tolls in acceptable currency at various points along the trade routes passing through Unyamwezi. It is also important to note that in addition to ivory, slaves, copper, and gold, the Nyamwezi also traded in salt, iron, crops, and livestock, and tobacco. While most of the salt came from the Uvinza brine springs on the lower Malagarasi River, iron is said to have been smelted in various places between the lower Malagarasi and Bujumbura (in Burundi). A more systematic archaeological investigation of these areas is awaited, to determine the antiquity and volume of salt and iron exploitation by the communities there between the fifteenth and the nineteenth centuries. According to missionary sources, crops, livestock, and tobacco were also important items of the Nyamwezi caravan trade. These items were sold at exorbitant prices to famine-stricken areas especially in Ugogo. Tobacco, which was also referred to as 'the soothing weed,' is said to have come from Ukutu and achieved a widespread reputation in the interior and at the coast.

The Yao occupied a large tract of land that extended from the southeast of Lake Malawi across the River Ruvuma into southern Tanzania. Before they were drawn into long-distance trade, Yao trade had been confined to exchanges with their neighbors of iron hoes, tobacco, livestock products, salt, and bark-cloth. But with the development of the eighteenth- and nineteenth-century long-distance trade, the Yao traders aggressively participated by controlling most of the trade routes in the southern interior of Tanzania, Malawi, and northern Mozambique. The principal items of their trade were ivory and slaves. Yao country was particularly endowed with great herds of elephants and a dense human population. In the Shire Valley of Malawi, for instance, was a marsh in which David Livingstone in the 1850s saw 'nine herds of elephants, [which] sometimes formed a line two miles [3.2 kilometers] long' (Livingstone, 1960). Elephant-hunting among the Yao was not organized in specialized guilds, but was tied to the political structure of the village and chiefdom in such a way that hunting expeditions had to get clearance from the chief or headman before they could go hunting. Yao traders went as far as Central Africa in search of slaves and ivory and, by so doing, controlled the southern trade route that sprang up from the southern end of Tanzania to Lake Malawi. So prosperous was their trade with the coast, that by the mid-eighteenth century Yao trade in ivory formed the backbone of the economy of Mozambique. According to contemporary sources, Yao traders alone carried approximately

400 to 500 bales of ivory per year to Mozambique, constituting more than 90 percent of that traded overland to Mossuril and Cabaceiras and about 65–70 percent of the ivory which entered Mozambique Island itself each year (Alpers, 1975: 104). Slaves were also an important trade commodity for the Yao. Like ivory, Yao slaves from the interior ended up not only in Mozambique but also in the northern coastal towns, especially Kilwa, which they knew from ancient times as Mchiwi Mchilwa. According to Abdallah's (1919: 30) version of the Yao traditions, coastal traders encouraged Yao traders to take interior products to the coast in order to make substantial profits:

> When they went to the coast they were told 'Next year you must bring ivory and slaves from Yaoland, and you will make your fortune. You will get the powder you want so much, and milandawala (i.e. guns) you will also obtain. You will get anything you want if you bring these two things, ivory and slaves.'

These traditions are supported by information from a French adventurer, Jean-Vincent Morice (Freeman-Grenville, 1965: 82), who in 1776 described the trade between Zanzibar and the coast as follows:

> When the ships from India arrive in December, January, or February, all the Moors from Kilwa, Mafia, Mombasa, Pate, &c., go to Zanzibar to buy cargoes and distribute them subsequently in their districts in exchange for ivory tusks, provisions and slaves, &c. In March and April all the Moors and Arabs come to the kingdom of Kilwa to trade there for slaves, for Kilwa is the assembly point for all the slaves who come from the mainland.

As Alpers (1975: 132) has observed, if this pattern of trade was operating before Morice's time, it is possible that by the 1750s Kilwa may already have been a place of considerable commercial activity at the beginning of each dry season, when all these traders were gathered there to bargain for the ivory and slaves with which the Africans of the interior arrived.

The Makua of southern Tanzania and northern Mozambique were not only active participants in the long-distance trade in slaves and ivory between the East African interior and the coast but also bitter rivals to the Yao. As farmers, the Makua got most of their subsistence requirements from their farms. What was lacking, however, was salt. The need for salt was in this way a major factor in bringing together the Makua and their neighbors, particularly those from the coast. These strong connections are reflected in the fact that the Makua word for coast, *maka*, also means salt (Alpers, 1975: 10). Although the Makua had secret societies for hunting elephants and buffaloes, their idea of hunting was traditionally for food and for territorial expansion and not for ivory which could be traded with the coast. Like other interior communities already discussed above, the Makua only started to hunt for ivory and slaves after they learned from the Arab and Swahili traders on the coast that the two items were in great demand and would fetch them a good deal of wealth. By this time the Makua had established themselves as far into Tanzania as Western Ugogo and the general region of Kilosa. Armed with new weapons, firearms, they took immediate advantage of these new opportunities. Within no time the name 'Makua' had become a generic name for itinerant professional elephant hunters throughout the interior of Tanzania (Roberts, 1970: 69) and Malawi. They also became undisputed middlemen in the interior trade with the Portuguese who were in Mozambique.

Before the introduction of long-distance trade in the interlacustrine region of East Africa in general and in present-day Uganda in particular, local trade was based on two principal items, salt and iron. The main salt-producing centers were at Kibiro on the eastern shore of Lake Albert in Bunyoro and at the salt lake of Katwe on the northern side of Lake Edward. Archaeological evidence from the 'salt-gardens' at Kibiro (Connah, 1996), shows that salt production and trading probably date back to early in the present millennium. Kibiro salt was of a high level of purity and was supplied to the whole of Bunyoro and Buganda in the south, as well as to Acholiland and Alurland in the north. According to Emin Pasha (Schweinfurth et al., 1888: 176), 'The salt deposits of Kibíro, therefore, constitute one of the most valuable portions of Kabréga's dominions [referring to the ruler of Bunyoro].' Katwe salt was of a slightly inferior quality compared with that from Kibiro. All the same, due to the great demand for it, Katwe (with a population of 2000 people by 1889) also became a regional center in the salt trade. According to H.M.Stanley (1890: Vol. 2, 311–16), this bustling center was being frequented by the banyAnkole, banyaRuanda, and baToro, who brought in grains, bark-cloth, vegetables, and iron tools to exchange for salt. So far as iron was concerned, while Bunyoro had excellent deposits of iron ore, other parts of Uganda seem to have been deficient in this material. The Banyoro thus became the principal suppliers of iron ore as well as iron hoes, spearheads, and arrowheads to their neighbors. Iron hoes were used for tilling the land, while spearheads and arrowheads were principally used in hunting, and occasionally in settling interethnic disputes that had resulted in war. In addition to salt and iron, trade items included bark-cloths, coffee, and tobacco. Buganda had a vigorous and prosperous bark-cloth industry, whose plain and dyed products were exported to Karagwe, Rwanda, Busoga, and Bunyoro, as well as to parts of present-day western Kenya. Coffee and tobacco were luxury crops. Coffee as a stimulant was an established trade item well before the eighteenth century among the Haya states, who exported it to Karagwe. Clay tobacco pipes have been found in the seventeenth-century occupation layers at the Ankole capital site of Bweyorere (Posnansky, 1961:

193). This area is said to have grown the best tobacco, for both local consumption and for export to Karagwe and Bunyoro (Schweinfurth, 1888: 112; Grant, 1864: 158–9).

Ivory and slaves were not important trade items to the communities in the interlacustrine region of Eastern Africa until the coming of coastal Arab and Swahili traders. This is indicated by Emin Pasha, who observed that when Arab traders traded with the rulers of Buganda and Bunyoro they usually left with ivory worth five times the value of the goods they had brought (Schweinfurth, 1888: 115). James Grant substantiates this statement by citing a case in which a trader, by the name of Jumah, was asked by Kabaka Mutesa to surrender clothing, brass wire, beads, and two flintlocks, and was in return later given 700 pounds of ivory, seven women, and 50 cows, together with the same two flintlocks (Grant, 1864: 163). With the coming of Arab and Swahili traders in Buganda and Bunyoro, via Karagwe, firearms were introduced into the region and used in the systematic slaughtering of elephants for their ivory tusks, which were known on the coast as being 'the whitest, softest, largest and heaviest in central Africa' (Burton, 1860: 184; Beachey, 1967). The Kabaka of Buganda established his own expeditions of elephant hunters whom he paid with cattle and women. He also gave guns to certain chiefs in his kingdom for collecting royal ivory. The primary collecting center for ivory from Lango, Acholi, and Busoga, was Buddu in the south-west. From there, ivory and slaves who were mostly war captives, were taken to Zanzibar via Tabora. By 1882, Rubaga, the capital of Buganda (in what is now Kampala), had become the most northerly depot for the trade in ivory and slaves. From here, slaves were transported across Lake Victoria in the Kabaka's canoes, in batches of 200 and more at a time, before reaching the main slave and ivory depot at Tabora *en route* to Zanzibar. Arab and Swahili traders even brought dhows to Buganda to replace the Kabaka's sewn canoes. These were built at Kirumba, near the Mwanza Gulf on the southern side of Lake Victoria, by workmen imported from Lamu and Mombasa. In addition to dhows, the Arab and Swahili traders also introduced luxury items such as cups, plates, spoons, glasses, and cotton cloth, as well as cowrie shells as a standard currency for trade (Stanley, 1878: 383). In contrast with West Africa, however, cowrie shells in the East African interior were seen by some traders as only having an ornamental value and were thus not readily accepted as a form of currency by everybody. Emin Pasha in 1883 observed that in Buganda cowries were widely current and even the smallest transactions could be made with them, but in Bunyoro the majority of the people stuck to barter even after the Zanzibaris arrived with their cowries. Baker (1866: 182) made a similar observation in Bunyoro, and describes his experience as follows:

Every morning shortly after sunrise, men might be heard crying their wares throughout the camp – such as, 'Tobacco, tobacco; two packets for

either beads or simbis!' (cowrie shells). 'Milk to sell for beads or salt! Salt
to exchange for lance-heads!'

Finally, it needs to be pointed out that in as much as the Arab and Swahili
traders used hinterland and interior communities as has been demonstrated
above, they also traveled along already-established routes and broke the
monopoly of interior middlemen so as to maximize their profits. In Kenya and
northern Tanzania they did this by concentrating on three principal routes: the
southern route, the central route, and the northern route. The northern route
incorporated the centers at Mombasa, Tanga, Rabai, and Pangani, and ran
toward Mt Kilimanjaro to the Taita–Taveta region, where it split into two. The
first of these became the north-western route which went across the Rift Valley
over to Mt Kenya and northwards to Lake Turkana. The second route went
through Masailand to Uganda via the Eastern shores of Lake Victoria. By the
end of the nineteenth century these routes were operating as far inland as
northern Uganda and eastern Democratic Republic of Congo, with Arab and
Swahili traders going as far as Bemba and Bisa, in northeastern Zambia, in
search of ivory.

CONCLUSION

The precolonial trading networks of the East African interior have a great
antiquity and can best be understood by a multidisciplinary approach. This
trade brought together different human groups at both local and international
levels. The long-distance trade was commercial in character, involving large
trade caravans that traveled over long distances to acquire ivory and slaves.
These were transported to the coast from where they were subsequently
shipped overseas to satisfy industrial and labor demands. The development of
this trade was gradual and its impetus does not appear to have depended on a
local indigenous initiative from the interior. The introduction and use of
firearms was a characteristic feature of this trade. In the interior, a large
proportion of the trade was in the hands of rulers who monopolized the profits
at the expense of their people, as exemplified by Buganda, Bunyoro, and
Ankole, where the kings retained one tusk in every pair collected and had
purchasing rights to the remainder (Baker, 1866: 248). From the evidence
discussed above, it would appear as if the transformations brought about by the
precolonial long-distance trade of the East African interior were ultimately
destined to destroy the economic infrastructures of the communities involved,
because many of the able-bodied young men and women had been sold into
slavery while traditional industries were often abandoned. It is no wonder,
therefore, that while this trade may have benefited some coastal and overseas

traders, it only laid the foundations for underdevelopment in the interior of Eastern Africa.

BIBLIOGRAPHY

Abdallah, Y.B. (1919) *The Yaos*. Translated by M. Sanderson, Zomba, Malawi.

Abungu, G.H.O. (1989) Communities on the River Tana, Kenya: an archaeological study of relations between the delta and the river basin, AD 700–1890. Unpublished PhD thesis, University of Cambridge.

Alpers, E.A. (1975) *Ivory and slaves in East and Central Africa*. London, Heinemann.

Baker, S.W. (1866) *The Albert N'yanza, Great Basin of the Nile, and explorations of the Nile sources*. 2 vols. London, Macmillan.

Beachey, R.W. (1967) The East African ivory trade in the nineteenth century. *Journal of African History* 8(2): 269–90.

Beckwith, J. (1964) *Early medieval art*. London, Thames and Hudson.

Burton, R.F. (1860) *The Lake Regions of Central Africa*. 2 vols. London, Sidgwick and Jackson.

Burton, R.F. (1872) *Zanzibar: city, island and coast*. 2 vols. London, Sidgwick and Jackson.

Chami, F. (1994) *The Tanzanian coast in the First Millennium AD*. Studies in African Archaeology 7. Uppsala, Sweden, Societas Archaeologica Upsaliensis.

Chittick, N. (1984) *Manda: excavations at an island port on the Kenya coast*. Nairobi, Memoir 9, British Institute in Eastern Africa.

Connah, G. (1996) *Kibiro: the salt of Bunyoro, past and present*. London, Memoir 13, British Institute in Eastern Africa.

Cutler, A. (1985) *The craft of ivory: sources, techniques and uses in the Mediterranean world: AD 200–1400*. Washington, DC, Dumbarton Oaks Library.

Freeman-Grenville, G.S.P. (1962) *The East African coast: select documents from the first to the earlier nineteenth century*. London, Clarendon Press.

Freeman-Grenville, G.S.P. (1965) *The French at Kilwa Island*. Oxford, Clarendon Press.

Freeman-Grenville, G.S.P. (1981) *The book of the wonders of India by Captain Buzurg ibn Shahriyar of Ramhormuz*. London and The Hague, East–West Publications.

Grant, J.A. (1864) *A walk across Africa*. Edinburgh and London, Blackwood.

Gray, R. and Birmingham, D. (1970) Some economic and political consequences of trade in Central and Eastern Africa in the pre-colonial period. In Gray, R. and Birmingham, D. (eds) *Pre-colonial African trade: essays on trade in Central and Eastern Africa before 1900*. London, Oxford University Press, pp. 1–23.

Hay, M.J. (1972) Changes in Luoland: Kowe, 1890–1945. Unpublished PhD thesis, University of Wisconsin.

Hitti, P.K. (1956) *History of the Arabs*. 5th edn, London, Macmillan.

Horton, M.C. (1984) The early settlement of the northern Swahili Coast. Unpublished PhD thesis, University of Cambridge.

Horton, M.C. (1996) *Shanga: the archaeology of a Muslim trading community on the coast of East Africa*. London, Memoir 14, British Institute in Eastern Africa.

Horton, M.C. and Mutoro, H.W. (1987) Tana Ware. *Newsletter of the Historical Association of Kenya*, Nairobi.

Krapf, J.L. (1850) Description of a voyage from Mombasa to the southern extremity of the Imam of Muscat's East African dominions. 12 (CMS: CA 5/0/16/175).

Krapf, J.L. (1860) *Travels, researches and missionary labours during an eighteen years' residence in Eastern Africa*. London.

Lamphear, J. (1970) The Kamba and the northern Mrima coast, In Gray, R. and Birmingham, D. (eds) *Pre-colonial African trade: essays on trade in Central and Eastern Africa before 1900.* London, Oxford University Press, pp. 75–101.

Last, J.T. (1883) *Church Missionary Society* 16.

Leakey, L.S.B. (1931) *The Stone Age cultures of Kenya Colony.* Cambridge, Cambridge University Press.

Leakey, M.D. (1943) Notes on the ground and polished stone axes of East Africa. *Journal of the East Africa and Uganda Natural History Society* 17: 182–95.

Livingstone, D. (1960) *Private journals 1851–53,* ed. Schapera, I., London, Chatto and Windus.

Mutoro, H.W. (1987) An archaeological study of the Mijikenda Kaya settlements. Unpublished PhD thesis, University of California, Los Angeles.

Mutoro, H.W. (1995) A site catchment analysis of the Mijikenda Kaya settlements. *African Urban Quarterly* (Nairobi) 10(3 and 4).

Onyango-Abuje, J.C. (1977) A contribution to the study of the Neolithic in East Africa with particular reference to the Nakuru-Naivasha Basins. Unpublished PhD thesis, University of California, Berkeley.

Pinder-Wilson, R.H. and Brooke, C.N.L. (1973a) Ivory. In Arts Council of Great Britain (ed.) *The arts of Islam.* London.

Pinder-Wilson, R.H. and Brooke, C.N.L. (1973b) The reliquary of St Petroc and the ivories of Norman Sicily. *Archaeologia* 104: 261–305.

Posnansky, M. (1961) Pottery types from archaeological sites in East Africa. *Journal of African History* 2(2): 177–98.

Roberts, A. (1970) Nyamwezi trade. In Gray, R. and Birmingham, D. (eds) *Pre-colonial African trade: essays on trade in Central and Eastern Africa before 1900.* London, Oxford University Press, pp. 39–74.

Schweinfurth, G., Ratzel, F., Felkin, R.W. and Hartlaub, G. (eds) (1888) *Emin Pasha in Central Africa: being a collection of his letters and journals* (translated by Mrs R.W. Felkin). London, George Philip & Son.

Sheriff, A. (1987) *Slaves, spices and ivory in Zanzibar, integration of an East African commercial empire into the world economy, 1770–1873.* London, James Currey.

Siiriäinen, A. (1971) The Iron Age site at Gatung'ang'a, Central Kenya. *Azania* 6: 199–232.

Sinclair, P. (1982) Chibuene – an early trading site in southern Mozambique. *Paideuma* 28: 149–64.

Soper, R. (1967) Iron Age sites in North-Eastern Tanzania. *Azania* 2: 19–36.

Soper, R. (1979) Iron Age archaeology and traditional history in Embu, Mbeere and Chuka areas of Central Kenya. *Azania* 14: 31–59.

Stanley, H.M. (1878) *Through the dark continent.* New York Scribner.

Stanley, H.M. (1890) *In darkest Africa, or the quest, rescue and retreat of Emin, Governor of Equatoria.* 2 vols. London, Sampson Low, Marston, Searle and Rivington.

Vansina, J. (1965) *Oral tradition: a study in historical methodology.* Translated by Wright, H.M. London, Routledge and Kegan Paul.

Vita-Finzi, C. and Higgs, E.S. (1970) Prehistoric economy in the Mount Carmel area of Palestine: site catchment analysis. *Proceedings of the Prehistoric Society* 36: 1–37.

CHAPTER 9

CITY STATES OF THE EAST AFRICAN COAST AND THEIR MARITIME CONTACTS

George H. O. Abungu

The East African coast is dotted with numerous abandoned settlements which formerly comprised independent city states. These city states, which were mostly confined to the offshore islands and mainland coast, date back to the first century AD, although so far archaeological records only point to the latter part of the first millennium AD.

Early documents, including the first century Periplus of the Erythraean Sea, *and the second century Ptolemy's* Geography, *describe these city states in detail, including names, people, and economies; Rhapta, Opone, and Hafun are depicted very clearly as rich metropolises, trading with the outside world. Although the geographic locations of these places as described from these documents have been unclear, the description leaves no doubt that they were located on the East coast of Africa.*

However, from the late first millennium AD, the city states are represented archaeologically as well as in historical records. Although first seen as a result of outside influences, the present evidence points to an African foundation. These city states were, however, for centuries in contact with the outside world, such as the Arabian Peninsula, the Indian subcontinent, China and South-East Asia. Through these contacts there was both exchange of ideas and goods; there was also interaction of people involving among other things marriage and the spread of the Islamic religion. The city states were, therefore, to an extent influenced by external forces, including religion and architecture. However, the culture, the people and their cities remained intrinsically African. The city states were part of Africa, with their foundation rooted firmly on the continent. The cities' founders and inhabitants were the Swahili, who were a specialized African community, who by virtue of their locality became middlemen in the Indian Ocean maritime trade. This chapter deals with the gateway communities whose lives were shaped by the trade between the African hinterland and the wider Indian Ocean trade network. These city states prospered, and by the fifteenth century AD reached a stage which has been referred to as 'The Golden Age of Swahili Civilization.'

Until the colonial period in Africa, little was known of the city states or urban settlements that are spread along much of the east coast of Africa. While the empires and city states of West Africa were known to the European world due to the extensive trade contacts between the two regions (especially from around the thirteenth century) the same was not the case with Eastern Africa. To many people in the 'outside world,' especially Europe, Africa was the 'Dark Continent' with no history and no civilization. It therefore came as a surprise to the first Europeans to visit East Africa, notably the Portuguese, to find well-established civilizations with well-developed urban settlements along the East coast of Africa.

While these settlements were observed, recorded, and described by the Portuguese as early as the fifteenth century, European scholars who followed as late as the mid-twentieth century found it difficult to attribute the origins of these towns to the African inhabitants. To them such an advanced civilization could only have originated from outside the continent; thus the creation of myths about the foreign foundation of Great Zimbabwe in the south and theories on the 'Arab cities' of the East African coast.

The east coast of Africa, as discussed in this chapter, is the strip of land stretching from Somalia in the north to Mozambique in the south; it also includes the Indian Ocean islands of Comoros and Madagascar (Fig. 9.1). The Swahili towns of this region had for many centuries been in close contact with the wider Indian Ocean trade circle, notably the Arabian Peninsula and Indian Subcontinent, China and South-East Asia.

Along the Kenyan coast alone there are over 120 archaeological sites, the majority being of abandoned Swahili settlements (Fig. 9.2). Some have ruins of one or two stone structures, while others contain numerous standing stone structures and occupy large areas. Some of the earliest Swahili sites along the East African coast are found in the Lamu Archipelago, dating to the eighth century AD; these include Manda (Chittick, 1984) and Shanga (Horton, 1984, 1986, 1996). It should however be noted that the existing standing structures were built around the fourteenth and fifteenth centuries. Many of these Swahili towns were abandoned in the seventeenth century; this was due to a combination of many factors, such as drought, disease, wells drying up or becoming saline, or wars. Although Mombasa, Lamu, Pate, Mogadishu, and Zanzibar are vibrant 'living' towns to this day, the greater part of this splendid civilization lies in ruins.

Through written records, it is known that trade existed between the East African coast and foreign countries as early as the first century AD. This trade with the Persian Gulf, the Near and Far East and, eventually, Europe, reached such great heights by the fifteenth century that this period has been referred to as 'The Golden Age of Swahili Civilization' (Kirkman, 1964: 28).

Archaeological investigations have produced abundant evidence which shows that the inhabitants of these towns were wealthy maritime traders, farmers, and merchants, whose possessions included fine imported cloth,

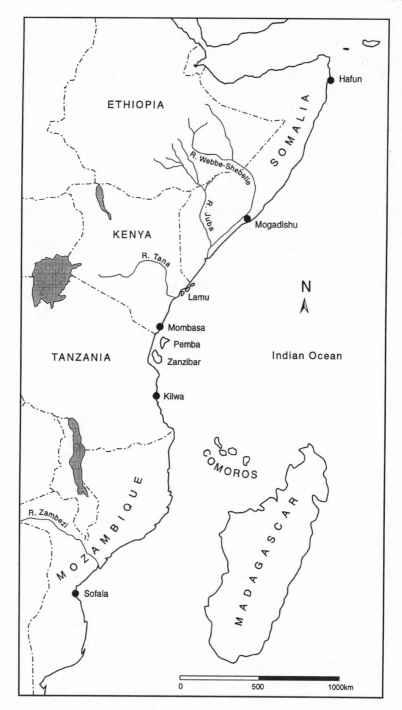

Fig. 9.1 The East African coast.

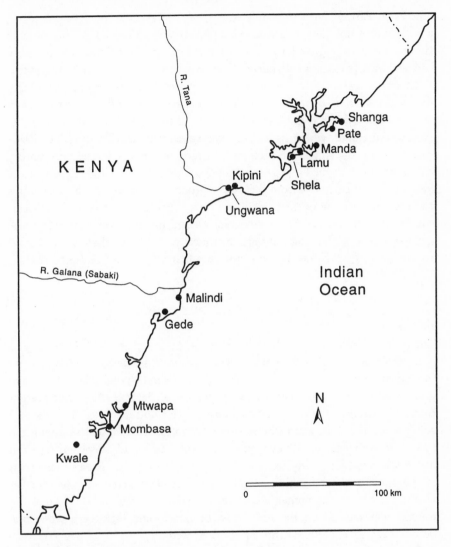

Fig. 9.2 The Kenyan coast.

ceramics, beads, and other jewelry. The significance of these sites lies in their rich past as trading centers with a very rich cultural and architectural history.

ORIGINS

The city states of the East African coast are the creations of the Swahili people. Although Swahili history, and especially origins, has been an issue of much debate, it is now accepted that their origins lie in Africa. The Swahili can be seen as an African, Muslim people who speak KiSwahili as their first language, are often (but not always) urbanized, and have a maritime way of life. Swahili culture spreads along the East African coast, from southern Somalia to northern Mozambique, and to the islands of Comoros and north-western Madagascar.

Over the centuries the Swahili have intermarried with other groups, notably the Arabs, due to their long-standing trade contacts, and as a result many Swahili also have Arab ancestry. The origins of the Swahili, however, lie in the African hinterland, where Early Iron-Age settlements and Pastoral Neolithic–Pastoral Iron-Age sites have been found dating to the first and second century AD. It has been argued elsewhere (Abungu, 1994–95) that the origins of the Swahili should be traced from the above groups. The evidence for the origins and the development of the Swahili and their towns is, however, still not clear-cut; the period between the second century and the eighth century AD is still unknown both archaeologically and historically. However, there are historical records dealing with this region during the first and second centuries AD.

HISTORICAL EVIDENCE

The earliest written historical evidence on the East African coast is the *Periplus of the Erythraean Sea*, a first-century AD navigational guide to the Red Sea and the Indian Ocean (Casson, 1989). It should, however, be noted that others have given a later date for the *Periplus* (Mathew, 1975; Chittick, 1981). The present chapter is based on the early dates by Casson. This document describes the city states along the coast and includes names, peoples, and economies; among the towns mentioned are Rhapta, Opone, and Hafun, all depicted as rich metropolises trading with the outside world. Although the names mentioned in the *Periplus* are difficult to correlate with modern geography (except for Hafun, located on the Somali coast), the descriptions leave no doubt that the towns were located on the east coast of Africa, and that there was trade between foreigners (Arabs) and the local Africans.

The next document is Ptolemy's *Geography* (Casson, 1989; Huntingford, 1980), written about AD 150 and revised 250 years later, which repeats many of the names mentioned in the *Periplus*. After this there does not seem to be any documentary evidence about the east coast south of Somalia from the third to the tenth centuries. In AD 956, however, a well-traveled Arab geographer and historian, al-Masudi, wrote his work, *Muruj adh-Dhahab* (Meadows of God), in which he occasionally mentioned the far lands of the Zanj. In it he described the area (the East African coast) and even mentioned an island called 'Qanbalu,' thought to be either present-day Pemba or Comoros. However, it was not until the twelfth century AD and after that the picture of the east coast of Africa and its inhabitants began to be clear; this period saw numerous Arab geographers and historians, like al-Idrisi (twelfth century) and ibn Battuta (fourteenth century), begin to write about the coastal towns (Freeman-Grenville, 1962; Kirkman, 1964; Trimingham, 1964, 1975).

The geographer al-Idrisi (1100–1166) wrote the *Kitab Rujar* (Geography of the World), in which he mentioned towns like Mombasa (Manbasa) and Malindi (Mlnda) by name (Kirkman, 1964; Guillain, 1856). The best regional account was, however, given by ibn Battuta, who visited some of the coastal towns including Mombasa, which he mentioned and described in his work. In all their works, these Arab scholars described the people (referred to as the 'Sahil:' people of the coast) as Africans who were different from themselves. They were described as good traders who dealt in many products, including ivory, rhinoceros horn, ambergris, frankincense, and other things. The Arab scholars were followed by the Portuguese at the end of the fifteenth century. By this time, however, the trade had widened to deal also with gold from the south and slaves, as well as the other traditional goods already mentioned.

ARCHAEOLOGICAL EVIDENCE

The earliest archaeological investigations along the East African coast were started in the late 1940s. The first excavations were carried out by James Kirkman at Gede in 1947 (Kirkman, 1954, 1957, 1960, 1963), which was followed by work on other Kenyan coastal sites (Kirkman, 1952, 1957, 1966, 1975). Kirkman was joined in the late 1950s by Neville Chittick, who concentrated first on the Tanzanian coast, especially on the site of Kilwa (Chittick, 1966, 1969c, 1974); he subsequently moved north to the Kenyan and Somali coasts, excavating the early site of Manda in the Lamu Archipelago from 1967 (Chittick, 1967, 1969a, 1969b, 1979, 1984).

During this period the early scholars managed to develop a reasonably good chronology of events, based on imported materials, mostly ceramics. From the start these sites yielded large amounts of imports; they also exhibited advanced architectural achievements in terms of buildings, mostly of stone (coral) masonry. In many cases these houses were situated in *mitaa* or wards, which in turn were grouped into a town. Because this kind of spatial arrangement and the architectural achievements were not known before to Europe and its scholars, the towns were thought to have been outside introductions. The Swahili's commercial contacts overseas, their Islamic faith, and the adoption of certain Arabic (and, later, Portuguese) loan words into the KiSwahili language, further strengthened the belief that the Swahili and their history were not all, or only partly, African. This was the argument up until the mid-1970s; since then, there has been a progressive shift in scholarly orientation that has led to acceptance of the fact that the Swahili are African, as are their achievements. It is, however, important to note that the Swahili have a long history of commercial and cultural contacts with other parts of the world, from where they naturally have borrowed in one way or the other; they have not lived in isolation. Nevertheless, their achievements have been built and nurtured in Africa.

The earliest archaeological evidence of the Swahili sites so far found at the coast dates to the eighth century AD, at the sites of Manda and Shanga in the Lamu Archipelago. At Shanga the primary levels yielded little imported material; and the few imports came from a wide variety of sources including the Persian Gulf, western India, and China. Local pottery made up the majority of artifacts, comprising 95 percent of the total pottery collection, but other craft activities represented included ironworking, bead-preparation, and shell-cleaning. Both round and rectangular houses were built, and the town arrangement included a central rectangular timber enclosure which Horton (1984, 1986) has interpreted as representing a cattle corral, either symbolic or actual. The resident population was initially non-Muslim, basically African farmers and traders, and the settlement arrangement has been compared to that of the Mijikenda Kaya of the immediate hinterland (Horton, 1984). The same kind of situation seems to occur at the sites of Manda and Ungwana on the Tana Delta, where the earliest strata have few imports, although they increase through time. At Shanga, as in other places along the coast, Islam arrived and spread gradually, just as did the trade in the different commodities. The gradual spread and acceptance of Islam by the local population is reflected in the increase in size and importance of the mosques through time; the same applies to the trade items which gradually increase in quantity and quality over the same period.

This period (the eighth century AD) coincides with the Abbasid period of the Islamic heartland, when the Indian Ocean trade initially opened up its focus on the Persian Gulf. This is apparent from the above documentary evidence for the existence of contacts between the East African coast and the Red Sea as early as the first century AD. However, just as there is a dearth of continuous documentation of such contacts through the late Roman and Sassanid periods and even during the first two centuries of the Islamic era, there is even less physical evidence of these contacts during these times (the eighth century AD) at the coast itself and on the islands. No East African Swahili site has yet been found to have been in existence between the first and eighth centuries AD. From the eighth century AD the picture changes, and the archaeological evidence of the late first millennium at several Swahili sites is matched by the above-cited travelers' accounts and other literary allusions, such as those of al-Masudi writing in the mid-tenth century. The subsequent years saw a lot of activities and developments along the East African coast and are represented in both the archaeological records (in terms of artifacts and permanent standing structures) and also in historical sources (as written documents). By the fifteenth century much of the East African coast, including the adjacent islands, saw the development of major town settlements whose widespread commercial contacts encompassed both the African hinterland and foreign lands.

OVERSEAS CONTACTS

HISTORICAL INFORMATION

Apart from the towns it mentions, the *Periplus of the Erythraean Sea* (Casson, 1989) also talks of the ongoing trade between the east coast of Africa and the other parts of the world. One of the items mentioned as being traded from Rhapta is ivory (Huntingford, 1980). It has been suggested by Cutler (1985) that the size of many surviving classical ivories, with their smallest diameter larger than 110 millimeters, indicates that African savanna elephant ivory was used. This ivory could have reached Europe through the traditional Southern Arabian route, a route which was probably in existence before the first century AD.

Although there appears to have been a decline in the ivory trade in the sixth century (Cutler, 1985), the eighth century saw a revival of this trade. Al-Masudi, in AD 916 (written AD 956), observed extensive hunting of elephants and export of ivory to Oman, India, and China, from the East African ports. In the late tenth century, ivory-carving became a major occupation and many workshops were set up in both Christian and Islamic Europe (Cutler, 1985). Due to the sizes of the tusks carved at that time, the sources surely lay in the exploitation of the larger-tusked African savanna elephant, rather than the much smaller African forest elephants or Indian elephants.

Other recorded trade items from East Africa carried into the international market included ambergris, slaves, and timber. The trade in slaves seems to have been very prosperous and most were sent to the swamps of the Shatt el Arab at the head of the Persian Gulf; there they reached such great numbers that they were even able to revolt by the year AD 868. While ivory and ambergris were sent to the Far East, the African teak and mangrove were extensively used at Siraf and probably in Sammara and Baghdad. These building materials, traded over the centuries, continued to form the bulk of the trade up until the mid-twentieth century.

East Africa was also known for its export of gold and copper, the former coming from southern Africa (possibly from the Mapungubwe, and subsequently Great Zimbabwe, kingdoms) through Sofala in Mozambique, and exported mostly from the port town of Kilwa in Tanzania (Freeman-Grenville, 1962). It was recorded by De Barros that the Arabs or the Moors exchanged with the people of Sofala cloth for gold and ivory (Freeman-Greenville, 1962). The overseas gold trade from Sofala through Kilwa is also described by both ibn Battuta in the fourteenth century and by the Portuguese in the late fifteenth to early sixteenth centuries; the latter took little time before demanding huge tributes in gold with dire consequences for the inhabitants of Kilwa when they tried to oppose this. The gold trade should be seen as a long-standing trade that started before the tenth century and involved long-distance trade into the interior of Africa.

ARCHAEOLOGICAL INFORMATION

The archaeological evidence along the East African coast, for the maritime contacts between that coast and the outside world, is plentiful. This evidence is found in the form of standing buildings, architectural features within them, remains of imported trade goods, and local artifacts with borrowed features.

A substantial length of the East African coast was dotted with town settlements; some of these are now in a ruinous state while others are now major towns. These settlements range in size from small sites of about 1 hectare, with only one or two stone structures, to large towns covering hundreds of hectares of land and mostly built of stone. Building in stone was perhaps a local innovation due to the availability of the building material; however, some of the houses found in these settlements incorporate borrowed elements introduced from outside Africa. Within some of the houses are found decorative motifs commonly used in the Islamic world; these include the niches that are common in Swahili houses, especially in the inner (or *ndani*) part of the house, associated with the women and therefore more private (the latter yet another Islamic characteristic) (Fig. 9.3).

Apart from the houses, there are mosques (Fig. 9.4) and tombs (Fig. 9.5); although the latter are not necessarily Islamic (and the ones found along the East African coast are basically African-influenced), some of the decoration, the inscriptions and the architectural styles are Islamic or Islamic-influenced. A mosque itself is, of course, synonymous with the presence of the Islamic faith; thus its presence in all the Swahili towns from at least the ninth century AD further confirms these contacts.

The greatest archaeological indicators of maritime contacts with overseas countries are probably the numerous trade items; these include pottery, glass, and glass beads. From the earliest occupational layers in these settlements are found trade items, although in small quantities. The trade items increase consistently from the earliest period of contact (the eighth century AD) up to the seventeenth century AD, representing the increase in trade and therefore contact between East Africa and other parts of the world.

As far back as the eighth century, trade items in terms of pottery seem to

Fig. 9.3 *Above:* The House of Niches at Shela, Lamu, sixteenth century AD. Photograph L. Abungu. *Below:* Decorative *Vidaka* (niches) in an eighteenth-century Swahili house (Swahili House Museum, Lamu). Photograph L. Abungu.

Fig. 9.4 Domed mosque at Mwana, near Kipini, fifteenth century AD. Photograph L. Abungu.

Fig. 9.5 Domed tomb of Mwana Ndia wa Msingi at Siyu, Pate Island.
Photograph L. Abungu.

come from diverse areas, notably from the Gulf, Western India, and China.
Within the archaeological context of these settlements are found pottery such
as Sassanian Islamic, Sgraffiato, different kinds of Islamic Monochromes,
Polychromes, Chinese White, Chinese Blue and White, Celadon, and Indian
Red. These finds are also indicators of times of prosperity and times of leanness,
depending on the amount and quality of the material at any given time. Glass
beads and glass are other items of trade represented in the archaeological
records on the East African coast. Some of the beads are from India, while
others came from Mediterranean Europe probably through the Red Sea or via
India. Glass was at first imported from the Gulf and later from Europe.

Numismatic finds are yet further evidence which confirms the widespread
coastal contacts. A number of coins, including some in hordes, have been found
in sites along the East African coast; these include gold and silver coinage. Both
the sites of Shanga (Horton, 1986) and Mtambwe Mkuu in Pemba (Horton and
Clark, 1985), have produced coins. Although some of these coins were made on
the East African coast, others came from outside, such as the Fatimid coins

found at Manda (Chittick, 1984) or the Fatimid dinars from the Mediterranean mint dated to AD 1066 found at Mtambwe Mkuu ; other coins were minted in East Africa using the local gold supplies. The fact that these coins could have been used in Africa at that time shows the incorporation of this region into the Indian Ocean regional trade network. Thus the Swahili settlements along the coast were part and parcel of the wider global trade and exchange network.

DISCUSSION AND CONCLUSION

The close contacts between East Africa and especially Asia are not only evidenced by historical and archaeological finds but also by the presence of a people of South-East-Asian origin in Madagascar. This, together with the presence of outrigger canoes (thought to be the invention of South-East Asia), and the introduced food crops such as bananas, sugar cane, coconut, and rice (all of South-East Asian origin) goes further to confirm the long-standing contacts between East Africa and Asia.

It is however important to note that, so far as the trade goods found in East African sites are concerned, neither archaeological nor historical evidence suggests that Africans had to go to China or India to get such trade items, or vice versa. To the contrary, the Arabs acted as middlemen in the transoceanic trade, moving up and down the coasts with the help of the yearly monsoon winds. From Africa, apart from the ivory, slaves and wood, other export commodities that the Arabs took back included rhinoceros horns, tortoiseshell, leopard skins, incense, iron, and grains.

The prosperity of the Swahili coast to a large extent depended on a very well-organized entrepôt system of exchange and trade. Established locations on the coast became centers for the exchange of goods with overseas merchants on the one hand and with the hinterland on the other. These then became nodes of state formation and urban development; a consistent development can be seen from the eighth century onwards, culminating in a great complexity as represented in material culture, architecture and social organization within the sites.

The Swahili communities, thus being at the crossroads between two worlds – the African hinterland and the outside world – also occupied a middleman's position which they were able to utilize effectively. They became gateway communities, controlling and monopolizing the exchange of the commodities from two worlds. Control of the trade by the Swahili was so real that, as ibn Battuta in his visit to Mogadishu pointed out, no foreign merchant was allowed to trade directly with other people, but only through his host (Gibb, 1962: 379; Freeman-Grenville, 1962: 27–8). In this way the Swahili were advantaged; as Africans, they had the support and confidence of their brothers in the interior with whom they traded and made alliances; on the other hand, as Muslims, their acquired religion put them on a par with their Muslim overseas trading partners. It was through this acumen for trade, control, and monopoly, that the Swahili were able to build numerous city states and join in the world trade arena, thus extending their contacts well past the shores of the African continent.

BIBLIOGRAPHY

Abungu, G.H.O. (1994–5) Agriculture and settlement formation along the East African coast. *Azania* 29–30: 248–56.

Casson, L. (1989) *The Periplus Maris Erythraei. Text with introduction, translation and commentary*. Princeton, Princeton University Press.

Chittick, H.N. (1966) Kilwa, a preliminary report. *Azania* 1: 1–37.

Chittick, H.N. (1967) Discoveries in the Lamu Archipelago. *Azania* 2: 37–67.

Chittick, H.N. (1969a) A new look at the history of Pate. *Journal of African History* 10: 375–91.

Chittick, H.N. (1969b) An archaeological reconnaissance of the southern Somali coast. *Azania* 4: 115–30.

Chittick, H.N. (1969c) The early history of Kilwa Kivinje. *Azania* 4: 153–8.

Chittick, H.N. (1974) *Kilwa: an Islamic trading city on the East African coast*. Nairobi, Memoir 5, 2 vols, British Institute in Eastern Africa.

Chittick, H.N. (1979) Early ports in the Horn of Africa. *International Journal of Nautical Archaeology* 8(4): 273–7.

Chittick, H.N. (1981) The *Periplus* and the spice trade. *Azania* 16: 185–90.

Chittick, H.N. (1984) *Manda: excavations at an island port on the Kenya coast*. Nairobi, Memoir 9, British Institute in Eastern Africa.

Cutler, A. (1985) *The craft of ivory: sources, techniques and uses in the Mediterranean world: AD 200–1400*. Washington, DC, Dumbarton Oaks Library.

Freeman-Grenville, G.S.P. (1962) *The East African coast: select documents from the first to the earlier nineteenth century*. London, Clarendon Press.

Gibb, H.A.R. (1962) *The travels of ibn Battuta 1325–54*. Vol. 2. London, Hakluyt Society Series 110.

Guillain, M. (1856) *Documents sur l'histoire, la géographie, et la commerce de l'Afrique Orientale*. 3 vols. Paris, Betrand.

Horton, M.C. (1984) The early settlement of the northern Swahili coast. Unpublished PhD thesis, University of Cambidge.

Horton, M.C. (1986) Asiatic colonization of the East African coast: the Manda evidence. *Journal of the Royal Asiatic Society* pt 2: 201–13.

Horton, M.C. (1996) *Shanga: the archaeology of a Muslim trading community on the coast of East Africa*. London, Memoir 14, British Institute in Eastern Africa.

Horton, M.C. and Clark, C. (1985) *Zanzibar archaeological survey 1984–5*. Zanzibar, Ministry of Information, Culture and Sports.

Huntingford, G.W.B. (1980) *Periplus of the Erythraean Sea*. London, Hakluyt Society.

Kirkman, J.S. (1952) The excavation at Kilepwa. An introduction to the medieval archaeology of the Kenya coast. *Antiquaries Journal* 32: 168–84.

Kirkman, J.S. (1954) *The Arab city of Gedi: excavations at the Great Mosque, architecture and finds*. London, Oxford University Press.

Kirkman, J.S. (1957) Historical archaeology in Kenya 1948–56. *Antiquaries Journal* 37: 1–5.

Kirkman, J.S. (1960) *The Tomb of the Dated Inscription at Gedi*. London, Occasional Paper 14, Royal Anthropological Institute.

Kirkman, J.S. (1963) *Gedi, the Palace*. The Hague, Mouton.

Kirkman, J.S. (1964) *Men and monuments of the East African coast*. London, Lutterworth.

Kirkman, J.S. (1966) *Ungwana on the Tana*. The Hague, Mouton.

Kirkman, J.S. (1975) *Gedi: historical monument*. 8th edn, Nairobi, Museum Trustees of Kenya.

Mathew, G. (1975) The dating and the significance of the *Periplus of the Erythrean Sea*. In Chittick, H.N. and Rotberg, R.I. (eds) *East Africa and the Orient: cultural syntheses in pre-colonial times*. New York and London, Africana Publishing Company, pp. 147–63.

Trimingham, J.S. (1964) *Islam in East Africa*. London, Clarendon Press.

Trimingham, J.S. (1975) The Arab geographers and the East African coast. In Chittick, H.N. and Rotberg, R.I. (eds) *East Africa and the Orient: cultural syntheses in pre-colonial times*. New York and London, Africana Publishing Company, pp. 115–46, 272–83.

CHAPTER 10

THE EUROPEANS IN WEST AFRICA: CULTURE CONTACT, CONTINUITY AND CHANGE

Christopher R. DeCorse

This chapter examines the characteristics and consequences of African–European interactions in West Africa. Emphasis is placed on the varied nature of the contact setting and the evaluation of culture change in African populations during the period of initial European contact, trade, and colonization. Archaeological data, documentary sources, and oral traditions are used to evaluate transformations in African world views. Although a general relationship between an expanding Eurocentric economic system and changing artifact inventories is recognized, inferences concerning the alteration of nonmaterial cultural systems are viewed as more difficult and challenging to assess. Acknowledgment of the varied way in which material remains represent cultures and how changes in shared beliefs or world views may be identified archaeologically is seen as fundamental to archaeologists' perception of the past. These issues are highlighted by recent work at the site of Elmina in coastal Ghana.

CULTURE CONTACT IN AFRICA

In the wake of an array of studies focusing on Columbian consequences in the Americas, archaeological studies in Africa afford a wide range of contrasting models of European-indigene interactions and archaeological evaluations of the contact setting. The European arrival on the West African coast in the late fifteenth century began the sustained economic and cultural interactions which culminated with the partition of Africa into colonies in the late nineteenth century. These events, however, were only one aspect of a complex tapestry of relations which linked West African societies and other regions. Contacts, which brought both technological and cultural innovation, were integral to African societies long before the arrival of the Europeans. The advent of the trans-Saharan trade during the first millennium AD brought metal goods, cloth, and beads to West Africa from the north, while the forest and savanna provided gold, salt, and slaves (e.g. Austen, 1979; Garrard, 1980; Law, 1980; Levtzion and Hopkins, 1981; Sundström, 1965) (Fig. 10.1). Linkages across the

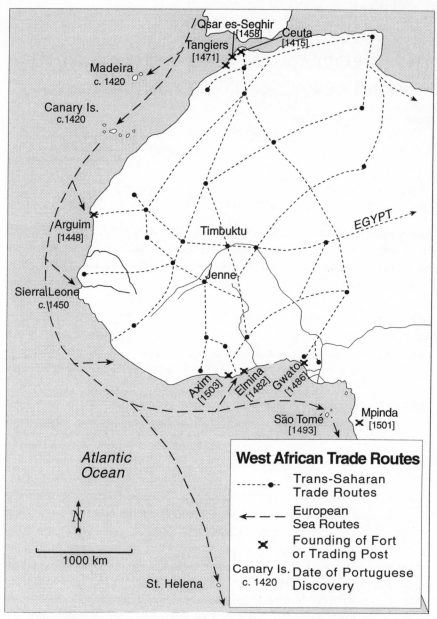

Fig. 10.1 Map showing long-distance trade routes in West Africa.

Sahara also brought Islam, which had extended throughout the societies of North Africa by AD 750 (Hiskett, 1984; McCall and Bennett, 1971; Trimingham, 1978). The earliest documentary accounts of West Africa are, in fact, provided by North African scholars such as ibn Battuta and al-Bekri, who left accounts of cultural traditions both foreign and strange to the eyes of Islamic visitors. West African cities such as Timbuktu and Jenne emerged as seats of Islamic learning by the middle of the second millennium AD.

There has been a tendency in West African studies to stress north–south connections and the trans-Saharan trade, yet east–west links were equally important. On the coast, movement through the rivers and lagoons between the Volta River and the Niger Delta facilitated an indigenous exchange system that complemented later European maritime trade (e.g. Law, 1983, 1991; Sutton, 1981). Ethnohistorical studies also reveal a web of connections throughout the interior hinterland. Iron, salt, beads, and exotic imports circulated throughout the West African interior centuries before the advent of the Europeans on the coast (Brooks, 1993; Goucher, 1981; Kopytoff, 1989).

These observations underscore the myth of the primitive isolate. Culture contact, the exchange of goods, and spread of ideas are endemic to human existence. The interactions initiated in West Africa prior to European contact set the stage for relations which are still going on. Hence, when considering transformations in West African societies during the period of European expansion, an understanding of the connections between the Islamic polities of the savanna and sahel, and the societies in the southern forest remain fundamental. Notably, much of the archaeological research in West Africa that has focused on the archaeological record of the past 500 years does not deal with the European presence, or does so in only a peripheral way. Emphasis has, instead, been placed on indigenous technological developments, archaeological perception of ethnographically identified cultural groups, indigenous social organization, and the effervescence of sociopolitical complexity.

EUROPEAN EXPANSION

The European expansion into Sub-Saharan Africa began in the fifteenth century (Fig. 10.1). The Madeira Islands off the north-west African coast were colonized a full seven decades before Columbus's voyages to the Americas. North Africa remained under Islamic rule in the early fifteenth century and the Christian Portuguese kings diverted the last crusades there. Cueta was captured in 1415, Qsar es-Seghir in 1458, and Tangiers in 1471. Portuguese exploration of the African coast culminated with the rounding of the Cape of Good Hope in 1488 and the circumnavigation of the globe between 1519 and 1522. Within a relatively short period of time, sea routes and Portuguese trade posts linked Africa, Brazil, India, and Asia.

Portugal claimed exclusive European trading rights in these regions, but this monopoly was to last for little more than 50 years. In West Africa, 'illegitimate' trade by other European nations had surpassed that of the Portuguese by 1530

(Blake, 1977). During the seventeenth and eighteenth centuries England, the Netherlands, France, Sweden, Denmark, and Brandenburg vied for the West African market. By 1800 more than 60 European forts and trading lodges had been established on the Gold Coast alone (Fig. 10.2). Gold was the primary objective during the fifteenth and sixteenth centuries but other commodities, including ivory, pepper, redwood, and hides, became increasingly important. The slave trade, shifting in focus and volume through time, had major consequences in many regions. An estimated 12,000,000 Africans were enslaved and brought to the Americas (Lovejoy, 1989).

European involvement in Africa culminated in the late nineteenth century with the partition of Africa into spheres of influence and the onset of colonial rule. With the Berlin colonial conference of 1884–5, France, Germany, Belgium, Italy, Portugal, Spain, and Britain formally divided Africa into areas of expansion. By the close of the century, France had at least nominally laid claim to most of West Africa from Mauritania to Cameroon. This vast area, spanning some 4,700,000 square miles (12,173,000 square kilometers) became Afrique Occidental Français, an area which is today divided into ten independent countries. The British eventually consolidated claims in the modern nations of Gambia, Sierra Leone, Ghana, Nigeria, and Cameroon (Pakenham, 1991).

The European trade, territorial claims, and colonization over the past 500 years had far-reaching effects on West African exchange systems, economies, and sociopolitical organization. However, direct interaction between Africans and Europeans was, for the most part, limited. There were some exceptions. European outposts extended far up the Gambia and Senegal Rivers, and many trade castles and forts were established in coastal Ghana. Nevertheless, the European population remained very small, even during the colonial period. Limited numbers of Africans were employed in the European forts or were married to Europeans. There was also open conflict between Europeans and different African polities. Yet prior to the late nineteenth century and the advent of colonial rule, European influence was primarily effected through the emerging commercial relations with the interior, including the trade in gold, slaves, and an increasing variety of other commodities during the nineteenth century. Even in the coastal trade posts the actions of the Europeans were frequently constrained by the perceptions, goals, and motivations of the African populations. Europeans had little direct control over the hinterland, or even the people within the purview of the trade post. Instances can be noted of people simply moving away when European policies became too antagonistic. In the Hueda and Dahomey kingdoms the Europeans were not allowed to fortify their trading lodges, and the presence of European traders was interpreted through indigenous ideology and social constructs. The early eighteenth-century Hueda located the European trading lodges under the walls of the palace, underscoring the power and authority of the king (Kelly, in press).

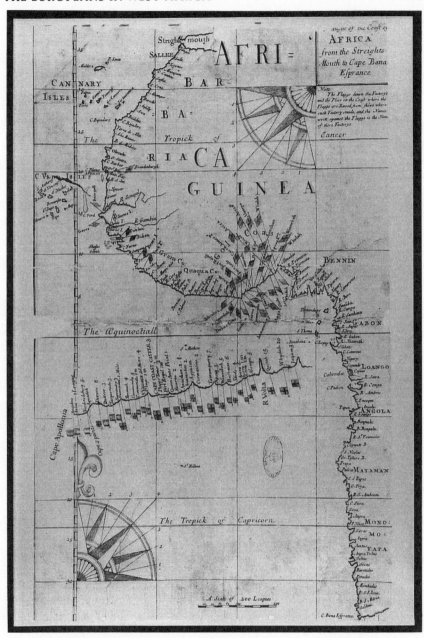

Fig. 10.2 Eighteenth-century map of the West African coast. The flags represent trade posts belonging to different European nations. The inset shows detail of the Gold Coast. Based on a British Crown copyright photograph (ref. MPK45) reproduced courtesy of the Public Record Office, Kew.

The Europeans acted within the African social framework or risked the cession of relations and the interruption of trade. The contact situations presented in these settings are very different from those in South Africa and even twentieth-century Kenya, where substantial European settlement and conscription of aborigines into the labor force was an integral part of the European presence.

A number of pragmatic considerations, including a variety of natural features, limited European settlement in West Africa. The coast offers few harbors or island arcs to shelter ships. The narrow continental shelf is pounded by surf and has dangerous currents, which made landings difficult. Until the advent of the steam launch and the construction of deep water piers in the late nineteenth and twentieth centuries, Europeans were dependent on African boatmen to land goods and supplies. Mangrove swamps extended along much of the coastal margin, while dense forest and the limited number of navigable rivers constrained travel in the interior. The threat of death and disease was another obstacle. Despite problems in assessing estimates of European death rates and the absence of corresponding information on African populations, the fact remains that a large number of Europeans newly arrived on the West African coast died (Curtin, 1961, 1968; Feinberg, 1974). The image of horrible death in the tropics became part of the Victorian European view of Africa as the dark continent, an unknown, unexplored and forbidding region. Finally, political and technological sophistication allowed many African societies to effectively manipulate European relations and resist incursions.

Because of the limited European presence, the 'impact' of Europe in both economic and cultural terms was often played out with little direct European involvement and within African sociocultural contexts. It is not surprising, therefore, that examinations of Europe in Africa have often been conceptualized in terms of changing trade relations and economic impact (e.g. Austen, 1987; Curtin, 1975; Daaku, 1970; Dike, 1966; Hopkins, 1973; Jones, 1983a; Kea, 1982; Polanyi, 1966; Priestly, 1969; Reynolds, 1974; Rodney, 1972; Wallerstein, 1986). It was trade that brought the Europeans and it was within this arena that their activities took place. Many models have been posited which chart these interactions. Among the best articulated is world-systems analysis developed by Immanuel Wallerstein (1980, 1986). For social scientists, this theory provides insight into the economic and political connections which have shaped the world during the past 500 years. Its potential for contextualizing the appearance of European trade materials in the archaeological record makes it particularly seductive to archaeologists examining the record of European expansion. Wallerstein identified several historical phases during which Africa was incorporated into the global economy. Prior to the eighteenth century he considers African economies to have largely functioned independently. European trade consisted mainly of nonessential commodities and demand was primarily dependent on European productive capacities and supply lines.

By 1750 the European economic core was expanding and portions of the coastal regions of Africa had been incorporated into the periphery of the European economic system. This period was, first and foremost, characterized by the growth of slave labor as an integral part of the European economy. The growth of the trade, Wallerstein argues, in turn precipitated changes in sociopolitical organizations within the slave-exporting regions. African states became dependent on the wealth and prestige derived from European trade. During the next 150 years, the rest of West Africa was incorporated into the economic periphery.

World systems theory affords a macroscopic view of one facet of the contact setting, offering a holistic model of the economic constraints which shaped European expansion. It affords a less satisfactory explanation of developments internal to African societies. Addressing variation in the contact setting, Wallerstein notes:

It is not that there are no particularities of each acting group. Quite the contrary. It is that the alternatives available for each unit are constrained by the framework of the whole, even while each actor opting for a given alternative in fact alters the framework of the whole. (1986: 101)

Yet it is reasonable to question, as John Thornton (1992) has, to what extent the same Eurocentric 'framework' constrained the whole. Although European interactions in West Africa can be painted in broad strokes, active agency on the part of African societies in shaping the nature of the contact setting and the diversity of the interactions which occurred need to be underscored.

It is the particularities of African–European relations and variation in the cultural response that I want to emphasize. Although the constraints of the economic system instigated certain structural changes and certain commodities were emphasized, the timing and nature of contact varied, as did the specific European policies initiated, the materials exchanged, and the volume of trade. African responses to contact were similarly diverse – some African polities forged close alliances with the Europeans, others vigorously opposed or regulated European activities. Portuguese settlements in North Africa, such as Qsar es-Seghir, can be viewed as ill-fated colonial experiments: cultural transplants and economic failures that remained isolated from the hinterland and the interior trade (Redman, 1986). In contrast, the lucrative traffic along the West African coast was at first conducted entirely from ships and this remained the predominate pattern in some areas. It is not coincidental that two of the areas of West Africa which saw the most intensive European activity were regions which afforded comparatively easy access to the gold-producing areas of the interior. Gold was found relatively close to the coast of modern-day Ghana and the Europeans established fortified outposts to secure trade and allow for the accumulation and storage of goods. In the Senegambia, European trade posts were located along the Gambia and Senegal river valleys. These enclaves were, for the most part, small military garrisons staffed almost entirely by men (Posnansky and DeCorse, 1986; Van Dantzig, 1980; Wood, 1967). Nevertheless, the trade relations they engendered had far-reaching effects. The trans-Saharan trade and trading towns of the forest–savanna ecotone declined, while new coastal states thrived along the frontier of opportunity provided by the European trade.

CULTURE CONTACT AND WORLDVIEW

The preceding discussion underscores variation in relations between an expanding European-centered economic system and the nonindustrialized world. It is important to identify the economic basis of European expansion and look for archaeological manifestations of it. What has not yet been considered is the role of noneconomic factors such as shared beliefs, cosmology, religion – in short 'worldview' – in delineating the form, character, and import of African–European relations. Materialist models such as world-systems theory consider economic structure and culture to be inextricably linked, if not one and the same, the latter being a consequence, tool, or expression of the former: '... for cultures are the ways in which people clothe their politico-economic interests and drives in order to express them, hide them, extend them in space and time, and preserve their memory' (Wallerstein, 1980: 65). This viewpoint fails to recognize the essentially extra-somatic cognitive nature of culture and affords a Eurocentric – or rather an economic-centric – perception of contact consequences. It was, in fact, the individual cultural responses that dictated the diversity of ways in which Africans and Europeans interacted. Explication of these distinctive, culturally mitigated conditions are germane to many of the questions and concerns central to our understanding of the changes which occurred in African societies in the era of European expansion.

A tendency among researchers examining the archaeological record of European expansion has been to view the advent of the European trade and merchant capitalism as coinciding with equally dramatic changes in non-economic aspects of non-Western cultures, marking the erosion of values, the circumvention of traditional beliefs, and the devastation of cultural norms in the face of mass-produced products, technological superiority, and hegemonic policies of industrialized societies. There is, in fact, excellent evidence that the expansion of the industrialized state was disastrous to many cultures. Bodley (1990) persuasively pictures the expansion of the industrialized world as a struggle between two fundamentally opposed sociopolitical systems: states and tribes. He perceives preindustrialized societies as victims of industrial civilizations' notions of appropriate resource use and economic progress. The industrial state conceives of development as beneficial: tribal peoples voluntarily reject their own cultures in favor of the benefits of 'modern' life. Such interpretations misconstrue the dynamic nature of the contact setting and underestimate the actions of the indigene.

Ethnographic studies vividly demonstrate the variable nature of the casual factors involved in change and the specific processes through which change occurs (e.g. Bascom and Herskovits, 1963; Curtin, 1972; Herskovits, 1962; Serageldin and Taboroff, 1994; Steward, 1972; Tessler, O'Barr and Spain, 1973). A multitude of non-Western cultures became linked through European trade to an increasingly global economy, but a particular stage of economic development — the core-periphery relations of world-systems analyses — did not correspond to a particular 'stage' of acculturation. Indigenes responded to and interacted with Europeans in different ways and shaped the consequences of these interactions to varying degrees. In this respect, the ideas of Levy-Bruhl (1910), Whorf (1956), Geertz (1973), McCaskie (1995), and the Sahlins of *Islands of history* (1985) resonate more with the spirit, if not the specifics, of what I would consider a useful approach in assessing the consequences of European expansion affecting indigene beliefs, cosmology, and worldview; the essential points here being the diversity of cultural phenomena, the importance of local context, and emphasis on the role of worldview in human action.

West Africa witnessed extensive change in sociopolitical and economic relations during the past 500 years. The trans-Saharan trade was supplanted by more coastal-oriented European exchange. States rose and fell, new trade entrepôts flourished, and twelve million Africans were enslaved and transported to the New World. Yet, survey of African cultures presents rich evidence of continuities in customs, artistic traditions and religious beliefs. In Sierra Leone the Kuranko still invoke the name of Mande Faburre, the Asante of Ghana still venerate numerous spirit shrines, and Ife in Nigeria remains the holy city of the Yoruba. Despite explicit colonial policies of cultural assimilation and extensive technological innovation in some regions, Africans are not cultural clones of Europeans. Perhaps the most salient observation to be made about historical and ethnoarchaeological studies examining change and transformation in West African societies during the past 500 years is the extent to which the beliefs, rituals, and worldview of many modern Africans populations can be seen and interpreted in terms of their *non-European* aspects.

THE ARCHAEOLOGICAL RECORD

Equally varied as patterns of African-European interactions and the nature of culture change, are the ways in which these phenomena are represented archaeologically. The material record affords a critical means for assessing European impact, providing both time depth and information not assessable through other means. This historical perspective presents a real, but as yet unrealized, potential for archaeology to contribute to anthropology as a whole. Historically, archaeological cultures have been conceived as suites of well-defined diagnostic artifacts distributed in time and space. Groupings such as stone tool traditions, pottery types, and distinctive settlement patterns reflect variation in past human behavior and as such are of critical importance to archaeological explanation. What has proven problematic is recognition of the inconstant reasons for the observed variations. Archaeological cultures have often been incorrectly conceived as 'actors on the historical stage, playing the role for prehistory that known individuals and groups have in documentary history' (Shennan, 1989: 6) – as material markers of cultural or ethnic identities.

Although anthropological archaeology has moved beyond a normative, whole culture concept, some archaeologists still advocate generalized methodological approaches which at varying levels equate the archaeological record with non-material belief systems, cultural identity, or worldview. In its most reductionist form, particular artifact classes are equated with ethnic or cultural identity. A corollary of this position is that change in the artifact inventory – changes in technology – are seen as representative of culture change. Such methodological approaches can be illustrated by Quimby's pioneering studies of Native American assemblages, which measured acculturation in terms of the addition of new items to the material inventory and the production of traditional artifacts using new materials (Quimby, 1966; Quimby and Spoehr, 1951). More recent quantitative studies of artifacts and artifact patterns have been used in varying ways to delineate culture or ethnic identities archaeologically (e.g. Farnsworth, 1987; South, 1977).

There is, in fact, no simple or general correspondence between material culture and non-material sociocultural constructs. Many cultures maintained non-Western values and beliefs and, in doing so, turned European trade items to new purposes and ends. This observation is equally true with regard to sociocultural precepts as it is to technological innovation. Ethnoarchaeological research in West Africa serves to underscore both the prospects and problems in the archaeological delineation of ethnographically discernible cultural boundaries and changes in worldview. Research has examined the role of artifacts within systems and the use of space as a means of archaeologically identifying worldview. Studies by Agorsah (1983, 1986, 1988) of Nchumuru sites in the eastern Ghana, and David's (1971) work on Fulani compounds in Nigeria, underscore the usefulness of identifying social system as a means of delineating broader cultural groups (DeCorse and Carr, 1996). Work on individual artifact classes such as pottery has also demonstrated that decorative motifs, styles, and vessel forms may also express cosmological and religious concepts. For example, surveying data on the Mafa and Bulahay of Cameroon, David, Sterner, and Gavua (1988), argue that distinctive decorative motifs – patterns of stamping, appliqué, rouletting, incising, and impressed decoration – on ceramics closely parallel decorations on the body. These represent a suite of symbols that express collective messages which provide a material indicator of Mafa and Bulahay group identity and worldview.

On the other hand, ethnoarchaeological studies have demonstrated the *lack* of correspondence between artifact classes or patterns and ethnographically discernible boundaries. Material remains do not necessarily correspond with observable sociocultural divisions. Variables such as topography, natural resources, and environment may be more important in determining settlement patterns, construction techniques, and other aspects of material culture than sociocultural phenomena such as kinship relations, cosmological precepts or ethnic identity. Traits ranging from pottery styles to foodways may crosscut ethnographically perceived cultural boundaries. Such is the case among the Limba, Yalunka, and Kuranko in northern Sierra Leone (DeCorse, 1989). Although clan groups can be discerned on the basis of house clusters, a holistic examination of settlement organization, house construction, ceramics, and other classes of material culture afford little indication of group identity. The primary material indicators of group identity that are present consist of shrines and sacred spaces located outside of settlements. Such shrines are insubstantial and would be difficult to locate archaeologically without the help of informants. Initiation bushes and sacred groves may be distinguished by their lack of human modification, their virgin growth contrasting with the secondary forest and farm bush of adjacent lands. While such sites might be located with the help of aerial photography and careful ground survey, their function and relationship to associated settlements would also be difficult to infer outside of ethnographically known contexts. Such interpretative difficulties make it challenging to assess beliefs or worldview on the basis of the archaeological record.

Archaeological evaluation of the change in worldviews must be approached even more cautiously. The possibility of archaeologically examining culture change in African populations during the past 500 years has been considered for some time. For example, Paul Ozanne (1963) noted that if the impact of the small European population in coastal Ghana on indigenous social institutions could be documented archaeologically, the study would have implications for the interpretation of archaeological variability in other parts of the world. Data collected by Ozanne in Accra and Shai, and more recent research by other scholars, seem to provide archaeological indications of the social and economic impact of European contact and trade (Ozanne, 1962, 1964; c.f. Kea, 1982; Kiyaga-Mulindwa, 1982; Bellis, 1987; DeCorse, 1993). Access to European trade goods had dramatic impact on some aspects of material culture. Indeed, the florescence of entire artistic traditions has been traced to the availability of European imports such as copper alloys and sheet brass. Pottery predating the middle of the seventeenth century is different in form, decorative inventory, and manufacturing technique from that in later assemblages. Greater standardization of wares and vessel forms are seen as evidence of a widespread trade in pottery and the industrialization of craft industries. Archaeological evidence from southern Ghana also indicates greater urbanization and state development during the seventeenth century. Settlement patterns in portions of the hinterland are characterized by the appearance of fortified sites. Similar transformations appear in artifact assemblages and settlements in other parts of West Africa (DeCorse, 1991).

These archaeological data have been interpreted in varying ways. The Atlantic slave trade, new diseases, changing economic relations, and other factors resulting from the arrival of the Europeans, as well as influences from the Sudan, have all been viewed as explanatory factors. While the culture history of many areas remains poorly known, it is clear that the social and cultural transformations represented are not the same in all settings. In some instances the changes in the archaeological record are associated with dramatic shifts in settlement population and movement of cultural or ethnolinguistic groups. Such appears to be the case in the Mandara highlands of Cameroon, which witnessed a substantial demographic and cultural shift as the Islamic Wandala state expanded and non-Muslim indigenes were either assimilated, enslaved, or forced to flee to refuges in the Mandara Mountains (MacEachern, 1993).

In contrast, the information on southern Ghana suggests that the transformations observed archaeologically were part of an ongoing system of change and not the result of substantial population movements or invasions by replacement populations. Despite fairly dramatic changes in settlement patterns and sociopolitical organization, historical and linguistic evidence alike suggest a great deal of continuity in worldview since the fifteenth century. As Paul Hair (1967) has shown, the distribution of ethnolinguistic groups in coastal Ghana from the late fifteenth century onwards presents a picture of continuity in population, rather than one of dramatic movement. The major linguistic division on the coast – between the Akan dialects of the central coast and Ewe in the east – was discerned. Some indications of more subtle dialectical differences are also apparent. The earliest indications of polities on the Ghanaian coast similarly are consistent with current distribution. While there were influxes of new ethnic groups, the history of southern Ghana is not characterized by invasions by replacement populations.

CULTURE CONTACT AND WORLDVIEW AT ELMINA

Culture continuity within the context of a great deal of sociopolitical and technological change can be illustrated by the African settlement of Elmina in the Central Region of coastal Ghana. The town site affords a unique opportunity to examine African–European interactions. Castle São Jorge da Mina, founded by the Portuguese in 1482 near an existing African settlement, was the first and largest European trading post built in sub-Saharan Africa. The Castle was captured by the Dutch in 1637 and it remained the headquarters of Dutch mercantile interest (Fig. 10.3). After the Castle was ceded to the British in 1872, tensions arose with factions in the African town sympathetic to the Asante. On June 13, 1873, when an ultimatum to deliver all guns to the Castle went unanswered, the British military contingent opened fire. The settlement was subsequently leveled and never reoccupied, the inhabitants relocating to the north side of the Benya Lagoon.

The African settlement of Elmina underwent dramatic changes between the fifteenth and the late nineteenth centuries (Ballong-Wen-Mewuda, 1984; DeCorse, 1992, in press; Hair, 1994; Feinberg, 1989; Yarak, 1990). At the time of Portuguese contact, the town was described as a sizable settlement, yet its population probably only numbered several hundred people. By the mid-nineteenth century, however, the population had swelled to 15,000–20,000 inhabitants (Fig. 10.4). Written sources, ethnographic data, and oral histories attest to dramatic changes in Elmina society between the fifteenth and the nineteenth centuries. European involvement in the sociopolitical organization of the town was far greater than on many parts of the coast. Dutch officials levied tolls, settled disputes, and recognized African rulers. The settlement's relations with neighboring polities were also transformed. Early documentary references suggest that Elmina town was, at the time of European contact, subservient to the neighboring Fante states of Commany or Fetu. By the seventeenth century, however, Elmina had emerged as an independent state which maintained its sovereignty with, or without, European support.

Archaeological data provide a view of some of these transformations. Excavation of more than 30 structures has produced over 100,000 artifacts. Fragments of imported ceramics and glass, metal goods, and trade beads vastly outnumber locally produced artifacts (Fig. 10.5). New artifact classes are also represented, as illustrated by *forowa*, small ritual vessels made out of European sheet brass. Stone construction, a building technique very different from indigenous West African timber and clay methods, became common in the African settlement after the seventeenth century. Buttons, buckles, slate pencils and writing slates are additional indicators of new behavior patterns.

What do these changes in the material inventory convey about changes in the worldview of the people of Elmina? Above all, they are indicative of

Fig. 10.3 Elmina castle and town viewed from Fort Saint Jago, as pictured in an 1869 watercolor four years before the town's destruction. At this time the settlement probably had between 15,000 and 20,000 inhabitants. Reproduced courtesy of the Stichting Cultuurgeschiedenis van de Nederlanders Overzee (CNO nr. 66).

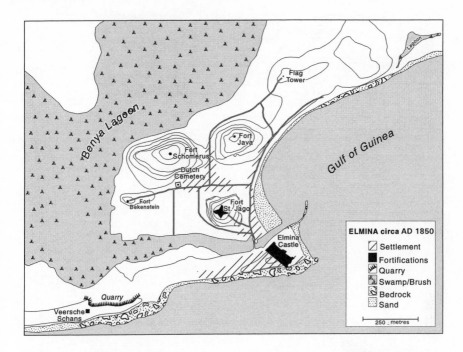

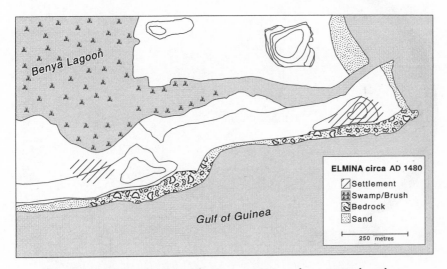

Fig. 10.4 Maps showing Elmina *c.* 1480 and *c.* 1850 based on documentary sources and archaeological data.

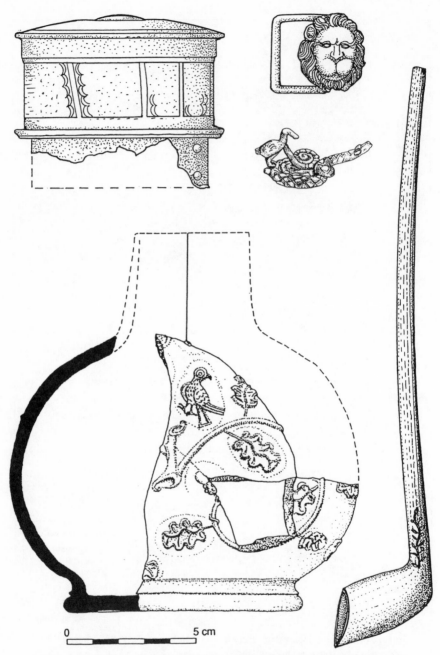

Fig. 10.5 Artifacts from Elmina. From upper left: a reconstructed *forowa, c.* 1800; a European lion's-head buckle, mid-nineteenth century; a figurative Akan gold weight dating to the nineteenth century; a nineteenth-century European tobacco pipe; fragments of a Rhenish stoneware jug or *krug, c.* 1500–50.

Elmina's pivotal role in Europe's mercantile relations with Africa: the coast's preeminent position at the economic intersection of Africa and Europe. The rapid growth of the settlement itself and the town's emergence as an independent polity illustrate the reorientation of trade toward the coast. The array of trade materials attest to the settlement's worldwide trade connections and the wealth of the town's African merchants. The tremendous change in the artifact inventory should not, however, be viewed as an *ipso facto* indicator of changes in worldview. Continuity in the beliefs of the African population at Elmina may be assessed by considering three categories of information: the built environment, the foodways system, and material indications of ritual behavior. Each of these aspects of the archaeological record have been used by archaeologists to assess a variety of phenomena, including group identity and worldview. Collectively, the cognitive context in which artifacts functioned – how the Elmina people thought about the trade materials they used, viewed the buildings they occupied, and conceived their religious life – suggests resilience rather than dramatic transformation, continuity rather than change in African beliefs and identity.

Among the most distinctive aspects of the Elmina settlement was its stone architecture. When the Portuguese arrived at Elmina, African houses were constructed with timber and clay walls, and thatch roofs. This technique is described in detail by a number of early visitors and it remains the traditional means of house construction on much of the coast. Writing in 1555, Martin Frobisher reported that: '... the howes abowt the said forte and castell [of Elmina] ... be made all of canes and reedes' (Blake, 1967: 359–60). Archaeologically, some indication of this method of construction may be represented by shallow depressions cut into the bedrock, that may have been used to support the timber house-posts.

This construction contrasts dramatically with the housing that came to characterize Elmina in the following centuries. Beginning in the seventeenth century, archaeological and documentary sources on Elmina attest to the appearance of stone-walled buildings, some with flat roofs. By the eighteenth century European travelers noted the town for its stone buildings, which some estimates numbered at over 1000 dwellings. Some of these structures boasted glass windows and external lighting fixtures. This represents a technological innovation probably learned from the Europeans. European influences can also be seen in the neoclassical features in the surviving nineteenth-century buildings in the modern town (Fig. 10.6). Some of these impressive structures were built by wealthy African merchants.

While new construction methods were adopted, in at least some instances, building plans and the use of space within dwellings corresponded to indigenous African ideals. Such is the case with the Locus B structure (Fig. 10.7). Built during the late seventeenth or early eighteenth century, the building

Fig. 10.6 Late nineteenth-century merchant house at Elmina.

consists of an unroofed courtyard surrounded by small rooms. Artifacts from floor contexts indicate that the rooms were multifunctional, including indications of cooking and food preparation, as well as masses of personal belongings. This pattern deviates little from the earliest descriptions of Fante housing and this use-pattern can still be seen in houses throughout the Akan area. Describing Fante housing in 1602 Pieter de Marees (1987: 76) wrote: 'They link together three or four such Huts, standing next to each other so as to form a square, so that women have a place in the middle where they cook' (see also Jones, 1983b: 86, 202; Agorsah, 1986: 33). The 'place in the middle' – the courtyard – is of particular significance. It serves as a semi-private area for cooking, eating, and a variety of other tasks. Typically, the small rooms are shared by individuals and serve as repositories for personal belongings. In ethnographic cases the only room which has a specialized function is a shrine. This use-pattern is not only found among the Akan, but also widely among other African groups. Rather than viewing African houses as small, it is more useful to conceive of them as reasonable size rooms surrounding a large multipurpose family room.

Another aspect of the material inventory which illustrates both continuity and innovation is the foodways system, a term which refers to the interrelated system of food conceptualization, procurement, preservation, preparation, and consumption. An array of new plant and animal species were brought to the

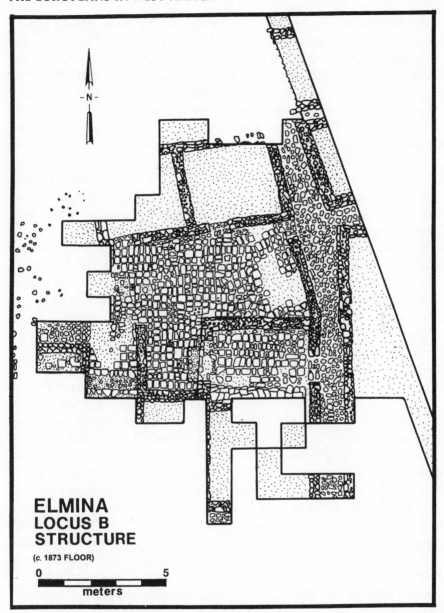

**ELMINA
LOCUS B
STRUCTURE**

(c. 1873 FLOOR)

Fig. 10.7 Plan of Locus B excavation, Elmina.

coast. Introduced cultigens common today include the onion, tomato, mango, pineapple, eggplant, peanut, guava, papaw, avocado, breadfruit, cashew, coffee, cocoa, sugar cane, coconut, cassava, orange, lemon, lime, sweet potato, wheat, maize, tobacco, bananas, and several species of bean (Alpern, 1995; Harlan, De Wet and Stemler, 1976; Mauny, 1954; Miracle, 1965). Varieties of sheep, pigs, cows and geese also complemented indigenous species. Although some of these introduced plant species may have been known in portions of Africa before the fifteenth century, the European sea-trade facilitated their spread throughout West Africa. Although the specific mode of introduction remains uncertain in many instances, many new crops were probably introduced during the Portuguese period. There is no doubt that *en masse* these introductions had a dramatic impact on West African diet. One possible consequence may have been an increase in foods available to support population growth.

Despite these introductions, several lines of evidence can be used to illustrate continuity in the foodways system. Animal bone from the site consists of domesticated species (*Bos* and ovicaprids), as well as a variety of wild species, including cane rat (*Thryonomys swinderianus*), wild pig (*Potomochoerus proms*), and duiker (*Cephalophus niger* and *maxiwelli*). This continued reliance on wild fauna reflects a subsistence pattern which extends back hundreds, if not thousands of years into the past. Despite the fact that evidence for plant and animal domestication in Ghana dates to the second millennium BC, sites later than this in the coastal hinterland bear testament to continued reliance on wild fauna. Faunal remains also demonstrate continuity in butchering practices. Bone from archaeological sites is typically shattered with occasional cut marks. Sawn cuts of meat are, in fact, still uncommon in Ghana today, the more common method of preparation being to chop meat apart with a cleaver. Bone is then boiled in soups and stews, the bones frequently being cracked to extract marrow during consumption. Ceramics related to food consumption, recovered archaeologically, including both imported and locally produced wares, are predominantly bowls: forms which would have been better suited for serving soups and stews which are typically eaten with the hand or a spoon. Collectively, these data indicate that the primary transformations in the foodways system during the European period was in the cultivation of plant species with greater caloric value, not in the manner in which food was procured, prepared, and eaten.

The built environment and the foodways system each illustrate continuity in the cultural system, yet these categories of information afford insight into only certain segments of the cultural system, segments which may not provide the most productive means of assessing past religious beliefs and ideology. However, continuity is also suggested by archaeological indicators of ritual behavior, including offerings, ritual vessels, and burials. Such categories of information provide more tangible material expressions of worldview. Ritual vessels found archaeologically exhibit continuity in form, as well as the context in which they functioned. Stylistically, some of these are very distinctive, including specialized shapes, surface treatment, and decoration. They include vessels which are today found only in shrine contexts or used for offerings (Fig. 10.8). Some archaeological examples were found upside down beneath house floors, their contents including the remains of offerings. Informants at Elmina and neighboring towns attested to the continued use of these vessels in specialized contexts today.

Insight into past ritual behavior is also illustrated by burials. This category of information is particularly important to archaeologists because mortuary behavior frequently provides physical expression of ritual practices, cosmology, and perceptions of the afterlife. Burial practices among the coastal Akan are not well-documented in either written records or ethnographic accounts. Specific patterns of interment clearly varied, including burial outside of settlements, beneath house floors, and probably in other specialized areas as well. Prior to the late nineteenth-century it was customary to wrap the body in a specially prepared cloth. Archaeological and ethnographic data indicate that brick tombs and coffins are late nineteenth-century innovations. At Elmina, all of the structures excavated produced interments from below house floors. Placement below the floor – rather than orientation – seems to have been the principal aspect of the burial pattern, despite the fact that in some cases only 30 centimeters of soil rested between the house floor and the underlying bedrock. In many instances the burials rested directly on bedrock, only a few centimeters beneath the house floor. In-house burial continued throughout the period under study, despite European attempts at prohibition. In fact, chiefs may still be buried within the house today. Grave goods, including specialized ritual vessels such as *forowa*, accompanied most bodies.

Collectively, these attributes are striking in their non-European character: insight into their context being informed, not by the presence of the Dutch or the Portuguese, but through reference to the Akan worldview. Methodologically, the most important point to be made is the fact that the various categories of information are not considered individually, but rather as part of a suite of characteristics which collectively present a picture of continuity in a shared set of beliefs, a perception of the afterlife and worldview. Archaeological observations can be validated by ethnographic observations of the modern community, as well as limited insights into religious beliefs provided by the documentary record.

CONCLUSION

This paper considers two conceptual areas with regard to European expansion in West Africa. The first of these is the economic context in which African–

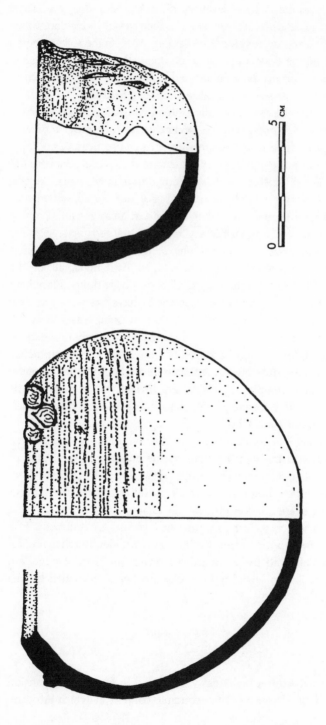

Fig. 10.8 Pottery from Elmina. The ritual function of the vessels is suggested by both their form and archaeological context.

European encounters took place. Although the advent of European trade stimulated certain structural changes in African sociopolitical institutions, the particularities of these economic relations varied in individual contact settings. In many instances the Europeans were confined to the coastal margins and developments occurred within African sociocultural contexts. Secondly, the extra-somatic nature of culture is emphasized. Although the European presence and changing economic relations may have precipitated changes in African belief systems, there is no direct corollary between particular levels of relations and acculturation. Indeed, a generalized model which seeks a univariate understanding of cultural developments in all settings is inappropriate.

Methodologically, archaeologists need to employ strategies to recognize and identify the variable ways in which these phenomena are preserved in the material record. Although archaeological assemblages are regarded as meaningfully constituted results of human behavior, their interpretation is not reducible to universal cross-cultural constructs. The presence of European artifacts and technological innovations in archaeological sites dating within the past 500 years are best viewed, initially, as indicators of change in the European mode of production and as markers of European expansion. They do not afford immediate insight into the specific nature of the contact setting or transformations within the populations with which the Europeans were interacting.

ACKNOWLEDGMENTS

My thanks to Jim Cusick and to Graham Connah for making useful suggestions concerning this chapter. I also wish to thank Zesha Skop for redrawing some of the figures.

BIBLIOGRAPHY

Agorsah, E.K. (1983) Social behavior and spatial context. *African Study Monographs* 4: 119–28.

Agorsah, E.K. (1986) House forms in northern Volta Basin, Ghana: evolution, internal spatial organization and the social relationships depicted. *West African Journal of Archaeology* 16: 25–51.

Agorsah, E.K. (1988) Evaluating spatial behavior patterns of prehistoric societies. *Journal of Anthropological Archaeology* 7: 231–47.

Alpern, J. (1992) The European introduction of crops into West Africa in precolonial times. *History in Africa* 19: 13–43.

Austen, R.A. (1979) The trans-Saharan slave trade: a tentative census. In Gemery, H.A. and Hogendorn, J.S. (eds) *The uncommon market: essays in the economic history of the Atlantic slave trade*. New York, Academic Press, pp. 23–76.

Austen, R.A. (1987) *African economic history*. London, James Currey.

Ballong-Wen-Mewuda, J.B. (1984) São Jorge da Mina (Elmina) et son contexte socio-historique pendant l'occupation Portugaise (1482–1637). Unpublished these de Doctorat. Paris, Centre de Recherches Africaines, Université de Paris.

Bascom, W.R. and Herskovits, M.J. (eds) (1963) *Continuity and change in African cultures*. Chicago, University of Chicago Press.

Bellis, J.O. (1987) A late archaeological horizon in Ghana: proto-Akan or pre-Akan? *Anthropological Papers of the American Museum of Natural History* 65(1): 36–50.

Blake, J.W. (1967) *Europeans in West Africa, 1450–1560*. Nendeln, Liechtenstein, Kraus Reprints.

Blake, J.W. (1977) *West Africa: quest for God and gold 1454–1578*. London, Curzon Press.

Bodley, J.H. (1990) *Victims of progress*. 3rd edn. Mountain View, California, Mayfield.

Brooks, G.E. (1993) *Landlords and strangers: ecology, society, and trade in western Africa, 1000–1630*. Boulder, Colorado, Westview.

Curtin, P.D. (1961) The white man's grave: image and reality, 1750–1850. *Journal of British Studies* 1(1): 94–110.

Curtin, P.D. (1968) Epidemiology and the slave trade. *Political Science Quarterly* 83(2): 190–216.

Curtin, P.D. (1972) *Africa and the west: intellectual responses to European culture*. Madison, University of Wisconsin Press.

Cutin, P.D. (1975) *Economic change in precolonial Africa: Senegambia in the era of the slave trade*. Madison, University of Wisconsin Press.

Daaku, K.Y. (1970) *Trade and politics on the Gold Coast 1600–1720*. Oxford, Oxford University Press.

David, N. (1971) The Fulani compound and the archaeologist. *World Archaeology* 3(2): 111–31.

David, N., Sterner, J. and Gavua, K. (1988) Why pots are decorated. *Current Anthropology* 29(3): 365–89.

DeCorse, C.R. (1989) Material aspects of Limba, Yalunka and Kuranko ethnicity: archaeological research in northeastern Sierra Leone. In Shennan, S.J. (ed.) *Archaeological approaches to cultural identity*. London, Unwin Hyman, pp. 125–40.

DeCorse, C.R. (1991) West African archaeology and the Atlantic slave trade. *Slavery and Abolition* 12(2): 92–6.

DeCorse, C.R. (1992) Culture contact, continuity and change on the Gold Coast. *African Archaeological Review* 10: 163–96.

DeCorse, C.R. (1993) The Danes on the Gold Coast: culture change and the European presence. *African Archaeological Review* 11: 149–74.

DeCorse, C.R. (in press) *Under the castle cannon: an archaeological view of African–European interaction on the Gold Coast, AD 1400–1900*. Washington, DC, Smithsonian Institution Press.

DeCorse, C.R. and Carr, E.R. (1996) Lost in space: archaeological perspectives of culture and the built environment in West Africa. Paper presented at the 95th Annual Meeting of the American Anthropological Association, San Francisco.

De Marees, P. (1987) Description and historical account of the gold kingdom of Guinea (1602). Translated and edited by Van Dantzig, A. and Jones, A. Oxford, Oxford University Press.

Dike, K.O. (1956) *Trade and politics in the Niger Delta, 1830–1885*. Oxford, Oxford University Press.

Farnsworth, P. (1987) *The economics of acculturation in the California missions: a historical and archaeological study of the Mission Nuestra Señora de la Soledad*. PhD thesis, University of California, Los Angeles. Ann Arbor, University Microfilms.

Feinberg, H.M. (1974) New data on European mortality in West Africa: the Dutch on the Gold Coast, 1719–1760. *Journal of African History* 15(3): 357–71.

Feinberg, H.M. (1989) Africans and Europeans in West Africa: Elmina and Dutchmen on the Gold Coast during the eighteenth century. *Transactions of the American Philosophical Society* 79(7).

Garrard, T. (1980) *Akan weights and the gold trade.* New York, Longman.

Geertz, C. (1973) *Interpretation of cultures.* New York, Basic Books.

Goucher, C.L. (1981) Iron is iron 'til it is rust: trade and ecology in the decline of West African iron-smelting. *Journal of African History* 22(1): 179–89.

Hair, P.E.H. (1967) Ethnolinguistic continuity on the Guinea coast. *Journal of African History* 8(2): 247–68.

Hair, P.E.H. (1994) *The founding of the Castelo de São Jorge da Mina: an analysis of the sources.* Madison, African Studies Program, University of Wisconsin.

Harlan, J.R., de Wet, J.M.J. and Stemler, A.B.L. (eds) (1976) *Origins of African plant domestication.* The Hague, Mouton. .

Herskovits, M. (1962) *The human factor in changing Africa.* New York, Alfred A. Knopf.

Hiskett, M. (1984) *The development of Islam in West Africa.* New York, Longman.

Hopkins, A.G. (1973) *An economic history of West Africa.* New York, Columbia University Press.

Jones, A. (1983a) From slaves to palm kernels. *Studien zur Kulturkunde* 68, Wiesbaden, Franz Steiner.

Jones, A. (1983b) German sources for West African history. *Studien zur Kulturkunde* 64, Wiesbaden, Franz Steiner.

Kea, R.A. (1982) *Settlements, trade and polities in the seventeenth century Gold Coast.* Baltimore, Johns Hopkins University Press.

Kelly, K.G. (in press) The archaeology of African–European interaction: investigating the social roles of trade, traders, and the use of space in the seventeenth and eighteenth century *Hueda* Kingdom, Republic of Bénin. *World Archaeology* 28(3).

Kiyaga-Mulindwa, D. (1982) Social and demographic changes in the Birim Valley, southern Ghana, c. 1450 to c. 1800. *Journal of African History* 23(1): 63–82.

Kopytoff, I. (ed.) (1989) *The African frontier.* Bloomington, Indiana University Press.

Law, R. (1980) *The horse in West African history.* Oxford, Oxford University Press.

Law, R. (1983) Trade and politics behind the Slave Coast: the lagoon traffic and the rise of Lagos, 1500–1800. *Journal of African History* 24: 321–48.

Law, R. (1991) *The Slave Coast of West Africa: the impact of the Atlantic slave trade on African society.* Oxford, Oxford University Press.

Levtzion, N. and Hopkins, J.F.P. (eds) (1981) *Corpus of early Arabic sources for West African history.* Cambridge, Cambridge University Press.

Levy-Bruhl, L. (1910) *Les fonctions mentales dans les sociétés inférieures.* Paris, Alcan.

Lovejoy, P.E. (1989) The impact of the Atlantic slave trade on Africa: a review of the literature. *Journal of African History* 30(3): 365–94.

McCall, D.F. and Bennett, N.R. (1971) Aspects of African Islam. *Boston University Papers on Africa, Volume 5.*

McCaskie, T.C. (1995) *State and society in pre-colonial Asante.* Cambridge, Cambridge University Press.

MacEachern, S. (1993) Selling the iron for their shackles: Wandela–*Montagnard* interactions in northern Cameroon. *Journal of African History* 34(2): 247–70.

Mauny, R. (1954) Notes historiques sur les plantes cultivées d'Afrique occidentale. *Bulletin de l'Institut Français d'Afrique Noire* 15(2): 684–730.

Miracle, M.P. (1965) The introduction and spread of maize in Africa. *Journal of African History* 6(1): 39–55.

Ozanne, P. (1962) Notes on the early historic archaeology of Accra. *Transactions of the Historical Society of Ghana* 6: 51–70.

Ozanne, P. (1963) Indigenes or invaders? *Antiquity* 37(147): 229–31.

Ozanne, P. (1964) Notes on the later prehistory of Accra. *Journal of the Historical Society of Nigeria* 3(1): 3–23.

Pakenham, T. (1991) *The scramble for Africa: 1876–1912.* New York, Random House.

Polanyi, K. (1966) *Dahomey and the slave trade: an analysis of an archaic economy.* Seattle, University of Washington Press.

Posnansky, M. and DeCorse, C.R. (1986) Historical archaeology in sub-Saharan Africa: a review. *Historical Archaeology* 20(1): 1–14.

Priestly, M.A. (1969) *West African trade and coast society.* Oxford, Oxford University Press.

Quimby, G.I. (1966) *Indian culture and European trade goods.* Madison, University of Wisconsin Press.

Quimby, G.I. and Spoehr, A. (1951) Acculturation and material culture. *Fieldiana* 36(6): 107–47.

Redman, C.L. (1986) *Qsar es-Seghir: an archaeological view of medieval life.* New York, Academic Press.

Reynolds, E. (1974) *Trade and economic change on the Gold Coast: 1807–1874.* New York, Longman.

Rodney, W. (1982) *How Europe underdeveloped Africa.* Washington, D.C., Howard University Press.

Sahlins, M. (1985) *Islands of history.* Chicago, University of Chicago Press.

Serageldin, I. and Taboroff, J. (1994) *Culture and development in Africa.* Washington, DC, World Bank.

Shennan, S.J. (ed.) (1989) *Archaeological approaches to cultural identity.* London, Unwin Hyman.

South, S. (1977) *Method and theory in historical archaeology.* New York, Academic Press.

Steward, J.H. (ed.) (1972) *Three African tribes in transition.* Urbana, University of Illinois Press.

Sundström, L. (1965) The trade of Guinea. *Studia Ethnographica Upsaliennsia* 24.

Sutton, I.B. (1981) The Volta River salt trade: the survival of an indigenous industry. *Journal of African History* 22(1): 43–61.

Tessler, M.A., O'Barr, W.M. and Spain, D.H. (1973) *Tradition and identity in changing Africa.* New York, Harper and Row.

Thornton, J. (1992) *Africa and Africans in the making of the Atlantic world, 1400–1680.* Cambridge, Cambridge University Press.

Trimingham, J.S. (1978) *Islam in West Africa.* Oxford, Oxford University Press.

Van Dantzig, A. (1980) *Forts and castles of Ghana.* Accra, Sedco.

Wallerstein, I. (1980) *The modern world system.* New York, Academic Press.

Wallerstein, I. (1986) *Africa and the modern world.* Trenton, Africa World Press.

Whorf, B.L. (1956) *Language, thought and reality.* Cambridge, Massachusetts, MIT Press.

Wood, W.R. (1967) An archaeological appraisal of early European settlement in the Senegambia. *Journal of African History* 8(1): 39–64.

Yarak, L. (1990) *Asante and the Dutch, 1744–1873.* Oxford, Oxford University Press.

INDEX